Gourmet's Guide to New Orleans

NATALIE V. SCOTT
CAROLINE MERRICK JONES

PELICAN PUBLISHING COMPANY

GRETNA 1980

Manufactured in the United States of America

Published by Pelican Publishing Company, Inc.
1101 Monroe Street, Gretna, Louisiana 70053

Gourmet's Guide
To New Orleans

Foreword

A FOREIGN critic once described America as a country which had one sauce and twenty different religions. Evidently he did not reach New Orleans in his travels, or else he would have discovered that its gravies are even more varied than its theology, and that good cooking is one of its religions.

In this thrice blessed city where the art of living has ever been esteemed the chief of the fine arts, and where dining is a function instead of a chore, cooking has reached a degree of perfection that it has not attained anywhere else in this country, and tourists come as definitely to New Orleans to eat as they go to New York to see the plays, or to Washington to behold the seat of government, or to Hollywood to gape at the movie stars.

Many things have contributed to make New Orleans a shrine to which gourmets make reverent pilgrimages. One is that it has what an old colored cook once described as the "ingrejuns" necessary to good cooking, for you cannot make omelets without having eggs. No other place in the world has such a market, for lying as it does with one hand in the marshes and bayous of its coastal region and the other hand grasping the packing houses of Chicago, as it were, and its head in a perennial market garden and its feet almost touching the tropics, it has a superabundance all the year round of sea foods par excellence, the finest cuts of butchers' meat, fresh vegetables and the exotic fruits that swift steamers bring in from Central American ports.

To properly prepare these gifts of the gods for human consumption there has slowly evolved through the past two hundred years a school of cooking that is part inspiration and sheer genius, and part a happy adaptation of the dishes of many races and lands. Founded originally on the French cuisine, it was pepped up, so to speak, by the Spanish, given body and strength by the New England influence, a bit of warmth by the hot breads of Virginia, and finally glorified by the touch of the old negro mammies who boasted that they had only to pass their hands over a pot to give it a flavor that would make your mouth water.

Thousands of hands have stirred and been subtle with onion and garlic, and pinched their thyme and bay leaves, and been spendthrifts with oil and miserly with vinegar, and have tested and tasted to make its incomparable sauces, and its oysters Rockefeller and its shrimp rémoulade, and its crabs timbale, and its gumbo filé and its courtbouillon, and it is the secrets thus discovered of these sophisticated dishes that this little book offers you.

Try them, and Heaven send you luck.

DOROTHY DIX.

i

INTRODUCTION

A gourmet, discerning admirer of fine food, is to New Orleans a native son, whatever his origin. New Orleans, offshoot of France, where culinary excellence was deemed worthy once of royal, even now of governmental, recognition, regards culinary creation and appreciation with a fine seriousness.

Here, old culinary traditions are treasured like old masters, and new ones are correspondingly acclaimed. In the following pages, the museums are thrown open, the chefs d'oeuvres stand for review. Only those that have met assured recognition have been chosen, many of them released here for the first time by jealous guardians.

Such a collection is only possible, of course, through the generosity of celebrated hostesses and renowned restaurants. But then, such hostesses and such restaurants are only possible in the atmosphere of sincere appreciation which New Orleans—all Louisiana—affords. See for yourself.

Go to Antoine's, and relish the ceremonial feeling that attends the offering of the matchless productions there. Meet Angelo Alciatore, grandson of the founders of that most famous restaurant.

Luxuriate at Arnaud's. There is no true artist who does not love his art, no true restauranteur without the fine perception of subtle flavors that makes the gourmet. Arnaud, the "Count," was such an example; transplanted from his native France he re-created it about him in his cuisine. The quietly busy rooms where he presided are delicately pervaded by an adulation, and habitues claim the presence of the master spirit.

Seek out the Galatoires in their sanctum, bright and shining. Perched high at one end of the room is the cashier, as in any proper French restaurant, while one of the members of the family stands nearby, suavely courteous, watching, unobtrusive but all-observing, as the deft waiters glide by with the trout Marguery, the canape, the gumbo. The maitre d' receives you deferentially and the room is full of the unique expansiveness which only a pleased palate can produce.

Linger at Broussard's, a New Orleans tradition since 1920. Dine inside or on the lovely patio, and taste all of the classic Creole cuisine, prepared with such savory individuality.

And note Bob LeFrois who serves at the Old Absinthe Bar on Bourbon Street, where notables have sipped absinthe frappes through the years.

Find your way to La Louisiane, where the ordered hosts of white tables await you. Regard the deferential waiter with appreciation, for he is to be the bearer of good things; the old traditions of New Orleans cooking find succulent embodiment here.

In this dominantly French atmosphere, you must note Kolb's, brilliantly asserting the German tradition, with Wienerschnitzel, pigs' knuckles, and sauerbraten, worthy of old Leipzig, or Munich, or Frankfurt. Italy is recognized with spaghettis and raviolis brought to their apogee by the Turcis, who once sang in the old French

Opera House here. Now relocated on Pleasant Street, Turci's retains their traditions.

Find a place for yourself among the enthusiastic habitues of the Vieux Carre, where the table d'hote offers as rich a variety as the a la carte; sample Chef Prudhomme's choice menu at K-Paul's or the seafood at Ralph & Kacoo's. In the business district try Maylie's, where the businessmen throng from their offices, and the air is full of relaxation. Or go to the Bon Ton, where Al Pierce has successfully transplanted the great Cajun cuisine, or any of the innumerable restaurants, and you will discover that within their scope they are equally loyal to the culinary traditions. In the residential districts there are many fine old restaurants such as Pascal's Manale and Commander's Palace, or numerous other favorite neighborhood restaurants where the menus feature the delights of the gourmet. Feast on any of the infinite variety of offerings at Pittari's or Masson's, or go to Christian's and Etienne's, where delicacies are offered that will surely please the most discriminating devotee of good food.

Travel the state and still find the same tradition. Hear businessmen tell about the miles they have driven to have a steak at Sig's in Port Sulphur, crawfish at Pat's in Henderson, or catfish at Middendorf's at Pass Manchac.

But the fine fire burns not alone in these numerous but sporadic spots. The home cooking has its own flame, as surely as have the restaurants in New Orleans, like Corinne Dunbar's on St. Charles. Or travel out U.S. 90 toward Houma and enjoy the creative and varied dishes that Mosca's prepares. There is such an infinite variety from which to choose, such as the fried chicken at Chez Helene's, gumbo at Dooky Chase's, red beans and rice at Buster Holmes. For lunch feast on a traditional po-boy or muffuletta sandwich, some of which are works of art. And the hotels, instead of the mere gradations of universal hotel fare, present you with distinctive New Orleans menus. The "piece de resistance" mile high pie at the Caribbean Room of the Pontchartrain Hotel and Begue's buffets at the Royal Sonesta are excellent examples of hotel fare.

You may note the fervor with which our most cultured voices pronounce upon the sacrilege of overboiling a fish, or of losing the juices of liver by piercing it with a fork. The erudite dwell lovingly upon their favorite dishes, discuss the various manifestations of them and their origins.

Thus, jambalaya, they tell you, is derived from the arroz con pollo, which has appeared on every proper Spanish menu from time immemorial. Quite often here, as in Spain, a touch—no more—of saffron is added for color and savor as well. A nationally renowned doctor will tell you that it is the ideal food, combining with beautiful accuracy perfect nutriment in perfect proportion (his logic is well supported by the inspired genius of his excellent cuisine!). Courtbouillon is so-called, according to tradition, because the earliest inspiration produced it as soup, then genius flashes again and it became 'courtbouillon,' a 'short soup' stew.

As to bouillabaisse, shades of Thackeray flutter at the name. That critic, so often difficult towards the United States, proclaimed that only in Marseilles and New Orleans could the dish be known in its perfection, a perfection that roused him to the supreme tribute of a poem. As for the name, the story is that in the first days of its glory, as the chefs hovered over it, when one saw that the rich brew was bubbling too rapidly, he shrieked a warning: "bouillit: baisse!" (it's boiling: lower the fire).

And there's the story of oysters Rockefeller. When our Jules Alciatore offered them with just pride for a group of his most favored patrons, one of them exclaimed: "Mon Dieu, how rich! How are they called?" The world was at that time just blinking its best at Rockefeller's new millions, and the chef retorted quickly, "Rich, are they? Eh bien, oysters Rockefeller you have."

Read the press of other cities, and you will find now and again an exiled New Orleanian deploring with genuine emotion the crimes against the delicate palate committed in the name of Creole cooking. The thin savorless water that proclaims itself Creole gumbo. The viscous mass made to travesty jambalaya. One such plaintiff arraigns the dictionary: 'a gumbo is any soup with okra in it'—yes, but not a Creole gumbo.

Creole cooking, it is true, is an art, and as such is mysterious in its origins and inspirations. But its technique can be acquired. Prime rule: each dish must be a harmony, its central feature predominant but subdued by the effect of its accompanying ingredients, so that not it, nor any one of them, is perceptible for itself—a blend to unity. And, in contrast to the white pastes of other parts of the country, and even to the excellent French originals, Creole cooking emphasizes rather the brown roux, point of departure in so many savory directions.

Almost all soups, to meet approval in New Orleans, must have a bay leaf, a wee bit of onion, and meat or chicken broth; garlic, and a bit of mace, are frequently included, garlic almost always.

Here it is common knowledge that the insipid carrots and peas of this country must be helped slyly with just a touch of sugar; that the least possible modicum of water must be used in cooking vegetables so that their flavor may be conserved. In fact, many deft lords and ladies of the cuisine steam their vegetables instead of boiling them, whenever it is possible. But enough for details, you must follow through the pages to come.

Thus the sources, thus the background. Our culinary history is old. Derived from France and from Spain chiefly, it is truly Creole. But it is never static, it grows. A language that is alive enriches itself by borrowings and adaptations. So must a lusty cuisine. Stranger dishes arrive among us; our chefs deal with them, and presto!— they are naturalized, the strangers are the same and more so, they are Creoles!

All, fellow gourmet, are yours —for he who reads may cook. It is no longer a handicap that New Orleans markets are not in reach of your streetcar line or limousine. With transportation and conservation what they are today, the Gulf of Mexico, for all practical purposes of markets, washes at every doorstep, and tropical plantations rise everywhere.

Joy is one of the duties of life. And the refined discernment that is culture makes any enjoyment more exquisite, more keen. The worthy one of good eating is here with us, and breakfast at Brennan's and dinner at LeRuth's are perfect examples of the choices that are the gourmet's in New Orleans. And so, bon appetit!

SIMPLE SYRUP

The simple syrup referred to in many of the recipes in this section is made by mixing sugar and water together in the proportions of two parts of sugar to one part of water. It may be brought to a good boil and kept indefinitely in the refrigerator.

MINT JULEP BEAUREGARD

    2   teaspoons simple syrup
    5   tablespoons whiskey
        sprigs of mint
        powdered ice

Have the mint fresh and dry. Let it soak in the whiskey an hour. Crush the ice to powder with a wooden mallet. Fill each glass to the top with ice, add the simple syrup, stir. Then add the whiskey. Stir again (never shake). Lastly, put a sprig of mint in the glass. Each glass should be made separately.

WHISKEY TODDY BELLE CHASE

    2   teaspons simple syrup
    ½   teaspoon orange flower water
    1   twist lemon peel
    1   jigger Bourbon, or rye, whiskey
        nutmeg
        ice

To a glass of cracked ice, add the simple syrup, orange flower water, and the lemon peel. Stir with a spoon till the glass is well chilled, never shake. Then add the whiskey, and a dash of nutmeg. Make each glass separately. Drink, and the world assumes a brighter hue.

COCKTAIL SELINA
Mrs. J. N. Roussel

    1   gal. whiskey
    1   punch-glass Peychaud bitters
        peel of ½ lemon
        peel of ½ mandarin
    1½ glasses simple syrup

Let stand three weeks, strain, and bottle. Be sure to use mandarins, not satsumas, as the flavor is entirely different.

GOLDEN DAWN COCKTAIL

    1   part orange juice
    1   part apricot brandy
    2   parts Calvados Gin
        dash of grenadine

Shake!

ALEXANDER COCKTAIL

    2   oz. London Dry Gin
    1   oz. Creme de cacao
    1   oz. sweet cream

Be sure to shake well with ice.

HONDURAS COCKTAIL

    8   ozs. gin
    5   ozs. vermouth
    5   drops bitters
    1   lemon, the juice
    1   dessertspoon sugar
    1   oz. absinthe
    1   oz. creme de cacao
    ½   oz. benedictine

Shake! Will serve eight.

BAYOU COCKTAIL

    1½ parts rum (or whiskey)
    1   part orange juice
    ½   part lime juice
    1½ teaspoon grenadine

Stir !

SAZERAC—HAVANA STYLE

    1   teaspoon sugar
    2   drops of absinthe
    1   glass rye or Bourbon whiskey
        dash of angostura
    2   drops of orange bitters

Put in glass with ice. Stir, but do not shake.

AUDUBON COCKTAIL

    2   parts whiskey
    1   part lemon juice
    ¾   part peach brandy
        dash of grenadine

Put in glass with ice. Stir, but do not shake.

ABSINTHE DRIP

    ¾   glass absinthe
    ¼   glass anisette

Never shake!

FLAMING YOUTH

    1   part honey
    2   parts cream
    2   parts gin (or whiskey)

Shake vigorously as for a gin-fizz. The result is smooth light cream gone snappy!

STRAWBERRY COCKTAIL

One part gin and one part fresh strawberry juice slightly sweetened. Shake well. Makes summer a triumph.

FLARE-UP

    2   parts gin
    1   part lemon juice
    ½   part light simple syrup
    2   teaspoons apricot brandy

Shake!

KICK-OFF

    2   dashes of anisette
    2   dashes of Angostura bitters
    2   dashes Benedictine
    ½   glass French vermouth
    ½   glass gin

Stir well and strain into a cocktail glass, twist lemon peel on top.

GIN FIZZ
Famous Ramos Style

The real art in making a Gin Fizz is in proper shaking. Don't just shake it up a few times and think you have done the job, because it is only started.

You need plenty of ice and you should shake until the contents of the Fizz have become so creamy that you won't be able to hear the ice tinkle against the sides of the shaker. Don't forget that, because your Gin Fizz won't be a real New Orleans concoction unless you follow these directions.

Here's what goes into a Gin Fizz: a dash of orange flower water; ½ jigger lemon juice; ½ tablespoon of simple syrup; 2½ oz. of London dry gin; 2 oz. of cream and half of a white of one egg.

These are the proportions of one drink, and of course you double up for each additional service.

GIN FIZZ "RAMOS"
Mr. S. A. Dobbs

    1   teaspoon powdered sugar
    ½   teaspoon orange flower water
    1   jigger Old Tom Gin
    ½   lemon, the juice
    ½   lime, the juice
    1   egg, white, beaten well
    ½   glass crushed ice
    2   teaspoons rich cream
    1   oz. seltzer water

Mix in this order: crushed ice, fruit juices, cream, orange flower water. Shake vigorously. Add beaten egg and shake until tired. Shake again!

APRICOT FIZZ au GEORGES

    1   oz. apricot brandy
    ½   lemon, the juice
    ½   lime, the juice
    1   lump ice

Fill glass with White Rock.

GREEN FIZZ

    1   teaspoon sugar
    1   lemon, the juice
    5   drops of creme de menthe
    1   white of an egg
    1   jigger gin

Shake with ice and serve in tall glasses.

A SUMMER SPECIAL

    2   measures gin
        a dash of simple syrup
        a dash of lemon juice
        mint, crushed

Put mint in a tea glass, then gin and other ingredients, plenty of crushed ice, fill with seltzer. Stir until glass is frosted as in a regular mint julep.

DIAMOND FIZZ

    1   jigger gin
    1   teaspoon lemon juice
    1   small lump sugar
        champagne

Fill a tall glass with ice cubes and pour in the above and stir. Now fill with champagne. This is a sure cure for weariness.

½ champagne and ½ Baccardi rum makes a delicious and potent cocktail!

CHAMPAGNE COCKTAIL

In a cocktail glass put 1 lump sugar, 2 dashes Angostura bitters on sugar. Fill glass with very frappéd champagne, twist a lemon peel on top and have the best of luck.

CHERRY BOUNCE
Mrs. George Villeré

    wild cherries
    alcohol
    simple syrup

Half fill jug with wild cherries, then fill it with alcohol. Cork it and leave for six months, then drain off the first cherry bounce, reserving the cherries in the jug. The cherry bounce may be sweetened, when ready to serve, with simple syrup. Creole tradition has it that the unsweetened cherry bounce is an infallible cure for intestinal difficulties.

PIQUET
Mrs. George Villeré

Into the gallon jug of cherries used for the Cherry Bounce pour simple syrup to fill it to the top. Cork and leave for 3 months. It will be ready to serve as it is, and is almost as good as the first thick Cherry Bounce.

BLACKBERRY WINE
Southdown Plantation

    1   gal. blakcberries or dewberries
    ½   gal. water
    3   lbs. sugar

Wash and mash the berries well. Let them stand with the water for 24 hours. Strain once or twice through cheese cloth, wringing as you strain. To gallon of juice add sugar and let stand in glass container for six weeks in a cool dark place. When all fermentation is over, bottle and seal well.

ZEPHYR

    1   part Italian vermouth
    1   part Dubonnet
    1   part orange juice

Serve with crushed ice. A refreshing apertif of the French mode.

BLACKBERRY CORDIAL
Miss Emily Bobb

1 qt. blackberries
1 lb. white sugar
1 pt. brandy, or
½ pt. whiskey
3 or 4 cloves

Strain the juice and dissolve the sugar thoroughly in it, and let it stand for about two hours with the cloves. Then add the brandy, or whiskey.

LIQUEUR DE MÉRISE
Mrs. J. T. Bringier

Among the papers of the gracious chatelaine of the live-oak guarded old plantation of Tezcuco is one in courtly French yellowed with age, beginning, "Madame and Friend, if you fear in any way whatever that you may not succeed in your first attempt, I can present to you all the quantity of liqueur de mérise that you desire. The doctor has always been so kindly to my mother that this little savoir faire is only a feeble tribute of my gratitude." And concluding, "with the respectful homage of a grateful person." You will find it worthy, for its concrete form was the following recipe:

1 gal. wild cherries
1¼ gal. rye whiskey
1¼ (or 1½) lbs. sugar

Wash the cherries in two waters, and be sure that they are free from stems or leaves. Then put them in an earthenware container. Iron or tin will not serve. Put the whiskey with them and let them soak 18 to 24 hours. Mash two cupfuls of cherry seeds in a mortar. Mash the cherries in the whiskey and add the seeds.

Boil the sugar in enough water to make a thick syrup. Let it cool, and add it to the alcohol mixture until the bitterness disappears. It must preserve, however, a piquant tang.

Strain the liquid three times through a closely woven cotton cloth.

CHILTAPIN
Mrs. J. H. Sutherland

1 part cognac
1 part apricot brandy
1 drop of bitters, or to taste
few drops of lemon juice

Put in cocktail shaker with crushed ice.

This has been imported from the Hotel Tasqueno in Tasco, where Genxaro, the handsome bar-keeper, reports it is a favorite.

O'JEN
Mrs. H. Waller Fowler

½ gal. alcohol, 198 proof
1 qt. boiling water
1 qt. simple syrup
120 drops oil of anise
12 drops oil of caraway

Drop the oils into the alcohol, and let it stand 24 hours in a gallon jug, so that the essential oils may have time to blend thoroughly. Mix the water and the syrup together. Then pour the alcohol into the syrup-and-water mixture, and shake it well. Allow to stand 48 hours.

Bottle, and age at least 60 days.

If the liquid becomes somewhat cloudy or murky, it makes no difference; when the ice is added to serve it, it always clouds.

When serving, a few drops of Angostura bitters may be added, if desired.

GUERRERO COCKTAIL

2 parts habanero
1 part orange juice
1 part lime juice
½ teaspoon sugar, or to taste

Add this to the habanero and put it in a saucepan on the fire until it steams.

Make a syrup of the sugar as usual. Put with other ingredients in a cocktail shaker with finely crushed ice, and shake well. It adds point to the good-neighbor policy.

VIVA MEXICO

2 parts tequila
1 part vermouth (dry)
1 part lime juice
½ teaspoon sugar, or to taste

Make a syrup of the sugar. Put all the ingredients in the cocktail shaker with finely crushed ice and shake liberally. A few of these would elicit a whoopee from Carrie Nation herself.

BERTA

Recently imported from Tasco is the Berta, sometimes known as the Dos Passos, as that writer conceived it in a moment of non-literary inspiration. It consists of adding a jigger of tequila to a strong limeade. The ambitious make it two jiggers. Lemonade gives results, also, though of lesser excellence.

SUGAR BOWL COCKTAIL

¼ sloe gin
¼ French vermouth
¼ rum
1 teaspoon sugar
1 dash Peychaud's bitters

Named after New Orleans' New Year's Day Football Classic.

From the "Mixed Drink 'Compilec-
tion'" of Lieutenant Winston
Folk, U. S. N.

GARDEN OF EDEN HIGHBALL

This is a creation of the author's
and is as good and refreshing as it is
simple. It consists of applejack and
sherry in equal parts, ice and soda.

An ordinary highball should have a
genuine jigger (1 or 2 ozs.) of spirits.
In this one, because of the relative
weakness of sherry, use ¾ of a jigger
each of the applejack and sherry. It
is a good idea to keep a bottle of the
applejack and sherry ready mixed.
Put two cubes of ice in the highball
glasses, three ounces of the mixture,
and fill with soda.

NEW ORLEANS COCKTAIL

    1   part whiskey
    1   teaspoon syrup
    2   dashes Peychaud's bitters
    1   dash absinthe

While these are getting acquainted
frappé an old fashioned glass, throw
out the ice and rinse glass with absinthe; then strain the cocktail into
it and serve with ice water on the
side.

AIRMAIL SPECIAL

Shake up your favorite **Side Car**—
say equal parts brandy, lemon juice
and triple sec. Use champagne
glasses and fill half full with **Side
Car.** Then fill with champagne.

Invented in Shanghai by some of
the aviators from the HOUSTON
when she was flagpan of the Asiatic
Fleet, and given us by "Zondie" who
guarantees it will create a furor.

UNIVERSITY COCKTAIL

    ½   brandy
    ¼   anisette
    ¼   French vermouth
    2   dashes Peychaud's bitters
    1   dash absinthe
    1   dash orange flower water

"Here's a song for the Olive and
Blue."

LOUISIANA COCKTAIL

    1   part Bourbon
    ¼   French vermouth
    ½   Italian vermouth
    1   dash curacao

And swing into that "Bengal
Swing".

ANCHORS AWEIGH

    4   applejack
    1   grenadine
    1   lemon juice

... "Army you steer shy-y-y." ...

NEW IBERIA COCKTAIL

    2   parts brandy
    1   part French vermouth
    1   part sherry
    2   or 3 drops Tabasco

CAMEO KIRBY COCKTAIL

    ½   gin
    ½   Italian vermouth
    2   teaspoons raspberry syrup
    ½   lime, the juice

Named for a famous Mississippi
River character.

VINEYARD COCKTAIL

        brandy
        claret
        sherry

Shake with ice.

An excellent before dinner cocktail that will not in the least spoil
one's taste for the wine.

FOLKLORE COCKTAIL

    ⅔   gin
    ⅓   French vermouth
    ⅙   applejack
    2   dashes orange bitters

Shake thoroughly with ice. Put a
pearl onion in glass before serving.

This is a Martini with a little applejack added, and is one of the author's
favorites.

* * *

TEA à la RUSSE

        tea
    4   oranges
    2   lemons
        sugar

Make a good strong tea, to serve
about eight glasses. Add the juice
of four oranges and two lemons,
sweeten to taste and add cracked ice.
Garnish with a few sprigs of mint.

A DRINK FROM THE TROPICS

    6   or 8 sprigs mint
    1½   cups sugar
    5   lemons
    ¾   cup water
    3   bottles ginger ale

Put the sugar and water on the
stove long enough to melt the sugar
thoroughly. Cool. Add lemon juice
and the crushed mint. Place in the
refrigerator. When ready to serve,
strain. Fill the glass with ice, fill
each glass a quarter full of the mixture, and fill the remainder with
ginger ale. Stir with spoon.

RUM TEA

The Finns always serve the Russian
type of rum tea with their Smorgas-
bord—hot tea, to which 1 teaspoon of
sugar, a little lemon juice and a teaspoon of rum have been added.

ICED TEA
Comdr. and Mrs. Phillip Yeatman

Heat teapot thoroughly. Add three teaspoonfuls of tea, and pour six cups of boiling water over it. Let it stand a minute, and then pour into a large bowl, add a little mint, and let it cool. When cold, add one small cup of sugar, the juice of three lemons, and plenty of ice. Just before serving, add one small bottle of ginger ale and a little cherry juice.

TAGLIO LIMONI

Place 2 tablespoons of lemon sherbet in an iced tea glass and add charged water to fill. Stir with spoon and serve with a straw. In Milan, whence we have imported this solace for a summer day's heat, they frequently add more seltzer until the sherbet is dissolved, and so prolong this most refreshing beverage.

GINGER ALE PUNCH
```
2   cups lime juice
4   cups lemon juice
2   cups pineapple juice
2   bottles ginger ale
```
In a large punch bowl put about 2 quarts of hard frozen pineapple sherbet. Pour over it the lime juice, lemon juice, and ginger ale.

CAFÉ BRÛLOT
Mrs. Stanley Arthur
```
1   cup cognac
2   lumps sugar per cup of coffee and
      20 over
40  whole cloves
½   orange, very thin peel
¼   lemon, very thin peel
2   sticks whole cinnamon broken
1   qt. coffee
```
Put the spices and the peel into the brandy in the brûlot bowl, with the sugar. Pour a little alcohol in the tray under the bowl and light it. Stir the contents of the bowl until it ignites. Let it burn only a few minutes, so that it may not destroy all the alcohol.

Pour in the coffee slowly.

Note:—If you have no brûlot bowl, you may light the contents of the bowl used in this way: take a tablespoon of the cognac, light a match, hold it underneath the spoon, and then light the cognac in the spoon, and light the contents of the bowl with the burning cognac in the spoon. The quantity of sugar may seem excessive: it is essential for the brûlot should taste like a very rich fruit cake.

CAFÉ BRÛLOT
```
1     after dinner coffee cup of coffee
1½    lumps sugar
2     cloves
2     allspice
½     after dinner coffee cup of cognac
      very thin piece of lemon rind
      very thin piece of orange rind
```
Use process above. Increase quantity as desired.

EGG-NOG
Mrs. Stephen Pierre Cottreaux
```
12    eggs
1     qt. best whiskey
1     qt. heavy cream
1     qt. milk
8—12-ozs. rum
12    tablespoons sugar
```
Beat yolks very light, sift in sugar and beat vigorously. Stir in whiskey, cream and milk. Fold in the stiffly beaten whites. Put in refrigerator until ready to serve. The rum may be left out if flavor is not desired.

ORANGE BRÛLOT
Mrs. Joel Harris Lawrence

Take a thin skinned orange, run a sharp knife around the center only cutting the skin. Insert the edge of a thin spoon between the skin and pulp, thus separating them. Then carefully roll the skin back from the pulp, turning it inside out, half making a cup, and the lower half making a stand. Fill cup with cognac, take a small lump of sugar, put in a teaspoon filled with cognac, light it, then put it with the cognac in the cup, setting fire to the whole thing. The heat extracts the oil from the orange peel, making a delicious liqueur.

Any one of these delicious brûlots will round out a perfect meal.

DRIPPED COFFEE CREOLE

A French drip coffee-pot is essential. Have a pot of boiling water on the stove; set the coffee-pot in another pot of hot water. Put into the dripper 2 level tablespoons of coffee to a cup, if you like your coffee strong. Pour the boiling water over the grounds, a gill at a time at generous intervals. Never let the coffee boil. A jealously guarded secret is that a tablespoon of cocoa or chocolate dissolved in a little of the coffee and then added to the rest gives a very special flavor.

PIERRE'S APPETIZER

1 Philadelphia cream cheese
1 small can anchovies, mashed
1½ teaspoon capers, mashed
½ teaspoon grated onion
½ teaspoon Worcestershire Sauce
2 or more tablespoons cream or milk
cayenne to taste

Cream cheese with cream. Add other ingredients. Serve on round salted crackers. This mixture keeps well.

CAULIFLOWER

Wash a fine white cauliflower. Place in ice water with ice for two hours. Break flowers apart and serve on tooth picks. Dip in highly seasoned mayonnaise that has an extra portion of lemon juice. Thin slivers of raw carrots or turnips may be used in the same way.

TOMATO CANAPÉ PLAZA

Cut rounds of thin bread, spread lightly with mayonnaise, place on top a piece of tomato not quite ripe. Salt well, cover with grated sharp cheese and dash of cayenne. Put on top of hot oven and allow to dry at the bottom, 20 to 30 minutes, then run in oven under flame to melt cheese.

ADMIRAL'S GOLDEN BUCK

1 lb. grated American sharp cheese
1 egg
1 tablespoon butter
½ teaspoon salt
1 tablespoon Worcestershire Sauce
½ coffee spoon cayenne pepper
2 doz. rounds of thinly sliced bread

Mix cheese, butter and raw egg together. Add seasoning, cover and put in refrigerator. When ready to serve, toast the rounds of bread to straw color. Spread the mixture on the rounds and run under the flame of the gas stove for 3 minutes until cheese melts. The mixture will keep for days.

It may be spread on the toasted bread rounds some time before serving if desired, and the whole heated just before serving.

BOUCHÉES D'ANCHOIS

pie crust
tube of anchovy paste

Make a nice pie or biscuit crust, cut into rounds with small biscuit cutter. Into each round, squeeze a small quantity of anchovy paste. Fold over the round and press down the edges with a fork. Prick the top with the fork and bake in a hot oven.

Serve immediately.

ANCHOVY CANAPÉS
Miss Julie Folwell

Make rounds of toast, spread with sweet butter, season with salt, pepper and mustard to taste. Arrange anchovy filets on these in form of a rosette or across. Garnish with finely chopped parsley. Press the yolk of a hard boiled egg, and some little of the white as well, through a sieve and arrange in a ring around the edges of the rounds.

CANAPÉ EGYPTIAN
Mrs. Edgar H. Bright

Chipped beef cut in small pieces, mix with 2 tsp. of catsup and 3 tsp. of mayonnaise, and a dash of cayenne pepper.

Serve on round pieces of toast or crackers.

BEURRE D'ANCHOIS
Mrs. Alfred T. Pattison

½ lb. best quality salt anchovies
(Use nothing but salt anchovies in brine)
½ lb. unsalted butter

Soak anchovies in water for half hour, changing water three times. Remove, wipe with a cloth to remove all scales. Split in half lengthwise and remove bones and fins. Wipe with a dry cloth to insure absence of fins, bones or scales. Put anchovies in a bowl and mash thoroughly until a perfect pulp is obtained. Then mix anchovies thoroughly with butter. Serve cold but not as hard as butter which is used at the table. It should neither be too soft nor yet too hard. Never use anchovy paste. The secret is in reducing the anchovies to a pulp and in having them free from bones and scales. This is a very recherché hors d'oeuvre in France.

BOUCHÉES SURPRISES

½ lb. chipped beef
4 New York cream cheeses
a few shallots, chopped fine
1 cup shelled walnuts, chopped fine

Get the chipped beef freshly sliced so it will not be dry.

Cream the cheese. Add the walnut and the white tender part only of the shallots.

Take a slice of chipped beef, lay it on the biscuit board, put in a small quantity of cheese mixture and roll. Trim off the ends. When finished, each roll should be the size of a thin finger. These are better after staying a few hours in a cold place.

If the flavor is preferred the cream cheese may be mixed with horse radish and cayenne pepper to taste.

DEVILED SARDINE CANAPÉ
Mrs. Frank H. Lawton

First skin and bone a can of sardines or better still use the boned variety. Place them in a well buttered tin, add ½ tsp. Worcestershire Sauce, ½ tsp. mustard and a pinch of cayenne. Cover with 1 tsp. bread crumbs.

Bake for 10 minutes and serve hot on toast rounds.

SHRIMP APPETIZER
Mrs. Frank H. Lawton

Toast small round slices of bread. Clean 1 lb. of shrimp, boiled. Skin out the back streak with knife. Cut up fine, add some finely chopped sour pickles. Mix with mayonnaise. Sprinkle thickly on the toast, cover with a very thick layer of grated cheese. Before serving put in oven and let cheese melt. Serve hot.

SHRIMP PIQUANT
Commdr. and Mrs. Phillip Yeatman

Two parts mayonnaise to 1 part Chili Sauce and one part whipped cream. Combine the ingredients in the order listed and chill in ice box before serving.

Boiled shrimp speared with toothpicks are offered at the same time with the sauce served in a separate bowl, and each guest dips his shrimp in the sauce.

ROQUEFORT CHEESE MICHEL
½ cup butter, unsalted
2 cups Roquefort cheese
2 tablespoons Worcestershire Sauce
3 drops Tabasco Sauce
4 white shallots, cut very fine

Cream butter until soft. Mash the cheese well and add. Mix well, then add Worcestershire, Tabasco, and finely chopped shallots. This mixture will keep well in the refrigerator. Serve on crackers.

CROQUETTES DE CAMEMBERT
3 ½ ozs. flour
5 ½ ozs. butter
5 ½ ozs. Camembert cheese
2 egg yolks
1 pinch cayenne
1 pinch paprika
1 egg

Mix the ingredients on a marble slab. Knead the paste three times and make it into a ball. Let it stand for 2 hours, then roll it out and cut into any desired shape. Dip the pieces of paste into the beaten egg and roll them in fine bread crumbs. Fry in hot fat and serve on a serviette.

They can be speared with toothpicks and served with cocktails and they are delicious too, with salads.

CELERY FARCI
Mr. Fred O'Tell

¼ lb. Roquefort cheese
½ lb. cream cheese
2 lemons
1 teaspoon Worcestershire Sauce
½ cup mayonnaise
paprika

Blend with a silver fork the cheeses and the mayonnaise. Add the lemon juice, the Worcestershire Sauce and the paprika. Put in a pastry tube and stuff in short tender stalks of celery, and your guests will drink their cocktails with more relish because of it.

MUSHROOM ROUNDS

1 doz. slices bread
1 ½ cups fresh mushrooms
1 tablespoon butter
2 teaspoons cream
salt, pepper to taste

Slice the bread as for Melba toast. Sauté the mushrooms in butter, chop them and add cream and seasoning.

Lightly butter the bread, spread it with the mushroom mixture, roll and hold together with tooth-picks, toast, and serve with tea or cocktails.

SWISS CHEESE BALLS
Mrs. Edward Rightor

1 ½ cups grated cheese
1 tablespoon flour
3 egg whites
2 tablespoons sherry
salt, pepper and paprika to taste

Mix the cheese and flour, sherry and seasoning, fold in the stiffly beaten whites. Make into balls. Roll in cracker crumbs. Fry in deep hot fat.

If served with cocktails, make balls small and place toothpicks in each. If made large serve with crisp broiled bacon and asparagus.

ROQUEFORT CHEESE

¼ lb. Roquefort cheese
2 teaspoons mayonnaise
½ cup pecans, chopped fine
rounds of rye bread cut very small

Mash and cream cheese with mayonnaise. Toast bread on one side, butter untoasted side. Cover with cheese, sprinkle nuts on top. Brown and serve at once.

CAVIAR CANAPÉ
Miss Julie Folwell

Make the canapé oblong in shape. If the caviar is too hard, work in a little lemon juice. Fill the center of the canapé with caviar, and lay a row of very finely chopped onion around the inside border and on top of the caviar.

GALETTES AU ROQUEFORT
Mrs. Walter Torian

1 cup butter
1 cup Roquefort cheese
2 tablespoons Worcestershire Sauce
5 drops Tabasco

Cream the butter and cheese together, add seasoning. Spread as appetizer on salted crackers. It can keep in the icebox for a week.

FRANKFURTERS VIENNES
Mrs. Emily Roosevelt

Cut sausage lengthwise leaving a hinge. Spread generously with Guldens Mustard, close, wrap with bacon, secure with a toothpick. When ready to serve place under the flames to broil. Turn from side to side until bacon is cooked. These snappy frankfurters can be cut in small rounds and speared with a toothpick and will give relish to a cocktail or for Sunday night supper.

PATÉ PAYSAN

calf's liver
hard boiled eggs
mayonnaise
salt, pepper, cayenne

Cook the liver and chop it very fine, chop the hard boiled eggs, mix both with the mayonnaise, season highly. Spread the mixture on thin crispy toasted rounds of bread, garnishing with powdered egg yolk.

It might be a twin to paté de foie gras.

PATÉ DE FOIE GRAS BISCUITS WITH BACON

small biscuits
bacon
paté de foie gras
cream

Make the biscuits very small and light, preferably the size of a quarter, or a half dollar.

Broil the bacon very crisp and chop.

Mix the paté de foie gras with a little cream to moisten it.

Open the biscuits and spread one side with bacon bits, the other with the paté. Press the halves together and it can share the honors of any cocktail.

PEANUT BUTTER APPETIZERS

Small rounds of toasted bread.

Spread thickly with peanut butter, creamed with butter. Add a dash of cayenne, place a small piece of bacon on top, run under the gas flames and brown.

MUSHROOM SAVOURY

1 lb. fresh mushrooms
1 cup cream sauce
¼ lb. grated cheese
1 tablespoon sherry
½ tablespoon salt
toast rounds
cayenne

Skin the mushrooms, stem them, and boil until tender. Mince them very fine. To the cream sauce add some of the mushroom broth, the cheese and the sherry, and with this bind the mushrooms together. Mound the mushrooms on toast rounds. Sprinkle with grated cheese and a little cayenne. Place in the oven until cheese melts and serve hot.

TOMATOES GARNIS
Miss Esther Dupuy

On a thin slice of toast place a slice of fresh tomatoes and heap with a generous mound of flaked salmon, lobster or shrimp, or top with a half egg stuffed with anchovy. Dress with mayonnaise and pour over Bonfouca salad dressing. (Refer to Sauces.)

PITTED OLIVES WRAPPED IN BACON

Wrap olives in bacon and broil. Oysters and shrimp can be treated in the same way—spear with toothpicks.

AVOCADO
(Alligator Pears)

Chill ripe avocados, cut in halves, remove seed and fill with very cold, tender, seedless, white grapes. Pour Madeira wine over them. This is an unusual cocktail and very delicious.

COD FISH BALLS

Make very small cod fish balls by recipe on page 22. Spear with toothpicks.

FRENCH FRIED BANANA CHIPS
Mrs. Grace Stevenson

Thinly sliced, not too ripe, bananas. Fry in hot oil or butter at 400° until golden brown. This goes well with cocktails, or as a garnish for meat.

BOUCHÉES SOUFFLÉ

Use very small muffin tins. Line each mold to height of ½ inch and bake. Half fill each with the soufflé mixture and run in the oven. Bake about ten minutes and serve piping hot. They will add grace to any cocktail.

"GUMBO Z'HERBES"

Mrs. J. T. Simmons

almost any fresh, tender greens
pod of cayenne
herbs, savories
seasonings
salt
3 tablespoons butter, lard or olive oil

Wash the greens, very, very, thoroughly to rid them of grit and insects (use salt water).

Drain, and strip them carefully of stems and tough midribs.

Put them in a large pot with enough water barely to cover them packed in loosely.

When the pot boils place it where it will simmer gently for about 20 minutes.

Remove, pour off the water, saving it. Remove the greens to a wooden bowl, and put the water back in the pot. Chop the greens very, very fine, adding the herbs, savories and flavoring, with salt, and chop again.

Replace in the simmering pot liquor, adding the butter, (lard, or vegetable oil), set back to simmer for about 2 hours.

If desired, one may add part or the whole of a chicken, or just the giblets, or a few strips of bacon, or diced ham, or diced fresh pork, browned in butter, or fried shrimp (this last is a favorite Creole dish for fast days.)

The ingredients may be chosen from the following:

Greens: spinach, mustard greens, lettuce, beet-tops, collards, carrot-tops, water-cress, radish-tops, turnip-tops, cabbage, kale, barecole, rape, Brussels sprouts, kohlrabi, endive, broccoli.
Savories: bay-leaf, sage, borage, thyme catnip, dill, taragon, chives.
Herbs: parsley, celery, green onions, sweet pepper, sorrel, dandelion, fennel, cress, celeriac, shallots, leeks, chili, roquette.

This Gumbo Z'herbes, so-called by the black slaves who served it to their Creole masters in the south's long-ago, probably originated in the Congo jungles of Africa. And no doubt it was modified by the friendly Cherokee and Choctaw Indians of the south, from their rudimentary knowledge of medicinal or "pot" herbs. Certainly many of the ingredients for making this delectable concoction were to be obtained from the Indian squaws who squatted with their baskets on the flagged entrance to the old French market.

Besides its savory taste, it has a highly salubrious quality, and, now that savories and simples are reappearing in favor, it finds a place in modern household magazines, recommended for its beneficial qualities.

"GUMBO Z'HERBES"

Mrs. Walter Torian

1 lb. pickled pork
1 Creole cabbage
2 large bunches spinach
1 bunch turnip tops
2 large onions
4 cloves garlic
1 pod red pepper
2 tablespoons vinegar (used in place of sorrel)
2 tablespoons flour
1 tablespoon, heaping, lard
1 bunch mustard green
   salt, pepper, to taste

Cover salt meat with water to boil until done. At the same time, break up the cabbage and stem the other herbs and put them in the pot with sufficient water to cover. When the herbs are done, put them in the colander to drain.

Turn them into the chopping bowl and chop fine.

Now put on the fire a deep iron pot. When hot, add lard and stir in the flour slowly to make a dark roux. Add chopped onions and garlic, and brown. Put in the chopped salt meat now, and add the greens. Allow to cook five minutes stirring all the time.

Next, add 1½ quarts of water, let cook slowly until it becomes a thick purée. Now, put in the vinegar, a pod of red pepper broken up, and salt to taste. Serve with yellow hominy.

Note:—For a lenten dish, put in the pot a heaping tablespoon of butter and cook the herbs in the butter, instead of in the pork; when ready to serve add another tablespoon of butter. In this way, the meat may be omitted without losing the richness of the dish.

CHICKEN GUMBO

1 chicken
3 onions
½ doz. crabs
1 doz. oysters
1 lb. shrimp
1 slice ham
6 large fresh tomatoes
1 pt. fresh okra
1 bay leaf
1 sprig parsley and thyme
1 pod of red pepper, minus seeds
1 large tablespoon lard, or 2 large tablespoons butter

Cut the chicken into pieces. Cut the ham in squares, chop the onions fine, also the parsley and thyme. Skin the tomatoes and chop fine, saving the juice. Wash and stem the okra, slice very thin. Put the lard or butter in a soup pot and when hot add the chicken, ham, crabs, oysters, and shrimp. Cover closely and let it simmer for about ten minutes, then add the chopped onions, parsley and thyme, also the tomatoes, and the okra and when well browned, add the juice of the tomatoes, which imparts a superior flavor.

The okra is very delicate and liable to scorch quickly if not stirred frequently—for that reason, lots of Creole cooks fry it separately in a frying pan, seasoning with salt, pepper, and cayenne, and then add it to the chicken.

The least taste of scorch spoils the gumbo.

When well fried and browned, put in boiling water, about 3 qts., and let it simmer gently for about 1 hour or longer.

Serve with nicely cooked rice.

The carcass of turkey may also be used in gumbo.

Crabs, shrimp, ham, oysters, veal or chicken—any one of the above may be omitted if not desired.

GUMBO FILÉ
Mrs. Walter Torian

1   4 lb. hen
1   tablespoon hog lard
2   tablespoons flour
1   tablespoon parsley, minced
2   large onions, chopped
2   cloves garlic, chopped
1   pinch red pepper
2   qts. stock from hen
½   tablespoon filé
2   doz. oysters
    salt, pepper to taste

Boil hen until tender. Cut the meat from the bones in medium sized pieces. Make a very brown roux. Add to this the stock from the chicken, and the meat, the seasoning, and the oyster liquor. Cook 30 minutes and just before serving add the oysters, allow to boil up—and last, the filé.

MADAME BEGUÉ'S BISQUE
—a l'ECRÉVISSE
Mrs. Walter Torian

40 nice crawfish
1   cup soaked bread
1   large spoon fried onions
    garlic, chopped parsley,
    salt, red pepper
Soup:
    butter
    flour
½   cup minced shallots
½   cup minced parsley
    sprigs of thyme
2   bay leaves, chopped fine
    salt, cayenne pepper

Wash the crawfish very thoroughly, cleaning them with a brush and purge in salt water. Boil them well,

remove from the fire, and drain. Clean the heads, keeping 30 of the shells and also the remains which you will set to boil in a quart of water.

Peel the tails and chop them fine.

Make a paste with the meat, together with the soaked bread, the fried onions, garlic, parsley, salt and pepper. With this, fill the 30 shells, and set them aside while the soup gets under way.

The Soup: Fry the onion in butter, add flour for thickening, then the green onions, parsley, thyme, and bay leaves. When browned, strain the stock from the crawfish remains and heads, and season with salt and pepper. Let it boil slowly for half an hour. Add more water if needed. When ready to serve, roll each of the stuffed heads in flour, fry them in butter until crisp all over, and throw them in the soup. Let boil three or four minutes, and serve with very thin slices of bread toasted.

This bisque was one of the reasons why a stretch of long bare rooms with sanded floors became one of the most famous and recherché restaurants in these United States.

CRAWFISH BISQUE
Mrs. C. A. Tessier

10 lbs. crawfish
6   large onions
6   slices dried out bread
2   cloves garlic
2   sprigs thyme
4   sprigs parsley
2   bay leaves
4   cloves
¾   gallon water
1   pt. chicken broth or consomme
    dash of cayenne
    salt and black pepper to taste

Purge crawfish in salt water 10 minutes, then wash until water is clear. Boil crawfish until they turn red (about 5 minutes), strain out of water and cool. Separate heads from tails. Now clean heads by pulling out the inside without losing too much of the fat. Place the heads in three quarts fresh water you are going to use to make your bisque. Break or crack each claw with a small hammer and boil with the heads to flavor your bisque. Let this come to a boil, then set aside and let stand while you prepare the stuffing.

Chop onions fine and cook in a heaping tablespoon of butter until tender. Soak and squeeze out six slices of bread, add to onions and mix thoroughly. Let cook ten minutes, add crawfish meat that has been chopped fine and season with red or black pepper, salt, garlic and parsley. You can be the judge of how long to cook. Make roux with two heaping tablespoons butter and flour. When golden brown, add a small can of tomatoes strained into roux. Gradually add bisque juice, thyme, cloves, bay leaves and chicken broth (or shrimp consomme if used on a fast day). Let this simmer for two hours.

Now go over the heads and clean thoroughly this time. When dressing cools, stuff heads and place in refrigerator over night (this will pack the dressing in the heads so that it will not come out into the juice). If you haven't time, then dot each stuffed head with butter and bake in oven ten minutes. Drop stuffed heads in bisque one-half hour before serving and heat slowly.

SHRIMP BISQUE
Mrs. Geo. W. Boutcher

2 lbs. boiled shrimp
3 slices stale bread
1 can condensed tomato soup
　bay-leaf, onion, parsley
　salt, pepper
　bacon grease

Peel the shrimp and cut them in half. Soak the bread in enough water to soften. Season highly with the bay-leaf, chopped onion and minced parsley, salt, and pepper. Put in the frying pan with the bacon grease and cook as you would a dressing for chicken. When well blended add the can of condensed tomato soup and an equal quantity of water. Then add the shrimp. If too thick a little more water may be added.

CRAB GUMBO

As prepared at the famous plantation home of Weeks Hall "Shadows of the Teche" in New Iberia.

1 doz. large crabs
2 lbs. okra
4 onions, medium size
4 cloves garlic, minced
1 pod red pepper
5 tomatoes (or 1 small can)
3 ears tender corn
1 tablespoon sifted flour
1 kitchen spoon lard
1 tablespoon vinegar
　salt to taste

Wash the crabs thoroughly, then boil them in just enough water to cover them, and cook until done, about thirty minutes after the water begins to boil, saving the water the crabs were boiled in.

Remove the shells, saving all the fat from the upper shells, and picking out all the meat of the crab.

Now put the lard in a large pot. Have the okra cut up in round slices and add it to the hot lard, to fry until dry. Add the onions, the chopped up tomatoes, and the minced garlic. Fry all this together, then add the water in which the crabs were boiled. Add salt to taste, and set it all to boil about 2 hours.

Meanwhile, add the flour to the corn, and about half an hour before serving, add the crab-meat and the corn with the flour.

The gumbo must be thick and highly seasoned. Just before serving, add one tbsp. of vinegar to prevent the gumbo from being ropy.

OYSTER GUMBO

2 to 4 doz. oysters
1 full kitchen spoon of olive oil
　or other shortening
1 tablespoon flour
1 tablespoon chopped shallots
1 tablespoon parsley
1 pt. oyster liquor
3 sprigs of thyme
2 bay leaves

Put oil in pot, slowly sift in flour, stirring all the time. Brown slightly, add onions. seasoning, oyster liquor, salt and pepper to taste. Let oysters simmer slowly for a few minutes in another pot, and just before serving, add to first mixture.

OYSTER BOUILLON
Mrs. Frank H. Lawton

4 doz. oysters
3 pts. breakfast cream
1 pt. oyster liquor
1 teaspoon salt
1 dash Tabasco
1 stalk celery, grated
½ small onion, grated
1 tablespoon parsley
½ cup whipped cream
　butter the size of an egg
　black pepper to taste

Cook oysters in liquor very slowly until they curl, add celery and onion. Heat cream and mix with oysters and let simmer one-half hour in double boiler. Season just before serving. Strain into cups, top with a teaspoon whipped cream.

OYSTER SOUP LAFAYETTE
Mrs. Walter Torian

2 doz. oysters and liquor
3 shallots
2 cloves garlic
1 tablespoon butter, heaping
1 tablespoon flour, heaping
1 sprig celery
½ cup minced parsley
2 eggs
　salt, red pepper

Melt the butter in a saucepan, and stir in the flour carefully, to make a light roux. Add the onions, celery, and garlic, chopped fine.

With the chopping knife, cut the oysters in three pieces, add salt and red pepper, and pour them into the roux. Cover, and let cook three minutes. Beat the eggs light, and pour the soup into them, whipping all the time. A color golden as the savor of this soup results. Note 1: 1 teaspoon of cold water in the eggs, and they will never curdle.

Note 2: Lessen the amount of liquor used and a delicious stew, instead of soup, results, that will do credit to a luncheon.

TURTLE SOUP
Mrs. Curran Perkins

1 small turtle
1 large onion
4 hard-boiled eggs, yolks only
4 bay leaves
1 qt. water
6 cloves
   flour
   sherry, 1 tbsp. each plate

Boil the turtle with cloves and bay-leaves till soft. Keep the stock. Take out the bones of the turtle. Fry the onion in butter, then thicken with a little flour. Pour the stock over it and add the meat. Cream the yolks of the eggs, and add them with the sherry when ready to serve. If there are many eggs in the turtle, the yolks of two hen eggs only need be used, mashed, and added.

ROYAL CONSOMMÉ
Mrs. Shaw Putman

1 turkey or chicken carcass
1 large soup bone
1 large veal knuckle
3 calves feet
   salt and pepper to taste

Boil these slowly with salt and pepper for 1½ hours. Skim. Add:

1 stalk celery
3 green peppers
6 onions
6 carrots
½ bunch parsley
10 cloves
2 bay leaves
½ teaspoon mace
1 teaspoon Kitchen Bouquet
1 teaspoon Creole Seasoning
2 lemons, the juice
2 lemons, the rind
1 orange, the rind
   several dashes of Tabasco

Boil two hours. Cool and skim carefully. Put back on fire, add shells of 3 eggs. Boil 5 minutes, remove and strain. When cold, strain through flannel bag dipped in ice water.

OYSTER PURÉE

4 doz. oysters
½ tablespoon butter
3 pts. breakfast cream
   pinch of mace, or grated nutmeg
   pinch of cayenne
   pepper, salt to taste
   bit of grated celery
   bit of grated onion

Heat the cream.

Plump the oysters in their own liquor at very slow heat until they curl; skin them, and use only the soft part Chop them very fine. Add the grated celery, onion and seasoning. Mix with the hot cream and serve.

BOUILLON ST. CHARLES

a large beef soup bone with
  plenty of meat on it
a small veal knuckle
1 stalk celery, cut fine
1 bunch carrots, cut fine
6 onions, chopped fine
1 qt. can tomatoes
   thyme, bay leaf, 8 cloves

Wash meat, cover with 1½ gals. cold water and allow to stand for an hour or longer. Then place on fire and bring to a quick boil and boil for fifteen minutes. Skim. Reduce the heat, simmer for two hours, then add the seasonings and the vegetables, salt and pepper. Simmer two hours longer. Strain and color, if desired, by adding two teaspoonfuls of sugar which have been carmalled. This is delicious hot or cold.

RED BEAN SOUP

1 lb. red beans (kidney beans)
1 whole onion
½ lb. sweet pickled pork, boiled
     separately until tender

Soak the beans overnight and in the morning discard the water in which they have been soaking. Put on to boil in a pot with two or three quarts of water. Do not salt at this point as the salt toughens the beans. Add more water if necessary and cook till the beans are very soft. There should be enough to serve six persons generously. Now pour through a colander mashing and pressing the beans through until only the skins remain. Place on the stove again with the cooked meat added and salt to taste. A few whole cloves will improve the flavor if liked. Just before serving add a glass of cooking sherry. Serve a thin slice of lemon and a slice of hard boiled egg in each bowl. This is a favorite lunch of New Orleans school children and is a hearty meal in itself with a green salad to balance.

BLACK BEAN SOUP

1 qt. dried black beans
2 tablespoons sherry wine
1 hard boiled egg
1 small shin beef bone
2 stalks celery, minced
1 large lemon
  few cloves, or allspice

Soak the beans overnight. Next morning, put the soaked beans on to boil with the beef shin and plenty of cold water. Boil till the meat leaves the bone. Take out the beans and mash them through a colander. Put the meat and the beans back into the pot and add the wine, the lemon, the egg, and the spice. Boil up once and serve.

TOMATO BISQUE

1 can tomatoes
1 onion, medium sized
1 teaspoon sugar
1 tablespoon butter
1 pt. boiled milk
1 tablespoon flour
  pinch of soda, salt, and red pepper

Cook the tomatoes and onion in a double boiler with the other ingredients, except the milk, until they are thoroughly done. Then press through a colander. Thicken with butter and flour rubbed together. In a separate pot bring the milk to a boil and combine with the first mixture. Do not boil again. Serve at once.

ICED TOMATO SOUP MEXICAINE

Use sufficient tomato juice to serve the required number. Season to taste with salt, pepper, pinch of cayenne, and a very little sugar. Shave into it a few slivers of fresh green bell pepper, white onion, and celery. Chill and serve in flat soup plates with a lump of ice in each plate. This is very refreshing and easy to prepare.

MOCK TURTLE SOUP
Mrs. Frank Hemenway

2 lbs. round steak or soup meat
2 onions
½ cup flour
2 quarts water
1 cup sherry
3 bay leavves, cloves to taste and thyme. Tie all in a cloth
  salt and pepper

Fry meat and onions in a little lard until brown. Remove them from the fat and stir in the flour and brown well. Return the meat and onions, add the tomatoes, stirring constantly to prevent lumping, till well blended. Add water and spices and simmer for three or four hours. Strain through a colander, add sherry, and serve a thin slice of lemon and a slice of hard boiled egg in each bowl.

OXTAIL SOUP à LUCIE

3 tablespoons, level, bacon drippings
2 ox tails
1 medium sized onion
1 carrot
2 sprigs parsley
1 bay leaf
1 stalk celery
1 quart cold water or stock
1 tablespoon pearl barley
1 teaspoon cold water
¼ cup sherry
  salt and pepper
  flour

Melt the fat and fry in it, the diced carrot and onion, then the ox tails which have been cut in pieces. When brown, add water and celery, parsley, and bayleaf tied together in small bag. When it comes to a boil, put in the barley and let simmer four hours. Remove the largest bones, and the bag of seasoning, and thicken the soup with flour, rubbed smooth with a tablespoon of cold water. Season rather highly, add the sherry, and serve.

BRAIN SOUP BONNE FEMME

2 sets calf's brains
1 qt. boiling water
2 tablespoons lemon juice
1 tablespoon salt
1 qt. milk
1 tablespoon butter, heaping
1 slice breakfast bacon
  salt, white pepper to taste
  crackers

Wash and skin the brains and plump in ice water for one hour.

Next, plunge them into boiling water with the lemon juice and the salt. Boil gently 30 minutes.

In another stewpan, put the milk with the butter, bacon, salt and pepper. Heat this.

When the brains are done, chop them up and pour the milk into the stewpan with the brains and the water in which they were cooked. Let all come to a boil and pour over toasted soda crackers.

MUSHROOM SOUP
Mrs. Erasmus Darwin Fenner

1 lb. fresh mushrooms
1 tablespoon flour
5 drops Cream of Teche Sauce
1 pt. milk
½ pt. whipping cream
  salt, pepper to taste

Boil the mushrooms 20 minutes. Strain them and grind them in a fine food chopper. Put the butter in a saucepan, blend in the flour, add the liquid in which the mushrooms were boiled, and cook until thick. Then add the mushrooms. Season, and add the pepper sauce. Just before serving, add the milk, boiling, and cream.

MUSHROOM SOUP

½ lb. fresh mushrooms
2 tablespoons flour
1 qt. milk
1 cup meat, or chicken, stock
   butter, size of an egg

Peel the mushrooms and cut them up fine. Put the butter in the frying pan and, when sizzling hot, add the chopped mushrooms, then the flour that has been well-mixed with a little butter. Let the milk come to a boil in double-boiler, add mixture and cup of stock and serve.

FRAPPÉED TOMATO SOUP

1 cup cream
3 cups tomato juice
1 onion grated
2 stalks celery grated
½ coffeespoon Tabasco
   salt to taste

Put in cocktail shaker filled with ice and shake well. Serve very cold in cups. This is delicious frozen.

CHICKEN SOUP ONORATO

1 three or four pound hen
½ lb. blanched almonds
1 cup cream

Boil the hen until tender and reserve the stock. Take the white meat and grind it, using the fine blade of the grinder. Grind the almonds. Combine both. Add to the meat and nuts the cream. Stir until smooth, add the stock in which the hen was cooked and boil gently for about an hour. Season, strain and serve poured over thin slices of toast.

PURÉE OF CHESTNUT SOUP

4 cups chicken stock, or consommé
2 cups chestnuts, boiled and mashed
1 slice onion
¼ teaspoon celery salt
2 cups cream
¼ cup butter
2 tablespoons flour
   salt, pepper

Cook the stock with the chestnuts, slice of onion and celery salt, for ten minutes. Rub through a sieve, add cream, and combine with the other ingredients. Season highly.

CREAM OF CORN SOUP
Mrs. William Westerfield

1 can corn (golden bantam)
⅓ can water
1 large whole onion
1 pt. milk
1 tablespoon flour, heaping
2 tablespoons butter
   dash of Tabasco
   salt to taste
   whipped cream

Add the water to the corn, then put in the onion, set in a double boiler and cook 1 hour.

Make a thin cream sauce with the milk, flour and butter.

Press corn through a sieve, add the thin cream sauce, Tabasco and salt.

Heat, serve with a spoon of whipped cream on each cup.

ONION SOUP
Served in Petits Marmites
Mrs. Herbert N. Cook

4 or 5 medium onions
2 tablespoons butter
1 qt. stock, chicken, beef, or
   vegetable
   bread
   Parmesan cheese, grated

Slice the onions and fry until light brown, in butter.

Put onions in well seasoned stock and allow to simmer twenty minutes.

Cut bread in thin rounds, and toast. Place one round in each marmite, sprinkle lightly with cheese. Pour broth with onions over this, then cover with another round of toast, sprinkling it also with Parmesan cheese. Run in the oven under flames long enough to melt the cheese. Place covers on marmites and serve very hot. Thin slices of imported Swiss cheese added just before serving are a pleasant addition.

BOILED FISH

    3   or 4 lb. redfish or red snapper
    3   bay leaves, thyme
    ½   onion
    2   tablespoons salt
    ½   lemon sliced with peel

Tie the fish up in a piece of bobinet. Into enough water to cover the fish, put all the ingredients. Let it come to a boil, put in fish and cook until thoroughly tender, about 20 to 30 minutes.

Remove and drain well. It may be served hot with egg sauce with capers, oyster sauce, drawn butter, or, cold with mayonnaise and garnished with quartered tomatoes, asparagus ringed with green peppers, or something of the sort.

BROILED FISH CHARPENTIER

    3   lbs. red snapper or trout,
          tenderloined
    3   tablespoons olive oil
    1   lemon, the juice
          salt, pepper, garlic

Rub the fish with the garlic and season with salt and pepper. Pour over the olive oil and the lemon juice. Place on the broiler and cook under the flame turning once and allowing ten minutes to each side. Serve with the following sauce;

    1   cup each shrimp and crab meat
    1   onion, minced
    1   tablespoon lard
    ½   cup sherry wine
          salt, cayenne pepper
          thick white sauce

Fry the finely minced onion in the lard, add the crab and shrimp meat. Season with the salt and red pepper. Add all to the thick white sauce and thin with the wine. Pour over the broiled fish and garnish with thin slices of lemon and fresh parsley. Serve very hot.

RED FISH—SHAH OF PERSIA
Marguerite Clark

    7   to 8 lbs. red fish
    2   quarts water
    2   onions
    1   stalk celery
          bay leaf, parsley, thyme
          red pepper and salt to taste

Make highly seasoned stock using two quarts water, celery, onions and all seasonings. Place fish on rack, lower into hot stock and cook 20 to 25 minutes until done, keeping tightly covered. Remove fish and reduce stock to about two cups. Separate all fish from the bones and arrange in warm casserole from which it is to be served. Cover and place in warmer. Serve with Sauce Marguerite, page 69.

FISH MARTINIQUE
Mrs. Shaw Putnam

    1   chicken carcass (Add water and
          boil down to 4 cups of broth)
    6   lbs. flounder filet
    1   can truffles
    1   can grapes, peeled and skinned
    4   tablespoons butter
    3   eggs
    1   can mushrooms
    1   cup cream
    ½   cup sweet white wine
    ½   cup dry white wine
    4   tablespoons flour
    ½   cup lemon juice
    ½   cup onion juice
          parsley, finely chopped

Soak grapes in wine for 2 hours before starting dish. Lightly brown mushrooms in butter, add flour. When smooth add the chicken broth and wine. Cream the yolks of eggs and butter. Add this and onion juice and the cream, and grapes. Cook only a few minutes. Remove from fire, add lemon juice to taste, salt and Tabasco. Lay in rows in a shallow pyrex baking dish the fillets of flounder which have been boiled and carefully cleaned of bones. Pour the sauce over fish, flooding generously. Slice the truffles and dot around in dish, pushing some down into the fish. Dot liberally with butter. Sprinkle lightly with powdered parsley. Do not let dish get cold. Run under hot flame only long enough to get a rich brown.

Serve with thin, crisp, sliced icecold cucumber salad with highly seasoned French dressing.

FISH TIMBALE

    5   lb. red snapper
    1   stick butter
    1   pt. cream
    6   eggs
          salt, Tabasco Sauce
          celery, bay leaf, cayenne

Boil the fish with a piece of celery, a couple of bay leaves, salt and cayenne in the water. Carefully remove all bones and beat with a wooden spoon until light. Add the butter, cream, yolks of eggs, salt to taste, and Tabasco. Beat thoroughly then fold in the stiffly beaten egg whites. Place in a well buttered mold, securely covered. Place in a pan of water, taking care that there is not enough water to seep into the mold, and bake ½ hour. This quantity will serve ten or twelve people. Serve with a medium thick cream sauce to which a cup of finely chopped mushrooms has been added.

FISH SOUFFLÉ

1 small red fish
½ lemon, sliced
2 bay leaves
1 pinch thyme
1 pod red pepper
1 large pinch salt
2 cloves garlic
1 large heaping tablespoon butter
3 egg whites, well beaten
2 tablespoons minced parsley
  a dash of cayenne pepper

Put the fish in a deep pan and cover with water. Add salt, red pepper, lemon, bay leaf, thyme, garlic, and salt to the water in which the fish is boiling. Cook the fish until done, about 20 minutes. Remove from water and take off the skin and bones and flake the fish. Put the butter in a sauce pan and add flour and a little salt and the milk. Add minced parsley and a dash of cayenne pepper. Cook about 5 minutes, then add flaked fish. When well blended, take off the fire and add two teaspoons of lemon juice. Stir well and add stiffly beaten whites of eggs. Put in a buttered casserole, sprinkle with bread crumbs and put a little melted butter on top. Put the casserole in another vessel of hot water and bake for 15 minutes.

SAUCE

4 tablespoons butter
2 tablespoons flour
2 cups fish stock, strained
2 egg yolks
¾ cup sherry wine
2 tablespoons chopped parsley
1 teaspoonful lemon juice

Blend butter with flour in top of double boiler, slowly add the fish stock and stir until smooth. Lower flame and add the slightly beaten egg yolks always stirring slowly, then add lemon juice. When sauce becomes quite thick, remove from fire and add the sherry and parsley. Pour over the fish and serve at once. This will serve ten people.

VOL-AU-VENT BERCY
Mrs. Edwin French

  large pastry shell
3 to 4 lb. sheepshead, boiled and boned
2 lbs. boiled shrimp
1 lb. crab meat
1 lb. broiled fresh mushrooms
  Sauce
¼ lb. butter
2 tablespoons flour
2 cups cream
1 cup vin Bercy or any other white wine or sherry

The fish should be boiled with ½ lemon, pod of red pepper, ½ cup freezing salt, bay-leaf, thyme, and ½ clove garlic.

Make a cream sauce, using a double boiler with the butter, flour and cream and cook it until it begins to thicken, then add the other ingredients, the wine last of all. Season to taste. Put all in pastry shell and pass through a hot oven for 3 minutes.

Noteworthy, even in this New Orleans millieu where there are so many noteworthy fish dishes.

"KEGAREE"
Mrs. Curran Perkins

  red snapper, salmon, trout or any other large fish, 3 or 4 lbs.
1 cup boiled rice
1 small onion, chopped
2 tablespoons melted butter
2 hard boiled eggs
4 bay leaves, 6 cloves, parsley

Boil the fish, with cloves and bay-leaves and break up the eggs, white and yolks together and mix well with rice, onion and parsley. A little mashed potato mixed with it is an improvement. Add the butter, then the fish. put in a baking dish and bake quickly. Garnish with sliced hard-boiled eggs.

KEDGEREE
Mrs. John May

1 cup salmon
2 tablespoons cooked rice
4 hard-boiled eggs
1 tablespoon butter
  seasoning

Simmer for about 10 minutes.

COD FISH CAKES
Mrs. Frank H. Lawton

3 cups shredded cod fish
3 cups mashed potatoes
3 teaspoons onion juice
2 eggs
½ stick butter (⅛ lb.)
  black pepper

Buy cod fish by the pound, soak in cold water. Put in fresh cold water and boil for several hours until easily shredded. Boil potatoes and mash, adding a half stick of butter.

Mix cod fish and potatoes, adding onion juice and eggs, beating in one egg at a time and black pepper, salt if necessary.

Both the cod fish and potatoes must be warm when mixed. Shape the cakes suitable for a portion. Flour well on both sides, set aside to cool and cook in deep fat. The cakes should be creamy inside and brown on the outside. Serve with crisp bacon and tomato catsup. Canned cod flakes may be substituted.

TROUT-WHITE-WINE-SAUCE

    3   lbs. trout
    3   tablespoons olive oil
    2   chopped onions
    6   tablespoons butter
    2   tablespoons flour
    1   lemon
    1   doz. shrimp, cut fine
    3   truffles, cut fine
    ½   can mushrooms
   12   oysters
    1   glass white wine

Skin and bone trout, cut in six pieces, fold over and put in pan with olive oil, a few onions, salt and pepper to taste. Place in oven to cook. Take another pan, blend flour, butter and lemon juice over fire, add shrimp, mushrooms, truffles, oysters and wine. Pour all over fish. Sprinkle with bread crumbs and cheese, dot with butter and run in stove again to heat very hot.

SCALLOPED OYSTERS

    2   dozen large oysters
    2   large tablespoons butter
    2   tablespoons Worcestershire Sauce
    ½   teaspoon Tabasco Sauce
    1   tablespoon minced parsley
    ½   lemon, the juice
    6   crackers, rolled fine
    2   tablespoons sherry wine

Drain all liquor from oysters and melt butter with Worcestershire Sauce, Tabasco Sauce and lemon juice. Roll crackers fine and roll oysters in cracker crumbs. Put alternate layers of oysters and butter sauce into the casserole until it is filled, having crackers on top layer. Put in hot oven and bake for 15 minutes or until brown. When done, remove from oven, pour over the oysters 2 tablespoons of sherry wine and serve immediately.

BAKED OYSTERS EMIL

Put oysters on half shell on platter or pie tin half filled with rock salt. Cover with thousand island dressing, then plenty of grated sharp cheese on top. Put in very hot oven 5 or 6 minutes.

POMPANO EN PAPILLOTTES
(To Serve Six)

    3   medium sized pompano, cut into
          six filets
    2   cups crab meat
    2   eggs, the yolks only
    1   pint fish stock, made by boiling
          the heads and bones of the fish
    1   large tablespoon butter
    4   onions, chopped
    4   truffles, chopped
    1   cup mushrooms, chopped
    2   ozs. white wine
    1   tablespoon flour

The filets are boiled for five minutes in salted water. The crab meat is sautéed in butter and a dash of white wine for five minutes. The sauce is prepared by cooking the chopped onions, truffles and mushrooms in the butter about five to ten minutes. The fish stock is added to them, a little being reserved to rub with the flour to a smooth paste. When the stock has simmered with the onions, mushrooms and truffles about ten minutes, the flour paste is slowly stirred in and it is allowed to cook down until quite thick, then add egg yolks. It is seasoned to taste with salt and pepper and the wine is added. It is immediately removed from the fire, not being allowed to cook after the addition of the wine. Each filet is then folded over with a generous spoonful of the sautéed crab meat in the fold and is placed in a paper cooking bag. It is liberally dressed with the sauce, some being placed within the fold as well as over the fish. The bag is securely folded and the whole baked for ten minutes in a hot oven. It is served piping hot in the bag in which it is cooked, which is cut open at the table.

TROUT MEUNIÈRE AMANDES
Arnaud

Filet of trout is dipped in milk, then seasoned with salt and pepper. After that it is dipped in flour so that both sides are well covered. The next step is a saucepan where butter has been heated. The trout is dropped into this, turned as it cooks, so that it may brown evenly on both sides.

Remove it from the saucepan to a warm platter, drop chopped almonds a moment into the butter where the trout was cooked, and sprinkle them thickly over the fish.

CREAM OF FISH
Mrs. Edgar Bright

    1   3-lb. trout
    4   ozs. butter
    2   eggs, the yolks
    ¼   pt. thick cream
        salt, pepper

Bone the raw fish and pound to a pulp. Add the butter and yolks, well beaten, pound again, and season with salt and pepper. Rub through a hair sieve into a bowl, work the mixture with a wooden spoon until quite light, adding the cream gradually. Put mixture in greased mold and set it into a pan of water to steam, but not to boil, for 20 minutes. Serve with mushroom sauce, with a few shrimp or oysters added.

BOUILLABAISSE
à la Nouvelle-Orléans

1	lb. red fish, red snapper, or trout
2	cloves garlic
4	tomatoes
1	tablespoon parsley
3	onions
½	cup olive oil
1	pinch saffron
	salt, pepper to taste

Put the olive oil in a saucepan, add chopped tomatoes, onions, garlic and parsley. Let all this simmer, then throw in a good pinch of saffron, season with salt and pepper to taste. Now put in sliced fish, cover with water and bring to a boil. Cover the saucepan well and allow the fish to boil gently for 10 to 12 minutes. Sprinkle the purée and fish with parsley. Serve on slices of French toast.

FISH ROE
Mrs. Walter Torian

Roll fish roe in cornmeal.
Fry in butter.
Fine for breakfast or light luncheon with biscuits and cup of coffee.

COD ROE AND BACON
Mrs. Alfred T. Pattison

1	tin fine cod roe
½	lb. butter
1	lemon, the juice
½	whole lemon
1	tbsp. parsley, chopped fine
12	slices very thin bacon

Remove roe from tin carefully so as to keep it whole. Cut into six thick rounds. Sprinkle with a little lemon juice. Fry in butter until a light brown, being careful not to break rounds. When done pour over these rounds a maître d'hotel sauce made with 3 tablespoons butter, 2 tablespoons lemon juice and 1 tablespoon chopped parsley. Serve with curls of bacon. Curls of bacon are made by rolling each slice of bacon into small roll and cooking as one cooks other bacon. Serve piping hot.

COURTBOUILLON BARATARIA

1	red snapper or red fish, 3 or 4 lbs.
½	dozen allspice, well mashed
3	sprigs thyme
6	sprigs parsley
1	bay leaf
1	large onion
1	clove garlic
6	large fresh tomatoes
1	qt. water, or more
1	lemon, the juice
3	tablespoons flour
3	tablespoons butter
1	cup claret
1	tablespoon Worcestershire Sauce
	salt, cayenne or Tabasco to taste

Prepare 6 slices of the fish, put a pint of water over the cut up head and boil it, adding onion, garlic, bay leaf, and tomatoes. When this is cooked down, pour in a deep skillet ½ cup of olive oil, put in the slices of fish, cover it with the liquid from the heads and add a pint of water. Meanwhile, make a roux of the flour and butter, stirring to a smooth paste, then stir into the fish, add the claret and lastly the Worcestershire Sauce.

This is pronounced in Louisiana "coobouillon" and is considered a rare delight.

FILET OF FLOUNDER À LA MARSEILLES

6	to 8 filets of flounder
1	onion
2	tablespoons butter
3	cups rich soup stock
2	tablespoons flour, sifted
½	cup thick cream
½	cup Parmesan cheese
½	cup chopped almonds

Cut the filet in narrow strips, roll each strip and fasten with a toothpick. Fry the chopped onion in butter, add the stock, cook the filet in this until done, when it must be removed to a baking dish. The sauce is then thickened by stirring in slowly the flour which has been stirred to a thin, smooth paste with a little water. After it has cooked a few minutes add the cream and pour over the fish. The cheese and almonds are sprinkled over the top and the dish run under the broiler to brown.

FILET OF FLOUNDER LOUIS 13th
Antoine's—Roy Alciatore

"Take some choice green onions, chop them very finely and sauté them in the finest butter obtainable. Then take some fresh mushrooms, chop very finely and add this to the green onions, cook for about five minutes and then add a wine glass full of the best dry white wine. Cook again for five minutes.

Then take a sole or flounder, remove the filet and cook in white wine, green onions, butter, and season with salt, pepper, and a bouquet of thyme, bay-leaf and celery. Moisten with oyster water.

Take a silver dish, fill the bottom with the mushrooms cooked with green onions and white wine. Lay the filet of flounder on top of this.

Then to the sauce in which the fish was cooked add some rich cream and allow to cook a while longer. Cover the sole with this sauce and on top of this sprinkle some grated Parmesan cheese. Pass this under the salamander (overhead fire).

Garnish the sides of the dish with Duchesse potatoes sprinkled with chopped pistachio nuts and serve."

FILET OF TROUT

```
6   or 8 filets of trout or pompano
2   cups béchamel sauce
1   cup stock
1   cup mushrooms
1   lb. shrimp
2   doz. oysters
    sherry
    chopped shallots
    salt, pepper, bay leaf, thyme
```

The fish is boiled with the seasonings. To the béchamel sauce is added the stock in which the fish was boiled, the chopped mushrooms, chopped shrimp, chopped oysters, and a dash of sherry at the last.

White wrapping paper closely grained and fairly thick is cut in double ovals (roughly fish shaped) somewhat larger than the filets; the paper is oiled and a thick layer of the sauce is placed on one of the double ovals, next the fish, and another thinner layer of sauce. The other oval is folded over, like a cover and the edges of the two ovals are folded together in order to seal in well the luscious contents.

Before serving, a little arc near the edge is cut into the top of the paper with a sharp knife, so that the guests may take out the fish. Judgment must guide the proportions of the ingredients. No dish has contributed so largely to the culinary fame of New Orleans.

TROUT MARGUERY

Clean, skin and bone your fish. Cut in filets, tenderloin and roll them. Put three tablespoons of olive oil in the pan with the fish; and season with salt and pepper. Add ½ glass of water, and bake in a hot oven. When cooked dress on platter. Use Hollandaise Sauce No. 1.

OYSTERS ROCKEFELLER
Broussard

Take out the oysters, wash them, and drain them. Put them back in the shells, set on a pan of hot ice-cream salt, and run them under flames of the gas stove for five minutes, then cover them with the sauce described below, and run under the flame until the sauce melts and browns.

SAUCE

```
2   bunches spinach
1   bunch fresh anis
1   bunch shallots
1   pt. oyster water
```

```
1   pt. plain water
2   lbs. best butter
1   cup ground bread crumbs, toasted
    and sifted
6   ozs. absinthe
    small sprig thyme
```

Grind all the vegetables in the meat grinder. Put the water and the oyster liquor together, and let boil vigorously until reduced to a pint, then add the ground vegetables and cook twenty minutes.

Stir in the butter, then add the toasted bread-crumbs and the absinthe. Put in jars and set in the refrigerator. It will keep two weeks or more. (The quantities given are for a large amount of sauce: smaller ones may be used in proportion).

OYSTER ROCKEFELLER SAUCE

```
1   bunch green spinach
2   small bunches green onions
3   bunches green celery
1   bunch parsley
1   head green lettuce
1   lb. butter
1   handful bread crumbs
3   tablespoons Worcestershire Sauce
3   tablespoons anchovy sauce
2   oz. absinthe
```

Chop all greens together very fine and mix the butter, the bread crumbs to thicken, Worcestershire Sauce and anchovy sauce. Season with salt and Tabasco, also absinthe, if available. Mix all together. Put this butter sauce over your oysters that are on half shell. Cover with Parmesan cheese and fine bread crumbs. Bake in hot oven until brown. Serve.

OYSTERS À LA POULETTE

```
2   doz. oysters
¾   cup sherry
3   beaten egg yolks
1   tablespoon chopped parsley
1   tablespoon chopped green onion
1   pod garlic
¼   lb. butter
2   tablespoons flour, heaping
1   dozen whole cloves
    salt and pepper to taste
```

First, drain oysters and save liquor.

Second, melt butter and stir into it the flour until smooth, gradually adding oyster water, salt, pepper, and cloves.

Third, add oysters and chopped garlic. Let simmer until oysters curl.

Fourth, take out some of the cream sauce (about ½ teacup) and add ½ of the three beaten egg yolks and part of the sherry. Stir well and add to the oysters. Then take more of the sauce in cup and add to the remainder of egg yolks and sherry, and then add to the oysters. Add, lastly, onions and parsley, and serve. A very fine old French recipe. Garlic can be omitted if flavor is not desired.

OYSTER à la POULETTE
Mrs. Edgar H. Bright

1   pt. oysters
1   tablespoon butter
2   egg yolks
2   tablespoons flour
1½ cups cream
½   cup oyster liquor
    dash of nutmeg
    salt, cayenne and black pepper

Set the oysters on the stove to heat in their own liquor. As soon as they come to a boil, skim carefully and turn them into a strainer.

Now make white sauce with liquor, the flour and 1 cup of the cream. Season with salt, pepper and a bit of nutmeg and a grain of cayenne.

Add ½ cup of cream or milk, to the well-beaten egg-yolks, add to sauce, place the oysters in the sauce and cook over hot water for three minutes, stirring all the while. Remove from the fire to prevent them from separating. Serve on puff-paste or on buttered toast. Add the juice of half a lemon as the oysters are taken from the fire.

STEAMED OYSTERS

3   doz. oysters
1   tablespoon butter
½   teaspoon salt
1   tablespoon parsley

Put the oysters in a colander, and let cold water run through. Then put them over a pot of boiling water and cover to steam until the edges curl. Then turn them on to a hot dish or platter, pour melted butter with parsley and salt over them and serve at once. They require about 5 minutes to cook. Serve with lemon.

OYSTERS WITH BELL PEPPERS
Mrs. Shaw Putman

4   dozen oysters
3   large bell peppers
1   pound American cheese, grated
1   pint oyster liquor
1   pint milk
2   egg yolks
2   tablespoons corn starch
1   cup butter
1   teaspoon Kitchen Bouquet
    Tabasco, black pepper

Strain the oyster liquor and put on to boil with the three green peppers ground through a meat chopper. After they have boiled until quite soft, add the oysters and salt to taste (and in correct salting, lies the success of the dish). Cook for five minutes and add milk, corn starch, eggs and butter which have been creamed smoothly together, Kitchen Bouquet, a generous dash of Tabasco, and three-fourths teeaspoonful of black pepper. When the mixture has thickened, put in the cheese. Stir constantly. The cheese should be dissolved and smooth in less than five minutes. Serve on thin slices of very crisp buttered toast.

OYSTERS & FRESH MUSHROOMS

3   doz. large oysters
1   cup milk
2   tablespoons flour
½   lb. fresh mushrooms
2   shallots
1   sprig parsley
1   tablespoon butter
1   cup oyster liquor
1   teaspoon salt
1   pinch cayenne pepper
½   coffee spoon black pepper
½   cup cream

Simmer oysters in own liquor until edges curl. Drain oysters. Make cream souce with one cup of milk, 1 cup oyster liquor, ½ cup cream, 1 tablespoon butter. Mince the shallots and parsley, and add salt and pepper. Smother the mushrooms with a little butter until tender and add to the cream sauce. Then add oysters and serve hot.

BOHEMIAN OYSTERS
Mrs. Shaw Putnam

4   dozen oysters
1   pound noodles
1   pint milk
1   pint oyster liquor
1   pound American cheese
2   egg yolks
2   tablespoonfuls corn starch
1   cup butter
1   teaspoon Kitchen Bouquet
    dash of Tabasco

Place a large iron skillet or iron pot on the fire, and let it get very hot.

Drain the oysters, and throw them into the pot so that they stick and appear to scorch.

Stir with a cake turner so as to scrape up that portion of the juice and oysters which have stuck to the hot pot, as this gives a delightful flavor to the dish.

Salt, and remember you are salting for the finished dish, not for the few oysters in the pot.

At the end of five minutes, when the oysters are at least partially cooked, add the pint of oyster liquor and the pint of milk. When this is hot, add the eggs, corn starch and butter, which have been creamed together, Kitchen Bouquet and a dash of Tabasco.

When the mixture is thick and creamy, remove from the fire.

The noodles, in the meantime, should have been boiled with salt until very tender, and drained. Have the cheese grated. (It is better to buy the cheese the day previous as it grates better when not too fresh).

In a large casserole, place a layer

of noodles, about an inch deep. Divide the oysters into three parts, and cover the noodles with one-third of the oysters. Flood liberally with the sauce, and then cover the layer thickly with grated cheese. Sprinkle with black pepper. Add another layer of noodles, a third of the oysters, sauce and cheese. Finally the third layer of noodles, the remaining third of the oysters, and enough of the sauce to flood the dish generously, sprinkle thickly with the cheese and dust with black pepper.

Put in the oven for 20 minutes before serving. All of the ingredients being cooked the dish should not be allowed to remain in oven longer than this, as the cheese otherwise bakes into a crust, whereas it should only melt. Twenty minutes is sufficient to make the dish very hot when served.

BAKED OYSTER BOURGINGNONE
"La Louisiane"

Shallots, very little garlic, few anchovies, fresh walnut meat, all chopped fine and sautéed in butter. Pour over oysters on half shell, bake and serve with a piece of bacon.

BAKED OYSTERS GRAND ISLE
    4   doz. oysters
    1   stick (¼ lb.) butter
    1   onion
    2   stalks celery
    1   coffee spoon garlic
    1   tablespoon flour, heaping
    3   tablespoons Worcestershire Sauce
    1   small can mushrooms
    1   can tomatoes, small
        cayenne pepper, salt to taste

Melt butter, add onion, celery, garlic and flour. Strain in tomatoes. Add salt and pepper to taste. Worcestershire Sauce, mushrooms and oysters last. Cook till the oysters curl. Put in baking dish, sprinkle with cracker crumbs, dot with butter and bake for 15 minutes.

FRIED OYSTERS

Take fine large oysters, free them from all small particles of shell. Put them into a colander and pour over a little water to rinse them. Place in a clean towel and dry them. Have ready some cracker dust, very fine, which season with salt and pepper and cayenne pepper of equal proportions. Beat as many eggs and cream mixed as will moisten all oysters. Dip each oyster in the eggs and cream and lay them in the cracker dust and pat with the back of a spoon. Pack the cracker-dust close to the oyster, lay them on a dish and so continue until all are done. Put in a frying pan an equal portion of butter and lard. Wren boiling hot, put as many oysters as the pan will hold without their touching and fry quickly a light brown on both sides. A few minutes will cook them.

OYSTER CROQUETTES
    4   to 5 doz. oysters
    2   tablespoons minced onion
    1   tablespoon parsley, finely chopped
    1   tablespoon butter
    4   eggs
    5   drops Tabasco
    2   level tablespoons Crisco

Drain the oysters and chop them very fine, removing the hard part.

Heat Crisco and cook in this the minced onion and parsley, then the oysters and cook a few minutes. Season highly.

Cool, add the eggs well beaten, the butter and a little cream. Mold in croquette form (if necessary add a little cracker crumbs) then put in the refrigerator to harden. Bake in the oven until light brown, serve with tartar sauce or mushroom sauce.

OYSTER PIE
    1   pint oysters
    4   hard boiled eggs
    ½   cup oyster liquor
    4   tablespoonfuls butter
    ½   cup milk

PIE PASTRY
    2   cups flour
    2   tablespoons lard
    1. teaspoon baking powder
        pinch of salt, milk to soften

Line a deep pan with thinly rolled out pastry and then put a layer of oysters in bottom with layer of sliced eggs next, dotted with bits of butter and salt and pepper and then repeat layers. Next pour in milk and oyster liquor and sift a light powder of flour over the liquid and then put on the top pastry making large cut openings to let the steam out. Bake in over 30 or 40 minutes or until pastry is nicely browned.

OYSTERS ALEXANDRIA
Mrs. Richard Franklin White
    3   dozen oysters
    1   tablespoon butter
    2   tablespoons flour
    1   medium sized onion
    1   small can tomatoes
    ½   cup oyster liquor, or more
        Parsley, green onion tops, sweet
        pepper, celery salt, pepper, cay-
        enne, Worcestershire Sauce

Brown the flour in the butter, with minced onion and cook a few minutes, then add the tomatoes, slowly, and stirring constantly. Add all green seasonings, chopped fine, also salt, pepper, cayenne, and Worcestershire. Add oyster liquor but do not make too thin as the oysters, which are added last will thin the sauce somewhat. Cook three minutes and serve

on a hot platter. Cover with crou-
tons.

This dish may be varied by using
one-third oysters, one-third crab meat
and one-third shrimp.

OYSTERS FARCIS
Mrs. Frank S. Walshe

    3   dozen large oysters
    1   cup shallots, minced
    1   cup parsley, minced
    ½   cup celery, minced
    1   stick of butter (or, better, bacon
            drippings
    1   tablespoon flour
    ½   cup dried bread crumbs
    1   egg
    6   large oyster shells
        cayenne, salt to taste

Heat the oysters until plump.
Drain and cut into small pieces. Melt
butter, cook onions, parsley, celery.
Add the flour, oysters and bread
crumbs. Season to taste. Remove
from the fire. Mix in the beaten egg.
When cool, fill shells, cover with
bread crumbs and dot with butter.
Put aside until a few moments before ready to serve, then run into the
oven to brown, and serve piping hot.

SWEETBREADS WITH OYSTERS

    2   sweetbreads
    2   dozen oysters
    1   cup white stock
    ¼   cup butter
    2   tablespoons flour
    1   wineglass cream
        pepper, salt, nutmeg, bayleaf

The sweetbreads must be soaked,
parboiled, aand trimmed. Place in a
saucepan with the white stock, strained oyster liquor and seasonings. Allow to simmer 20 minutes. Put the
butter in a saucepan and stir in the
flour slowly, add some of the stock in
which the sweetbreads are cooking,
slowly, stirring all the time to prevent lumping. Finally add the rest
of the stock and the sweetbreads.
After a few minutes cooking, add the
oysters and cook until they curl. Just
before serving add the cream. A
touch of luxury is attained by larding
the sweetbreads with truffles.

LOBSTER, CRABMEAT OR
CRAWFISH à la NEWBERG
Mrs. Alfred T. Pattison

    2   cups cooked lobster, crabmeat or
            crawfish cut into small pieces.
            Crawfish should be left whole.
    1   tea cup whipping cream
    3   egg yolks
    1   tea cup cooking sherry
    2   green onions or shallots
    1   saltspoon salt
        dash of cayenne and paprika
        heaping teaspoonful butter
        sprigs of parsley tied into a bouquet

Put meat, butter, salt, cayenne,
paprika and bouquet of shallots and
parsley in a double boiler, preferably

a chafing dish. Let cook for five
minutes. Add cooking sherry and
cook until sherry begins to simmer. Remove bouquet of shallots and
parsley. Mix egg yolks throughly
in cream. Add to mixture. Stir
constantly, without allowing to
boil. As soon as mixture begins to
thicken serve immediately, as the
sauce will curdle if cooking is con-
tinued too long after adding cream
and eggs. The secret of success is
in the seasoning.

FRENCH FRIED SCALLOPS
Mrs. Grace Stevenson

        scallops
        lemon juice
        egg
        garlic juice

Soak scallops in lemon juice, roll
in well beaten egg to which a dash of
garlic juice has been added, then in
well seasoned dry bread crumbs,
again in egg, and crumbs. Fry at
350° until golden brown. Serve
with tartar sauce.

CRAWFISH NEWBERG
(Or Crab, Shrimp or Lobster)
Mrs. E. T. Merrick

    1½ cups shrimp, crawfish, or crabs
    1   tablespoon butter
    1   cup heavy cream
    1   teaspoon salt
    ¾   cup sherry
    3   egg yolks
        few drops Tabasco

Place butter in pot. When melted
add the meat of the shell fish and
salt and Tabasco. Cover the pot
and let simmer 5 minutes, then add
sherry. Cook only 3 minutes, then
have ready the yolks of the eggs
stirred well into cup of cream.
Add this to the mixture in the pot,
and let thicken, which it will do very
quickly.

Serve at once on hot buttered
toast. If it stands or cooks too long,
it will curdle. Use a double boiler.

CRAB FRICASSEE

    2   sweet peppers, chopped
    8   large fat crabs
    1½ pounds peeled raw shrimp
    2   tablespoons butter
    3   cloves garlic, minced
    4   shallots, minced
    3   tablespoons parsley, minced
    2   stalks celery, minced
    3   tablespoons sherry
        season highly with red pepper, and
            salt to taste

Boil crabs 15 minutes without seasoning. Put butter in iron skillet,
melt, add flour and make a dark
roux. Add shallots, garlic, and
sweet peppers, and cook five minutes,
then add four crabs quartered and
two cups of the crab water, cover

and cook ten minutes. Now add two more cups of water, season highly and put in the raw shrimp and cook 15 minutes. Now add parsley and picked meat from crab claws and the white meat of the four other crabs and cook 5 or 6 minutes. When removed from fire put in sherry. Serve with boiled rice. This with a salad makes a delicious luncheon.

CRAB MEAT au GRATIN

1 pint crab meat
¼ pint sweet cream
2 eggs, the yolks
2 tablespoons butter
2 tablespoons grated cheese
  salt and pepper

Melt the butter in a pot, add the crabmeat with seasonings and cook for five minutes. Add the cream and the yolks of the eggs, slightly beaten. Cook, stirring constantly about four minutes more. Put the mixture in a deep baking dish, sprinkle with grated American cheese, dot with butter, and bake till a golden brown.

UPSIDE-DOWN CRABS
Mrs. H. C. Ehrenfels

1 lb. crab meat
1 cup bread crumbs (soak and drain)
1 large onion cooked soft in butter
2 eggs, well beaten
1 teaspoon Worcestershire Sauce
2 heaping tablespoons mayonnaise
  nutmeg, salt and pepper

Mix all together well and fill shells. Toast a little bread crumbs and spread over the top, patting firmly. Drop in deep hot fat to fry with filled side down. Then turn and do shell side. Will take about 5 minutes to brown well.

CRAB CHOPS à la NOUVELLE-ORLEANS

1½ dozen crabs, or 1 pound meat
1 cup sweet milk
4 tablespoons flour, level
2 tablespoons butter
2 egg yolks
1 teaspoon minced parsley
1 tablespoon Worcestershire Sauce
  salt, pepper to taste

Mix the flour with part of the milk. Put the rest of the milk to boil, then stir into the flour a tablespoon of butter. Cook until a stiff paste, add crab meat to get well heated. Have the egg yolks beaten well, then stir them into the hot mixture. Put back into double boiler, add another tablespoon of butter, the minced parsley, pepper, and salt. After it cools, place it in the refrigerator. When cold, form in chop shape. If too soft, use a little fine bread crumbs to help mold chops. Dip each one first in bread crumbs,

then in egg, then back in bread crumbs. They must stand several hours in the refrigerator to harden before frying. Pull the little claw with the teeth from the foot claw. Clean, and when your chops are fried stick a claw in each one. Serve with mushroom sauce. (A cup of crab meat may also be added to the sauce.) Lobster or salmon may be used in the same way.

CRABS ST. JACQUES
Miss Virginia Fassman

1 dozen large crabs
1 can mushrooms
1 tablespoon flour
1 tablespoon butter
2 egg yolks
1 teaspoon salt, pepper to taste
1 pint milk

Cream butter, flour, and eggs. Add gradually to hot milk in a double boiler, and cook until the mixture thickens. Cut the mushrooms in four and season with salt and pepper, a little butter, and boil them in their own juice. Pour this over the crab meat, then add the salt. Put in shells or baking dish, sprinkle with bread crumbs, dot over with butter, and bake until brown in a hot oven.

CRABMEAT RAVIGOTTE

2 lbs. fresh crab meat, chopped
6 green onions, chopped very fine
3 tablespoons butter
3 tablespoons cream sauce
4 egg yolks
6 tablespoons melted butter
2 lemons, the juice
  salt, pepper
  Hollandaise Sauce, No. 3

Put the butter into a saucepan. Fry onions.

When brown add crabmeat, season same with salt and pepper, add 3 for a few minutes. Make Hollandaise sauce No. 3. Add the crabmeat, then the yolks of 2 eggs, stir until thickened and serve hot on hot dry toast.

BAKED CRAB MEAT
Mrs. W. P. Bentley

1 stalk celery
½ green pepper
1 stick butter
1 pint crab meat
1 pint milk
1 tablespoon flour
  sherry, bread crumbs, butter

Chop the celery and the green pepper very fine. Put the butter in a deep skillet and add the celery and pepper, then put in the crab meat. Next the milk, then the flour, stirred in smoothly. Cook until creamy, then add the sherry. Put into a baking dish, cover with bread crumbs, dot with butter and bake.

CRABS FARCIS à la TECHE

1 dozen large crabs
3 hard boiled eggs
1 tablespoon butter, heaping
2 cloves garlic
2 tablespoons minced parsley
1 cup thin cream
2 tablespoons toasted bread crumbs
2 tablespoons sherry wine

Mash the yolks of the eggs to a cream with the butter. Toast thin slices of bread very dry and roll with a rolling pin to crumbs. Have the crabs well cleaned, boiled, and the meat picked out. Add the meat with all the other ingredients, fill the shells high with the mixture, sprinkle bread crumbs over the top of each, dot with butter and squeeze a little lemon juice over them. Bake until nicely browned, and serve with a sprig of parsley on each.

BAKED CRAB MEAT

1 lb. sharp American cheese
2 lbs. crab meat
½ stick butter
2 tablespoons Worcestershire Sauce
2 tablespoons flour
1 pint milk
salt, pepper to taste

Cream flour and butter, add milk and cook until it thickens. Salt and pepper, to taste. Add cheese, crabmeat, bake in oven 15 minutes. Fish or shrimp can be used in place of crabmeat.

CRAB PIE
Mrs. D. D. Curran

1 dozen crabs
5 slices stale bread
¼ lb. butter
1 cup cream or milk
salt, pepper, lemon

Boil the crabs with a little salt. Pick them. Slice bread very thin and butter on one side. Let it soak in cream or milk. Put a layer of this bread at bottom of baking dish, then a layer of crab meat, salt, pepper, bits of butter and very thin slices of lemon. On this, place another layer of bread, then crab meat as before, and repeat until dish is filled, ending with buttered bread. Just before putting in oven, pour over it a gill of milk.

CRABS À LA MME. DAUTERIVE

1 dozen large fat crabs
1 tablespoon butter, heaping
1 large onion, cut very fine
3 cloves garlic, minced
1 bell pepper, cut very fine
3 tablespoons minced celery
1 cup toasted breadcrumbs, moistened
    with three tablespoons milk
3 tablespoons minced parsley
2 tablespoons melted butter
    salt and pepper

Boil the crabs until well done, re-move from fire and allow to cool; remove all meat, fat, and juice, from the shells. Put the large tablespoon of butter on the fire to melt, add the minced garlic, celery, and pepper. Fry for five minutes slowly, mashing all the ingredients well while frying. Now add the bread crumbs which have been moistened in the milk. Cook a few minutes then add the crab meat, season with salt and pepper to taste, lower the burner and cook ten minutes. Remove from the fire and add the melted butter and minced parsley. Pour boiling water over the waiting shells to heat them, fill with the prepared mixture, put a slice of lemon on the top. Serve very hot.

BOILED RIVER SHRIMP

1 quart shrimp
1 quart water
½ cup coarse salt
2 pods red pepper
½ lemon, sliced
10 whole cloves

The shrimp must be thoroughly washed. Let the water with the sea-sonings and spices boil, then drop in the shrimp and let them cook 10 to 15 minutes. Drain and cool. To serve, cover with cracked ice.

The same procedure is followed for crabs, also for crawfish.

SHRIMP NEWBERG
Mrs. John Barry

3 lbs. shrimp
½ cup salt
1 bay leaf
1 pod cayenne pepper
1 pint scalded sweet milk
1 tablespoon flour
1 heaping tablespoon butter
1 wine glass sherry
1 raw egg
    sprigs of thyme

Boil the shrimp about 20 minutes with the salt, bay leaf, pepper and thyme. Remove the shells. Cream together the flour and butter, put in a double boiler and add the scalded milk very gradually, stirring con-stantly, and let it cool until it thick-ens. Add shrimp, salt to taste and a dash of red pepper. Remove from the fire and add the sherry. Just be-fore serving add the egg well beaten.

SHRIMP ARNAUD AND REMOULADE

From shrimp boiled as above may be prepared SHRIMP ARNAUD and SHRIMP REMOULADE. See index for these delicious sauces. Shrimp for salad are also prepared in this way.

SHRIMP PIQUANTE

Five pounds lake shrimp about two-thirds covered with vinegar and one-half cup water. Add three tablespoons black pepper, three tablespoons celery salt, rock salt, dash of cayenne pepper and bay leaves. Boil about 25 minutes, remove from stove and allow to stand in liquor for at least one hour. Remove and place on ice.

For river shrimp use same recipe, except substitute draught beer in place of vinegar.

SHRIMP PASTE

1 pound shrimp, cooked and peeled
½ pound butter
salt to taste

Grind shrimp fine in the meat grinder. Cream butter, and work in thoroughly into the shrimp. Salt to taste. Pack it in an oblong baking dish, and bake in a moderate oven until it leaves the side of the dish and is a little brown on top. Cool, and place in the refrigerator overnight before slicing.

Serve with hot boiled hominy.

TURTLE au GRATIN
Mrs. E. M. Choppin

4 lbs. turtle meat
½ cup butter, or lard
1 tablespoon flour
1 onion
1 clove garlic
1 cup chopped olives
2 dozen stoned olives
1 wine glass sherry
1 hard boiled egg
1 lemon
toasted bread crumbs
salt, pepper, parsley

Remove all the fat from the turtle meat and boil until tender. Make a roux of the butter (or lard) and the flour, sprinkling in the flour after the butter is hot, letting it brown thoroughly. Add the onion, parsley, and garlic, all chopped fine. Now put in the diced turtle meat, cover with water, add seasoning to taste, and let all simmer gently until very tender when the water will be reduced to a thick gravy. Soak the olives for chopping well in water, meanwhile, (otherwise the dish will be too salty), Add them to the simmering turtle meat with the sherry and pour all into a shallow pyrex baking dish.

Cover the top with toasted bread crumbs and decorate with the stoned olives, the sliced hard boiled egg and sliced lemon. Serve very hot.

NOTE: It is not necessary to soak the olives for stoning, as they are not used in the cooking. To stone them, take a sharp knife and cut around and around the stone, leaving the olive meat in a spiral.

SHRIMP SOUFFLÉ
Mrs. Chas. Crawford

1½ tablespoons shortening
1 tablespoon curry powder
1 tablespoon flour
1 cup milk
1 small onion
¼ cup canned tomato soup
½ teaspoon salt, pepper to taste
1 cup fresh shrimp, cut up
½ cup cooked rice
4 eggs

Melt shortening in saucepan, add chopped onion and brown lightly. Add curry and stir well. Sift in flour, stir well and slowly add milk, salt and pepper, shrimp, yolks, and rice. Heat, remove from fire. Add beaten whites. Pour in greased baking dish, bake in 350 degree.

FRIED SHRIMP

To one pound of boiled peeled, lake shrimp, add the yolk of one egg, one cup of cold milk. Put your shrimp in this preparation, take them out, dip in bread crumbs or corn meal. Fry in hot lard.

STEWED TERRAPIN
Mrs. D. D. Curran

3 terrapins
½ lb. butter
5 eggs, boiled hard
2 tablespoons flour
2 gills sherry
1 dessert spoon salt
cayenne to taste

Boil meat until tender; break into small pieces, adding liver and any terrapin eggs, the juices that have accumulated through the cutting up, and 2 gills of stock. Set in a china lined stew pan (or pyrex) over a moderate fire, rub flour and butter to a cream and stir it in. Rub the yolks of eggs to a smooth paste with salt, pepper and wine, then add the cream and serve immediately. It must not boil after the cream is added and must not stew more than 5 minutes after the time it begins to cook.

EGGS de LUXE

    2   ozs. Roquefort cheese
    1   dozen hard-boiled eggs
    ¼   cup finely chopped celery
    ¼   cup finely chopped onions
    2   teaspoons finely chopped parsley
    ½   cup bread crumbs
    1   raw egg
    ¼   cup water

Slice eggs lengthwise, remove yolks and work together with the cheese, onions, celery, parsley. Refill the egg cases with the mixture and press the halves together. Dip eggs into the beaten raw egg to which the water has been added. Roll in bread crumbs and fry in deep fat until light brown in color. Serve at once with a tomato sauce, and garnish with a pepper ring, stuffed olives and sprig of parsley. A rich treat.

SCRAMBLED EGGS BENOIT

Break 6 eggs into a bowl, yolks and whites together. Beat well for 5 minutes with an egg beater. Put a double boiler on the stove and, when, the water is boiling, put a tablespoon of butter in the inside pot. When hot, pour in the eggs and add two large spoonsful of sweet cream and a teaspoonful of butter. When eggs begin to harden on the sides of the pot, scrape from the sides and stir the mixture a little. When eggs are firm, pour on buttered toast and serve.

RUSSIAN EGGS

    6   eggs
    1   small jar caviar
    2   tablespoons anchovy paste
    1   teaspoon butter
    1   cup Hollandaise sauce
    6   rounds lightly toasted bread

Poach eggs until firm. Butter toast, spread it with anchovy sauce and put an egg on it. Cover with the Hollandaise sauce and top with caviar.

EGGS à la BENEDICTINE
Mrs. Rafferty

        eggs
        cream sauce
    2   beaten egg yolks
    ½   cup grated cheese
    1   wine glass sherry
        pepper, salt
        thin wafers of Virginia ham
        slices of tomato

Have ready as many small buttered jelly molds as there are eggs required. Drop an egg in each. Make a sauce by adding to the cream sauce the grated cheese, the beaten yolks and the sherry, pepper and salt. Use a long, oblong serving dish with a 1-inch rim if possible, otherwise any platter will do. Cover the bottom with dainty pieces of buttered toast. Broil the slices of ham and place a

piece on each piece of toast; then fry slices of tomato, placing one slice each on top of the ham. Meanwhile, place the molds in boiling salt water till the eggs are poached. Turn out an egg on each piece of toast, and pour sauce over all till just the egg appears, and serve. A pride and pleasure of New Orleans homes and restaurants.

HOT DEVILED EGGS
Lt. Comdr. and Mrs. S. W. Wallace

        eggs
        crumbs
        fat

Devil as many eggs as desired. Fasten halves together by placing toothpicks through diagonally Roll in egg and crumbs, fry in deep fat until brown. Remove tooth picks and serve with "Epicurean Sauce."

EGGS á la KING

    1   teaspoon lemon juice
    2   tablespoons butter
    ¼   lb. sliced mushrooms
    ½   green pepper, shredded
    2   tablespoons flour
    1½   cups rich milk
    2   beaten egg yolks
    ½   cup cream
    8   hard boiled eggs, sliced

Melt the butter, add mushrooms and pepper, and cook slowly until softened a little. Add flour and salt and mix, then the milk, slowly stirring until creamy. Add sliced eggs and stir carefully until very hot. Put lemon juice in as it is taken from the stove.

EGGS BEAUREGARD
Mrs. Curran Perkins

    5   eggs
    2   level teaspoons butter
    2   level teaspoons flour
    ½   pint cold milk
    1   teaspoon salt, pepper
    6   slices of bread

Put the eggs in a pan of water at the boiling point, pushed to the back of the stove where it cannot boil, but will keep hot, for thirty minutes. (This makes the yolks very soft, mealy, and digestible, and the whites easily crumbled.) Remove the eggs and cover them immediately with very cold water. Remove the shells and press the whites through a vegetable press, keeping them separate from the yolks.

Rub the flour and butter together, add the cold milk and stir this over the fire until it just reaches the boiling point, then add the salt, pepper, and the whites of the eggs. Heat over hot water.

Toast the slices of bread and arrange them neatly on a platter. Pour the mixture with the whites of eggs over them, sprinkle the top with the grated yolks of the eggs and stand them at the oven door for two minutes until thoroughly heated.

EGGS and CHEESE á la CRÈOLE
    4   tablespoons grated cheese
    ½   pint cream sauce
    6   eggs
        cayenne pepper

Take a wide flat pyrex or casserole dish, butter it well, and pour in half the sauce. Next, break in the eggs separately and carefully sprinkle with cheese, and pour sauce over; then more cheese, and then sauce, alternately, till all is used up —the cheese should be on top. Bake in a hot oven until the eggs are set and the cheese melted.

EGGS AND TOMATOES
    6   eggs
    1   large can tomatoes
        minced onion, celery, parsley
        salt, pepper

Cook the tomatoes with the seasoning. Pour them while hot into a deep baking bowl. Then carefully drop in the raw eggs, and bake in the oven until the eggs are cooked.

EGGS FLORENTINE
    1   bunch of boiled spinach
    2   eggs
        grated cheese
        cream sauce
        little cream or butter

Grind spinach up fine, add little cream or butter. Poach eggs, add salt, pepper to taste. Put one tablespoon of butter in pyrex or earthenware pan, add spinach. Dress eggs over the spinach, cover with cream sauce, add little grated cheese.

EGGS á la PURGATOIRE
Mrs. J. N. Roussel
    4   hard-boiled eggs
    4   pieces buttered toast
    1   cup tomato ketchup
    2   tablespoons Worcestershire Sauce
    1   teaspoon pepper-vinegar
    ½   teaspoon salt
    ½   teaspoon black pepper
    1   tablespoon butter
    1   teaspoon mustard

Hard boil eggs, peel and stand on ends on hot buttered toast ½ inch thick with a hollowed center. Pour over this a sauce of tomato ketchup, Worcestershire Sauce, pepper-vineger, salt, and black pepper. Add butter and mustard. This must be poured over the eggs and toast while very hot. Delicious and so simple.

CREAMED EGGS á L'ANCHOIS
Take as many hard-boiled eggs as the number of your guests necessitates. Halve the eggs, remove the yolks and mix well with anchovy paste, salt, pepper and Worcestershire Sauce to taste. Fill whites and pour over them hot cream sauce.

EGGS IN RED WINE
    ½   glass red wine (claret)
    ¼   glass water
    1   clove garlic
    1   tablespoon flour
        salt to taste

Put all on to boil and when boiling long enough to consume some of the liquid (not very long) poach eggs in same, hard or soft, as many as necessary.

Garnish with triangles of buttered toast and mushrooms. Small pieces of ham may be added if desired.

OYSTER OMELET
Mme. Ludo d'Arcis
    4   dozen oysters
    1½   tablespoons each celery, onion,
         parsley
    2   tablespoons butter
    2   tablespoons flour
    1   cup rich milk
    1   cup oyster liquor
    7   eggs
         salt, pepper to taste

Heat the oysters in their own liquor till they curl. Remove them, saving a cup of the liquor, and plump them by throwing them into a pan of cold water. Skin them, and remove hard part. Fry the celery, onions, and parsley, chopped fine, in the butter till onions are golden brown, then make a cream sauce, adding the flour slowly and stirring the while till it is smooth and bubbling, then add the milk and the oyster liquor slowly. Cut the oysters in halves, setting a third of them on the back of the stove. Beat the eggs, yolks and whites separately, mix with two-thirds of the oysters, pour into a hot skillet with 1 tablespoon melted butter in it, add salt and pepper, and let it cook slowly on the bottom, then for a second run it into a moderate oven. When it comes to a golden brown, double it over, turn it on a hot platter, pour over it the sauce to which the remaining third of the oysters has been added, and send it at once to the table.

OYSTER OMELETTE A LA PASCUAL MANALE
John Wyeth Scott
    9   eggs well beaten
    ¼   cup cream
    ¼   cup water
    1   dozen oysters
    1   onion
    2   cloves garlic
    8   shallots, the green part
    ½   stick butter

Boil the oysters in water until they swell. Take them out and drain thoroughly and chop, not to fine. Chop the onion, garlic, and shallot tops, very fine, and fry them in butter. Next add the chopped oysters, taking care that they do not burn. Finally, add the well beaten eggs, to which have been added the water and the cream. Mix all well and quickly and allow to cook for the minimum of time required to set. Turn out in omelet form on a hot platter and garnish with finely cut parsley.

OYSTER OMELET
Mrs. Walter Torian
2 dozen oysters
1 tablespoon butter, heaping
4 shallots, the white parts
2 cloves garlic
2 tablespoons minced sweet pepper
3 tablespoons minced celery
2 bay leaves
1 large sprig thyme
4 eggs
2 tablespoons chopped parsley
  salt, red pepper to taste

Melt the butter, in the saucepan, and add the minced garlic, bayleaves, thyme and sweet pepper. Drain the liquor from the oysters, halve the oysters and put them in the butter with the seasoning, lowering heat at once, and let them cook three minutes. Beat the eggs together, add the salt and pepper, and turn them into the saucepan with oyster mixture, but do not stir. When lightly browned, turn onto a hot platter, and garnish with chopped parsley.

CRAB OMELET
8 eggs
3 teaspoons water
1½ cups milk
2 cups crab meat
1½ tablespoons flour, scant
1½ tablespoons butter
½ teaspoon onion
1 teaspoon minced parsley

Make a cream by mixing flour, butter and milk and cooking in double boiler. Add crab meat, salt, pepper, a little grated onion and minced parsley. Beat eggs separately, add water to yolks and fold in whites. Turn into a hot skillet, reduce heat. When done, pour over it, one-third of crab meat and sauce. Fold over and turn on hot platter. Pour balance of crab meat and sauce over omelet.

MUSHROOM OMELET
1 cup large button mushrooms,
1 tablespoon butter
½ cup cream, or milk
1 teaspoon flour
8 eggs

Clean the mushrooms and cut them fine. Melt the butter and add the mushrooms with salt, pepper, and cream. Thicken with flour dissolved in a little water or milk, and set to boil gently for 10 minutes. Make a plain omelet, and just before folding, pour some of the mushrooms in the center. Serve hot, with the rest of the mushroom sauce poured over.

OMELETTE au FOUR
1 cup soft breadcrumbs
1 cup milk
6 eggs
  salt, pepper to taste

Soak the crumbs in milk five minutes. Beat the eggs until light, add seasoning, then the crumb and milk mixture. Bake in a greased shallow pan in a moderate oven, for 25 minutes. Serve with jelly, or with creamed mushrooms, or meat. Yesterday's bread here comes to a noble end. Or one may mix a little grated cheese with melted butter, sprinkle it over the omelette just before it is done, and let it brown before serving.

OMELETTE AU CROUTONS
Cut one large thick slice of white bread in small squares and fry lightly in butter. Take good meat gravy and put the bread in it and allow it to drink up as much as it will. It should simmer gently on the back of stove. More gravy may be added if necessary. It should not be quite dry. Beat the bread up till it is fairly smooth. Add salt and pepper to taste. Place this in a bowl and break four whole eggs into it beating well between each egg. Cook in a well greased pan, carefully, as it burns easily. Serve in omelet form.

SNOWDRIFT EGGS
Use a glass or porcelain baking dish about two inches deep. Butter it generously. Beat the whites of eggs to super stiffness, add salt and pile in the dish with as many hills and valleys as possible. Allow one tablespoon of cream to each egg and pour gently over the egg whites. Now slip the yolks into the crevices where they fit best. Run into the oven until the yolks are just set and the whites tipped with brown. This is a particularly good way to serve eggs to an invalid as they are attractive to look at and most digestible, being prepared without grease of any kind.

CANAPÈ MARGUERY
Miss Betty Hooker

¼ pound white tuna, chopped
1 medium sized ripe tomato, chopped
2 hard-boiled eggs, chopped
8 anchovies, chopped
½ green pepper, chopped
1 cup Russian dressing

Mix well, stir in Russian dressing. Page 65.

This may be left on ice for almost any length of time. Just before serving, put a heaping tablespoon of butter in a heavy frying pan, blend with a tablespoon and a half of Worcestershire Sauce, heat the mixture in this, mixing all together with fork. Serve immediately on hot toast made by frying bread in the butter and Worcestershire mixture or just plain toast. The important thing is to have it as hot as possible. It can be made at the tables as crêpes Suzette This is very filling and called a canapé only as a compliment—its beauty lies not only in its flavor but also in the fact that it can be prepared long in advance.

JAMBALAYA
Miss Virginia Fassmann

1 lb. rice
1 slice ham, turkey or chicken
2 doz. oysters or 1 lb. shrimp
1 tablespoon lard
salt, pepper to taste

Wash the pound of rice, soak in cold water two hours. Cut up the cold roast chicken, or the remnants of turkey, and a slice of ham; fry in a tablespoon of lard. Dry and fry rice until it is slightly straw color.

Now stir into the meat slowly and at the same time add a pint of hot water. Cover your pot and set where it can cook slowly; should you add oysters, cook them in their own liquor for a few minutes on a slow fire until they curl, then add to the Jambalaya and serve. If desired, add a dash of saffron.

JAMBALAYA au VALOIS
Mrs. Walter Torian

2 links smoked sausage
1 tablespoon lard
2 onions
½ cup tomato juice
2 cups rice
minced garlic and parsley
salt, pepper

Cut the smoked sausage in half pieces, and fry in hot lard. Add the chopped onions and the tomato juice. Wash two cups of rice, and let it fry, stirring often.

Cover liberally with hot water, and cook on a slow fire.

Before serving add the parsley and garlic.

MACARONI PIE
Mrs. Charles A. Farwell

½ lb. spaghetti
½ lb. boiled ham
pepper
pastry

Line a baking dish with pastry. Boil the spaghetti until tender. Grind or chop the ham fine, and add the pepper. Fill the pastry shell with alternate layers of the macaroni and the ham. Dot the top with the butter. Cover with pie crust and bake in a hot oven for a half an hour. This is good hot or cold.

BIG HOMINY CROQUETTES
Mrs. S. G. Steiner

Melt three tablespoons butter in saucepan, add ¼ cup flour and grating of one onion, cook together few minutes without browning. To this add one cup milk; stir until sauce boils then add one cup grated American cheese and yolks of two eggs. As soon as cheese melts, add two cups finely chopped cooked big hominy, one teaspoon salt, ½ teaspoon pepper. Pour on platter and let cool, then shape, dip in beaten egg, fry in deep fat, using frying basket. Serve with tomato sauce.

FRENCH FRIED ASPARAGUS
Mrs. Grace Stevenson

freshly cooked or canned asparagus
2 tablespoons cream
2 tablespoons flour
1 egg

Drain asparagus well and roll in batter made from the other ingredients. Fry at 380 degrees until golden brown.

SPAGHETTI—SUPREME
Mrs. Stephen Seyburn

1 lb. spaghetti
2 pounds ground meat
2 large cans tomatoes
4 large onions
1 clove garlic
1 lemon, sliced
1 can mushrooms
1 can tomato paste
1 teaspoon allspice
1 teaspoon cloves
3 bay leaves
2 cans water, the same amount as tomatoes
1 tablespoon Snowdrift

Fry onions in lard, add tomatoes, water, ground meat, and let come to a boil. Now add pinch of soda and let boil hard 1½ to 2 hours, and add garlic, salt and pepper to taste, and other seasoning, and boil for 1 hour, and then add tomato paste and mushrooms and cook ten to fifteen minutes longer.

Boil Skinners spaghetti 20 minutes, put in colander and drain. Serve with the above poured over it.

SPAGHETTI ROLLINO
Mrs. Stanley Arthur

    1   large onion
    ½   cup olive oil
    1   clove garlic
    1   qt. can Italian tomatoes
    1   small can tomato paste
    2   teaspoons salt, thyme, cayenne
        pepper
    1   cup dried mushrooms
    1   cup boiling water
    1   lb. Parmesan cheese
    1   lb. spaghetti

Boil the spaghetti in 2 quarts of salt water. Drain, and put back in same boiler until ready to use.

Soak the mushrooms for a minute in a cup of boiling water or stock. (If you can not get the dried mushrooms, a small can of button mushrooms may be used). Drain and chop them fine.

Chop the onions, cook five minutes in the olive oil, add the tomatoes and tomato paste, salt, pepper and other seasoning. This is the sauce. Add mushrooms 10 minutes before serving.

To the drained spaghetti, add one-third of the cheese, then pour over it one-third of the sauce, mix thoroughly and heat piping hot, pour in hot platter or round dish, then pour over it the rest of the sauce.

The rest of the grated cheese is served on the side.

The sauce may be made in the morning, and heated again at night.

ITALIAN SPAGHETTI
Mme. Ludo d'Arcis

    ½   lb. spaghetti
    ½   lb. fresh tomatoes, or ½ can
    1   tablespoon butter
    1   large sliced onion
        bay leaf, garlic, cloves, sage, thyme,
        red pepper, salt, black pepper to
        taste
        grated Italian cheese

Boil spaghetti in salt water. Drain.

Put the butter into the pot and stir into it the seasonings, letting it all brown slowly. Mash into this the tomatoes, and let all cook together for half an hour, stirring frequently. When it is cooked, press it through a sieve.

Mix the sauce well with the spaghetti. Just before serving, add grated cheese sufficient to make a thick consistency, and stir well. A thin layer of grated cheese may be sprinkled on top for decoration.

WHITE HOUSE SPAGHETTI

    1½ cups spaghetti
    ¾   lb. Swiss cheese
    1   tablespoon white pepper
    1   tablespoon salt
    1   pint milk
    2   tablespoons butter
    1   tablespoon flour

Boil the spaghetti in salted water, then drain it, and make a white sauce, by creaming the butter and flour in the double boiler and adding milk in the usual way.

Butter a pyrex dish, and put in a layer of spaghetti, then a layer of cream sauce, then a layer of grated cheese, and continue until all of the spaghetti, sauce, and cheese have been used, having sauce and cheese on top. Run in the oven and bake until creamy. A dish fit for kings,—and a president's favorite!

NOODLE RING
Lt. Comdr. and Mrs. S. W. Wallace

    6   ozs. noodles
    3   eggs
    ½   cup catsup
    ½   cup milk
    1   cup grated cheese

Boil noodles ten minutes. Drain, adding all ingredients. Bake in ring mold which has previously been well buttered and placed in refrigerator. This makes it much easier to remove. Place ring in pan of water one-half depth of ring. Bake forty minutes at 325° F.

NOODLE RING

    1   package noodles
    1½ tablespoons butter
    1½ tablespoons flour
    1¼ cups milk
    1½ teaspoons salt
    2   eggs beaten separately
        dash of pepper and of mace

Let the noodles cook in boiling salt water then drain them. Heat the butter in a double-boiler, adding the flour and milk very gradually, to make a cream sauce. Add salt, pepper, and mace (or nutmeg), then the eggs well-beaten. Combine all this with the noodles.

Butter a ring-mold, place the noodles in it and set it in a pan of hot water to bake in a moderate oven, until firm, about 40 minutes. Turn out on a hot platter and fill the center as desired: with creamed fish, with a filling made after the recipe for Crabs St. Jacques; with meat, creamed shrimp or crab, what you will. Hot asparagus tips placed about the edges make a pretty and savory touch.

FROMAGE
Mrs. W. J. Bentley

    1   lb. grated cheese
    2   eggs, the yolks
    ½   pt. milk and cream
        cayenne, salt

Beat the eggs very light, and add the cream, then the cheese. Pour into buttered ramikins and bake 15 minutes.

CHEESE TAPIOCA SOUFFLÉ
Mrs. Charles M. Peaslee

1 cup scalded milk
3 tablespoons minute tapioca
1 cup grated cheese
3 egg yolks, well beaten
3 egg whites, stiffly beaten
½ teaspoon salt

Cook tapioca with milk in double boiler for fifteen minutes or until clear, stir frequently, add cheese and stir until melted. Add well-beaten yolks and then fold in the stiffly beaten whites. Turn into a well greased casserole. Bake about 30 minutes. Soufflé is done when it shrinks a trifle and is brown.

CHEESE SOUFFLÉ

1 pint milk
4 eggs
2 tablespoons butter
2 tablespoons flour
5 tablespoons grated cheese
1 teaspoon salt
1 pinch cayenne pepper
½ level coffee spoon soda
¼ coffee spoon paprika

Mix flour, milk and butter thoroughly and boil, stirring until the mixture becomes creamy. When cool, add the well beaten yolks, then the cheese and seasoning; fold in the stiffly beaten whites. Turn into a well buttered baking dish and place in hot water in moderate oven twenty to twenty-five minutes until it sets. Fish, shrimp, ham, or chicken may be added.

CHEESE TOAST TROIS FILLES
Mrs. Walter Torian

3 slices of bread about 1-inch thick
4 eggs
butter
grated American cheese
pinch of cayenne

Cut the crusts off the bread and spread the slices lightly with butter. Beat the eggs and add enough grated American cheese to make a thick paste. Now cayenne pepper, liberally. Spread the paste on the bread to the thickness of an inch. Put a slice of fat bacon on top. Run under the blazer, and serve piping hot.

QUAKER CROQUETTES
Mme. Ludo d'Arcis

½ package Quaker Oats
milk
1 tablespoon onion, and parsley, chopped fine
pepper, salt to taste
lard

Add to the Quaker Oats enough milk to make a paste and allow to soak all night. The next morning, if it seems too thin, add a little flour; if too thick, add an egg. Mix in the chopped onion and parsley, add pepper and salt to taste.

Drop a tablespoonful at a time into deep hot lard in the frying pan and fry until brown. To be served with a thick tomato sauce or a brown sauce with mushrooms au Madère.

RISOTTO

4 ozs. rice
6 ozs. cheese
1 onion, sliced
1½ pints water
salt, pepper

Fry the onion in a little fat until browned. Add the rice and the water and cook until the rice is quite soft. Then add grated cheese, pepper, salt, to taste.

Turn it all into a buttered pie dish and put it in the over to bake for 15 or 20 minutes.

ARTICHOKES SARDOU

8 artichokes
8 eggs, poached
½ lb. boiled ham, ground or chopped
2 tablespoons butter
16 anchovies
8 rounds of buttered toast
salt and pepper to taste

Boil artichokes, when cold scrape the tender part of leaves, remove the hearts and mash. Season with butter, salt and pepper, heat and put on buttered toast. Place poached egg on top, cover with anchovies and grated ham, and pour over all Golden Sauce Cote d'or. Refer to Sauces.

ARTICHOKES and SWEETBREADS
Mrs. Felix J. Puig

6 artichokes
1 lb. sweetbreads
1 cup cream sauce
1 tablespoon chopped green onion
1 tablespoon parsley
1 small can truffles, sliced thin
2 tablespoons butter
a sprig of thyme

Boil artichokes, remove center choke, scoop out heart, scrape tender part of leaves. Brown green onions, parsley, and thyme in a little butter, add to artichokes. Cream boiled sweetbreads with artichokes and truffles. Fill center of artichokes with this mixture, sprinkle with bread or cracker crumbs, dot with butter and heat very hot. Mushrooms add to this delicious dish.

MUSHROOMS UNDER GLASS

1 lb. fresh mushrooms
butter
salt, pepper to taste
Newburg Sauce

Cook mushrooms in butter ten minutes. Season with salt and pepper.

Add mushrooms to Newberg Sauce, put on piece of toast, cover with glass and serve.

SWEETBREADS AND FRESH MUSHROOMS
Mrs. A. T. Pattison

1½ lbs. sweetbreads
6 small shallots
1 sprig parsley
2 teaspoons butter
1 tablespoon flour
½ lb. fresh mushrooms
½ cup thick cream
1 egg yolk

Soak sweetbread in cold water to blanch, then boil until tender. Remove all skins from them. Keep the stock.

Make a roux with the butter and flour and cook until golden brown. Then add sweetbreads, the shallots chopped very fine, and the parsley. Add the stock, and let simmer very slowly until the sauce is quite thick. The mushrooms must meanwhile be smothered in butter. When ready to serve, add them, with the cream in which the yolk of the egg is beaten. Be careful not to let the mixture boil, once the cream and yolk of egg have been put in.

CALF'S BRAINS BIENVILLE

1 set brains
2 teaspoons Worcestershire Sauce
½ can mushrooms
2 hard boiled eggs
1 cup thick cream sauce, highly seasoned
½ cup warm boiled rice
1 raw egg
   bread crumbs

First plunge brains in salted water to get the skin off. Then boil the brains in well-salted water. When cold, mince well.

Have the mushrooms minced fine, the rice, and the cream sauce, and then hard-boiled eggs, the yolks creamed and the whites finely chopped.

Cool, and shape in croquette form Roll in fine bread crumbs, then in raw egg. then again in crumbs.

Have the lard sizzling hot, and drop them in to turn a golden, delectable brown. Or place on buttered baking sheet and bake. Drain.

BRAINS au FROMAGE
Mrs. William Westerfield

2 calves' brains
4 tablespoons flour
2 teaspoons dry mustard
1 cup milk
4 tablespoons Parmesan cheese
   lard, or oil
   cream sauce

Put the brains in cold water and skin them. Mix the mustard with the flour and dredge the brains in the mixture.

Fry them till they are light brown, then add the milk, and let cook an hour. Put the brains on toast. Add to the cream sauce 2 tablespoons of Parmesan cheese, and pour this over brains, then sprinkle with the rest of the cheese. Run this under the broiler until light brown.

CALF'S FEET RAVIGOTE
Arnaud

"The calf's feet are thoroughly cleaned, then boil with bay-leaf, chopped onions, one or two carrots, thyme, and hot seasoning—a red pepper or two, and salt.

When ready to serve, over them goes a sauce: mayonnaise, with cream stirred into it, finely-minced shallots, and bayleaf."

This dish is offered by Arnaud, known as the 'Count' in the gourmet's rendezvous over which he presides. He presented it first in New Orleans some years ago apologetically. "It has been known for centuries along the Normandy coast," said he, "but perhaps it appeals not to your Anglo-Saxon consciousness."

ITALIAN CHEESE

1¼ lbs. veal
1¼ lbs. liver
½ lb. bacon
1 small onion
1 tablespoon sage
1 tablespoon marjoram
1 tablespoon thyme
1 tablespoon savory
2 tablespoons chopped parsley
1 tablespoon salt
¼ teaspoon pepper
   dash of cayenne

Grind veal, liver, bacon, and onion, all together. Add marjoram, thyme and savory, salt, pepper, and cayenne. Place all in a covered mold which has been well buttoned. Steam three hours. Open the steamer carefully and pour off the liquid and add to it 1 tablespoon gelatin which has been hydrated. If necessary, add enough water to fill the space in the steamer. Place in the ice box to harden.

ONION PIE
Mrs. Charles H. Behre, Sr.

2 cups white onions, chopped
4 tablespoons vegetable oil
1 or 1½ cups sour cream
4 eggs, beaten, salt
   pastry, bacon

Make a plain pastry for a bottom crust only. Bake. Cook onions until soft with vegetable oil. Do not brown. Add salt. Remove from fire. When cool add sour cream and eggs and fill pie shell. Bake in moderate oven. When firm remove. Sprinkle top with bits of bacon. Replace in oven until bacon crisps and pie is a light brown.

CHICKEN au LAIT

    5 lb. chicken
    1 pt. milk
    1 stick butter
       salt, pepper

Rub the chicken with a little butter, salt, and pepper. Put the rest of the butter into a baking-pan.

Place the chicken on it. Bake, basting at intervals with milk. It should cook an hour, or more, depending on the tenderness of the fowl.

FRIED CHICKEN à MERVEIL

    1 chicken, disjointed
       salt, pepper to taste
       flour, sifted
       hog lard
       butter, size of egg

At the last minute, wash chicken in cold water. Do not wipe, but salt and pepper, then dip in sifted flour. Have a large aluminum pan with very hot hog lard ready. Add butter.

Drop chicken in, never touching a fork to it; cover, and let it cook on slow fire twenty minutes.

Turn with spatula, cover and cook about twenty minutes more.

CHICKEN FRICASEE WITH DUMPLINGS
Mrs. J. B. Simmons

    1 tender young hen, capon or 2 fryers
    2 cups vegetable oil
    1 tablespoon sifted flour
    ½ cup each of chopped onions, parsley,
       celery and green pepper
    5 tomatoes, large, ripe (or 1 qt. can)
       hot water
       dumplings
       salt, pepper
       sprig of thyme

Disjoint the chicken, cutting as for frying. Put the oil into a large iron skillet, and when it boils, add the chicken (which has been rubbed with salt and a little pepper. Add the giblets if desired). Let brown to rich café au lait color. Remove from the fire, pour off the surplus oil (about ½ the original quantity. It can be strained and kept for future use.) Now add the chopped ingredients, thyme, and bay leaf to the oil remaining in the pot, stir in slowly and carefully the flour and allow to cook, stirring constantly, until the chopped ingredients begin to melt into a rich brown gravy.

At this point, add the tomatoes. Set the pot on a slow fire until the tomatoes begin to be absorbed in the bubbling gravy. Add enough hot water (1 qt. or more) to cover well and let the pot simmer gently for at least 2 hours, stirring occasionally to prevent sticking.

Next the dumplings (rich biscuit dough, cut into any shape desired), dropped in to plump in the fragrant gravy.

Serve hot. Long to tell of, but easy in performance, and most savoury.

ROASTED CHICKEN, BREAD SAUCE AND CURLS OF BACON
Mrs. Alfred T. Pattison

    1 tender and large roasting chicken
    1 lb. thinly sliced bacon
    ½ onion chopped fairly fine
    1 cup very stale white bread crumbs
    1 lb. small sausages
    1 lump butter
    1 cup milk

Roast chicken as usual. Take giblets and boil in a pint of water with a small piece of onion and of parsley. When gizzard is tender remove giblets and pour this stock to which you have added a little coloring matter—say a drop or two of caramel—in the pan in which chicken has been roasted. In the meantime boil the milk with chopped onion, then add bread crumbs until whole is a thick mass. Season to taste. Make curls of bacon as for garnish of Cod Roe, these curls and the sausages are cooked in the same pan as the chicken. Remove chicken, bacon and sausages before adding giblet stock. Place chicken on platter, garnish with sausages and bacon, strain sauce in pan in a sauce bowl. Then into another sauce bowl, put bread sauce to which you add a small lump of butter stirring all the while, before removing from fire. Serve all piping hot.

SCALLOPED CHICKEN
Mme. Ludo d'Arcis

    3 lb. hen
    2 tablespoons butter
    2 tablespoons flour
    1 pint rich milk
    1 can mushrooms
    2 eggs
    1 tablespoon Worcestershire Sauce
       salt, white pepper to taste

Boil the chicken, and cut it up in pieces of desired size. Melt the flour and butter together, and add the milk very gradually, stirring constantly until the mixture thickens. Add the chicken, mushrooms, salt and pepper to taste and last of all, the egg yolks, stirring constantly. This is best done in a double boiler. When the eggs have thickened the sauce, add the Worcestershire and fold in the beaten whites. Stir for another moment or two and serve at once.

CURRY LUNCHEON
"Barbara Brooks"

A perfect one-dish meal.

    4 lbs. chicken or duck
    ½ pound rice
    2 tablespoons flour
    2 tablespoons butter
    1 tablespoon brown sugar
    4 tablespoons curry powder
    1 small onion
    1 green pepper
    ½ cup seedless raisins
    4 or 5 cups stock from fowl
    1 tablespoon vinegar
       black pepper, cayenne, bay leaf, salt

Simmer fowl until tender, in salted water with a stalk of celery, bay leaf and 1 tablespoon of vinegar. When done, remove skin and bones and cut meat in medium small pieces. Reserve 4 or 5 cups of stock for sauce.

SAUCE

In a large iron skillet, melt the butter and lightly brown the onions and pepper, finely chopped. Add curry powder, sugar and flour, blend together until smooth, and add hot stock, cup by cup. Let boil gently for about five minutes, until about the consistency of thick cream. Add raisins and cut up fowl, and simmer until ready to serve. Add more hot stock just before serving if necessary.

Put the rice on to cook in three quarts of rapidly boiling water, boil twenty minutes, drain and steam until light and fluffy.

To serve heap the rice on a large hot platter, make a depression in the middle of the pile and fill with the curry sauce. Serve individually in hot soup plates, with any or all of the following sambals: chutney, chopped roasted peanuts, chopped bacon, picalilli, grated cocoanut, chopped fresh pineapple, and shrimp. These are stirred into the rice and curry sauce and the mixture eaten with a fork and large soup spoon.

CHICKEN CADIEN
Mrs. Charles O. Noble

    1   hen
    2   small onions
    1   stalk celery
    1   doz. eggs, boiled hard
    1   cup green peppers, minced
    1   large onion, cut fine
    1   large can mushrooms
    6   medium sized tomatoes
    1   cup very thick white sauce, made
        with ½ cup milk and ½ cup
        chicken broth
    ½   cup butter or chicken fat
        Tabasco, Worcestershire, red and
        black pepper, salt
        cracker crumbs

Boil the hen until tender with the small onions, leaves and outer stalks of the celery and seasonings. Dice the meat, melt the butter and brown in it the minced pepper, the rest of the celery, chopped, and the large onion. Turn in the tomatoes and white sauce, then the chicken, with salt, pepper, Tabasco and Worcestershire, to taste. Last of all add the hard boiled eggs. Stir as little as possible after the eggs are added. Arrange in a casserole, sprinkle toasted crumbs on top, dot with butter then set the casserole in a pan of hot water in the oven and bake about ten minutes. Whereupon your luncheon party or Sunday night supper is an assured gastronomic success.

CHICKEN BÉCHAMEL
Mrs. Frank Hemenway

    2   chickens, large fryers
    1½   sticks butter
    2   onions, clove garlic, bay leaves
    2   cans consomme
    2   cups white wine
    1   can mushrooms
    2   tablespoons flour
    1   pint cream

Melt butter in a large pot. Put chicken in, cut as for frying. Brown well with the onions and garlic, sliced fine. Cover with boiling water, drop in the bay leaves, and consommé, boil 15 minutes, add white wine. Simmer 20 minutes. Fifteen minutes before serving add the can of mushrooms with the juice. Remove chicken to the serving platter and add to the sauce two tablespoons of flour, one pint of cream, and cook. Just before serving add two egg yolks that have been well mixed. Delicious.

CHICKEN DE LUXE
Mrs. Ludo d'Arcis

    4   large fryers, cut for frying
    1   wine glass sherry
    1   wine glass brandy
    1   lb. fresh mushrooms, cut fine
    3   shallots, chopped
    ½   lb. butter
    4   egg yolks
    1   pint cream
    1½   cups chicken stock
         salt and pepper

Use breasts and second joints only, reserving other parts for a family dish. Boil giblets, necks, feet and heads in water, highly seasoned, to make stock.

Sauté chicken in butter or oil, after rubbing with salt and pepper. Remove to another pan, add more butter, pour over sherry and brandy and simmer till very tender.

Put another lump of butter in the first pan and turn in the mushrooms and shallots to fry lightly. Cover with the chicken stock and allow to cook slowly till tender. Combine with the chicken.

Heat the cream in a double boiler at the last minute and stir in the parsley and the egg yolks, that have been well beaten. Cook until thick, stirring constantly.

Pour over the chicken and serve at once.

CHICKEN MACARONI

1 cup macaroni or spaghetti
4 lb. chicken
1 cup grated cheese
  cream sauce
  chicken stock

Boil the macaroni in salt water. Boil the chicken until tender.

Take the breasts only, and cut each chicken breast in 3 strips; lay them in the bottom of a pyrex pie dish, make a rich cream sauce, add the chicken stock and the grated cheese. Mix in the macaroni and pour this over the chicken. Brown in the oven.

CHICKEN TERRAPIN

1 large or 2 small chickens
1 cup cream
½ teaspoon salt
1 cup sherry
1 teaspoon mustard
2 hard-boiled eggs
  flour
  butter, size of egg
  pepper to taste

Boil the chicken and dice.

Chop the egg yolks and mix with the mustard, add the chopped whites, cream, sherry and butter. Mix these with the chicken and put in a saucepan or in the chafing dish with salt and pepper and cook 20 minutes. If it seems too dry, add more cream.

CHICKEN CROQUETTES WITH BRAINS AND MUSHROOMS
Mrs. Wm. J. de Treville

2 cups minced boiled chicken
1 small set brains
1 small can mushrooms
3 tablespoons flour
1½ cups milk
1 teaspoon Worcestershire Sauce
1 tablespoon chopped parsley
1 teaspoon salt, or to taste
½ teaspoon black pepper
1 large spoon of butter

Scramble brains dry in butter. Cut mushrooms fine, mix well with chicken. Make a thick white sauce, creaming butter, flour and milk. Cook well and then add other ingredients.

Then fold in mixture of chicken, brains, and mushrooms. Set aside to cool. Mold into shape, roll in fine cracker crumbs, then in beaten egg, again in cracker crumbs and fry in deep fat.

CHICKEN PIE
Mrs. Frank H. Lawton

The day before the pie is to be made, dress and wash thoroughly a 4 or 5 lb. chicken. Leave whole. Place in saucepan and cover with hot water. Boil a few minutes and add 1½ tablespoons of salt, pepper if desired. Cook until tender, let stand in stock overnight.

Line baking pan with ⅛ in. layer of biscuit dough, place a teacup in center. Cut the chicken into nice pieces. Leave in the bones. Lay the pieces, alternating dark and white meat, about the cup. Remove the stock. Melt it and thicken with 1 level tablespoon flour to each cup of stock. Let cool and pour over chicken. Over this place about 6 pieces of butter the size of a walnut. Over all place biscuit dough to cover, ½ inch thick, with slits for steam to escape.

Bake in a moderate oven until crust is well risen and brown. Test with toothpick to be sure it is cooked on under side. Heat remaining stock and serve as extra gravy.

CHICKEN PIE CRÉOLE
Mrs. J. T. Grace

1 large chicken
  Sauce:
3 tablespoons butter
4 tablespoons flour
3 cups of chicken stock
1 cup cream
½ teaspoon salt
¼ teaspoon pepper
  Crust:
2 cups flour
4 teaspoons baking powder
1 teaspoon salt
2 tablespoons melted butter
1 egg
1 cup milk, scant

Cut up the chicken and boil until the meat can be easily removed from the bones. Arrange in a baking dish.

Sauce: Blend together the butter and flour in a double-boiler, and add very gradually the warm chicken stock, the cream, then the salt and pepper. Cook to a creamy consistency and pour over the chicken in the baking dish, reserving enough sauce for a gravy bowl.

The Crust: Sift together the flour, baking-powder and salt, then add the melted butter, the egg well-beaten and the milk. This mixture should be thick enough to drop from the spoon over the chicken and sauce in the baking dish.

Bake 15 to 20 minutes, and serve with the reserved sauce.

COQUILLES DES VOLAILLE
Mrs. Chas. F. Buck, Jr.
3   or 4 lb. chicken
1   cup milk
1   tablespoon flour
1   can mushrooms, chopped
1   small can truffles, chopped
½   cup sherry
1   tablespoon minced onion
    bread crumbs

Boil the chicken until tender and remove meat from the bones and cut into pieces, not too small. Season with salt and pepper and pour over the sherry. Make a cream sauce with the milk, flour and butter and add the minced onion. Add the mushrooms and truffles to the chicken and combine all with the cream sauce. Put into baking shells, cover with bread crumbs, dot with butter and set in the oven to brown very lightly.

CHICKEN LOUISIANE
"La Louisiane"
1   medium sized fryer

Unjoint and fry the chicken to a golden brown. Keep it hot. Make a sauce by combining the following ingredients:

2   tablespoons butter
1   tablespoon flour
1   pint consommé or stock
6   stoned olives
12   large fresh mushrooms, chopped
4   artichoke hearts
    salt, pepper and sherry to taste

Pour over the chicken and dress on a hot platter.

CHICKEN SOUFFLÉ
Mrs. W. P. Bentley
2   tablespoons flour
2   tablespoons butter
1   wine glass sherry
1   pint milk
½   cup stale breadcrumbs, grated
2   cups chicken meat, chopped
    parsley, chopped
    mushroom sauce

Melt the butter, add the flour, then the milk gradually, and the breadcrumbs and cook 2 minutes. Salt, and pepper. Then add the chopped chicken meat, allow to cool. Now add the yolks, beaten light, the chopped parsley, and fold in the well-beaten whites. Cook in a buttered dish 35 minutes. Serve with mushroom sauce.

HOT JELLIED CHICKEN
Mrs. Paul Gorham
3½   pound hen
1   can mushrooms, chopped
½   to 1 cup stock
1   cup cream sauce, thick
2   tablespoons parsley, chopped
1   tablespoon onions, minced
8   eggs
    salt and pepper to taste

Dice chicken, add mushrooms, par-

sley, onions and seasoning. Marinate with cream sauce and stock. Stir in eggs but do not beat. Put mixture in well-greased mold, place in hot water and steam very slowly until it sets. Turn out on hot platter, fill center with mushroom sauce and serve.

GALANTINE OF CHICKEN CONTI
3   pound chicken
1   small onion
1   package gelatine
1   cup cold water
2   or 3 cloves
    bay leaf, sprig of parsley
    stalk of celery
    pinch of mace
    salt
    olives

Dress the chicken and boil until tender, without disjointing it. Stick the cloves into the onion. When the chicken is partly done, add the onion with cloves, parsley, celery, bay-leaf and mace.

When the chicken is thoroughly tender, remove the meat from the bones and throw away the fat, skin and gristle.

Skim all the fat from the liquid and strain it. Add salt, and boil down to a quart.

Soak the gelatine in a cup of cold water, and add this to the hot stock.

Pour this into the bottom of a mold to the depth of ½ inch and let it harden. Then spread over it a layer of the white meat of the chicken, and sprinkle it with diced tender celery. Melt the remaining liquid and pour another ½ inch layer over the chicken. Add a layer of dark meat garnished with olives, and then another layer of jelly.

BREAST OF GUINEA

Allow one guinea for each couple. An entire half breast is served for each portion. Roast the guineas until they are quite tender using exact method as in roasting chickens. When thoroughly done detach each breast from the breast bone and lay each half on thin slivers of broiled ham which you should have ready. Pour over the gravy and serve with any tart jelly. The unused portions may be reserved to make croquettes or stew the next day.

CHICKEN AVOCADO

Split avocado pears and remove seeds. Fill the cavity with creamed chicken or turkey. Run into the oven until the avocado is thoroughly heated This makes a delicious and unusual luncheon dish.

WILD FOWL

The Louisiana cook's usual dictum about wild fowl is, "De less you meddles wid' em, better dey be". In general she looks with disapproval on sauces that modify the flavor,—except in the case of certain very fishy ducks, when an onion may be inserted in the carcass during the baking process, to be removed later.

As is universally known, no fowl should be cooked fresh from refrigeration. It should stand at least an hour in a warm place.

Duck is well larded. Often two or three pieces of fat bacon or salt pork are put on the breast. It is set in a very hot oven and basted every four or five minutes. Just before removing it is sprinkled lightly with salt and pepper. Fifteen minutes or even less is enough for rare duck. Half an hour will have it thoroughly cooked. Wild rice is a favorite companion dish.

Quail and snipe are usually broiled. Ten or fifteen minutes for the latter and longer for quail. When nearly done they are sprinkled lightly with salt and pepper, and are served on thin slices of toast, after soft butter has been spread over them. Very finely chopped parsley and a few thin slices of lemon are a proper garnish.

DUCKS AU MADÉRE
Mrs. R. G. Robinson

4 small ducks, preferably wild
1 teaspoon Worcestershire Sauce
5 drops Tabasco
2 cups sweet wine
½ lb. butter

Put the butter in the pot and let it get hot. Put in the ducks and brown them.

Add sauce and wine, salt to taste. Let the wine cook out of the ducks, or until it cooks down into the gravy and serve with the ducks.

Birds and venison may be prepared in the same way.

MALLARD DUCK
Mrs. Alfred T. Pattison

1 mallard duck
2 lbs. ground artichokes
2 tablespoons butter
1 salt spoon salt
1 tablespoon chopped shallots and parsley
dash of pepper

Season duck as for roasting. Scrape ground artichokes thoroughly and leave whole. Put butter in large pot with tight cover. When butter is hot add whole duck. Let brown lightly. Then add ground articokes, salt, pepper, and perhaps a little more butter if the quantity used seems to have been absorbed by the duck, then chopped shallots and the parsley. Cover tightly. Stir every few minutes, cooking on a slow fire. When duck is very tender to the prick of a fork and ground artichokes are very soft and brownish in color, the dish is done. It takes about an hour. Remove duck, cut it into 4 quarters. Pile in center of dish and put ground artichokes around it. This is also excellent with chicken.

CANARDS EN PAPILLOTES
Broussard

8 ducks
1 lb. can mushrooms
1 small can truffles
1 bunch shallots
2 cans peas
2 tablespoons olive oil
¼ lb. butter
3 quarts water
bay leaf, thyme, salt, pepper

With a sharp knife, cut all the filets off the ducks, leaving only the bones.

Make a stock, boiling the bones in the water until the quantity is reduced to 2 quarts. Grind the meat of 2 of the ducks, brown it in 2 tablespoons of olive oil, add the mushrooms and truffles, chopped fine, to brown; then the peas.

Pour all the ground ingredients and the olive oil into the stock, and cook 20 minutes, turning the fire very low.

Cut the ducks in halves, wipe with olive oil and broil under a very hot fire, or sauté in the saucepan with olive oil.

Make heart-shaped pieces of paper 18 inches wide by 12 inches long, grease them with oil or butter, having one for each half. Pour sauce on it, then place ducks breast down. Fold over the other half, sealing in the contents by folding the two edges together. Turn each one over, so that the sauce may run through the duck. Place under the flames to get very hot, before serving.

Note:—The whole of this, except the last step of browning the papillotes, may be done several hours before the time of serving.

CANARD á la PRESSE
Arnaud

Place the duck in a hot oven for 5 minutes till the skin is browned. Detach the filets and place them in a chafing dish in hot butter with seasoning, to finish cooking. Meanwhile pass the carcass thru the duck, press and squeeze the juice into the chafing dish. Stir while cooking, add a little cognac to it and curacoa and peel of orange. Take the filets, place one in each plate and cover with sauce from the chafing dish.

GALANTINE OF GOOSE
An old Fortier Recipe

```
10   lb. goose
 5   lbs. ground lean pork
 1   lb. dripped pork fat
 1   small hog's head
 5   lbs. skinned pork, without fat
10   or 12 hog's feet, cut at first joint
     lots of seasoning
     allspice, cloves
     salt, red pepper to taste
     jelly
```

Take a dressed goose, cut the wings and feet at the first joint, cut the neck high. Slit the goose down the back and bone it, removing the carcass and entrails with a small sharp knife. Sew the neck, wings, and feet at ends. Season highly.

Stuff the goose putting seasoned ground meat—1 layer, then strips of fat 2 ins. apart, and continue stuffing the goose. Sew up the back and place the stuffed goose in cheesecloth and sew it up. Then put it in well-seasoned water, enough to cover. Let boil until tender, testing with a fork. Remove from the water, take the cloth off, and place a heavy weight for 12 hours on the goose:

Jelly: Into 5 gallons of highly seasoned water, put the hogs' feet, skin, and head, and boil until very thick. Add water when it boils down. Strain through the cheesecloth. Set the goose in a mold and pour the jelly over it to set. (This makes a gallon, and there will be some left over to put in another mold to serve on the side). A gala dish for the holidays, and it lasts for weeks in the refrigerator.

GAENSEPFEFFER (GOOSE STEW)
Mr. Conrad Kolb

```
6   carrots, 7 onions
1   bunch celery, ½ bunch parsley
2   bay leaves, sprig thyme
1   tablespoon flour
6   allspice, 6 cloves
7   tomatoes and juice
    goose
    vinegar, water
```

Marinate the goose for 4 days with equal parts of water and vinegar, 3 onions, carrots, cloves, and allspice.

Sauté the onions and celery, both chopped fine, add the garlic, thyme, bay-leaf, parsley, flour, allspice, the tomatoes, chopped, and the juice. Boil ½ an hour.

Brown the goose and add it to the above. Cook until tender, and remove the meat. Add to the gravy some blood, always stirring, and serve over the goose.

To be served with potato balls, noodles, or mashed potatoes.

VENISON EN CASSEROLE
Mrs. Albin Provosty, Pointe Coupée

```
3   lbs. venison, loin
2   tablespoons olive oil
2   tablespoons sherry
2   tablespoons butter
1   teaspoon salt
1   teaspoon sliced onion
1   coffeespoon of black pepper
1   tablespoon parsley, minced
1   to 1½ pts. stock
    a pinch of cayenne
```

Venison is very good casseroled with mushrooms. Brown the venison loin in olive oil or butter. Add stock, mix about 2 tablespoons of flour in some of the stock, also a small can of chopped mushrooms, onion and seasonings. Let simmer an hour. Before serving, add butter and sherry. A small can of truffles will improve the flavor.

VENISON STEAK

```
2   venison steaks
2   tablespoons butter
1   tablespoon water
1   tablespoon olive oil
1   tablespoon salt—very scant
    pinch of cayenne
    pinch of black pepper
    garnish with parsley
```

Wipe steak off, brush with olive oil, brown quickly first on one side and then the other. Place in hot oven and cook as you do beef steak. Have platter very hot. Put butter and water in it, salt and pepper steak on both sides, put it into platter and turn it several times, mashing it into the butter. Serve with plum jelly or tart jelly or, best, sugared oranges.

QUAIL IN SHERRY

Take six birds, clean and put aside. Put in a deep pot one heaping tablespoon butter, one teaspoon chopped parsley and one teaspoon chopped onions. Fry until the onions are a light brown. Add one tablespoon flour, let brown lightly and add one can mushrooms, including the liquor, then one cup sherry wine, ½ teaspoon salt, pepper and Tabasco to taste. When thoroughly boiled, drop in the quail, breasts down and boil for one-half hour.

QUAIL WITH TRUFFLES

```
8   quail
8   truffles
2   tablespoons butter
½   cup olive oil
½   coffeespoon cayenne pepper
1   teaspoon salt
```

Dress quail, salt and pepper inside and out.

Slice truffles and fry in butter and put into quail and let stand 24 hours. Heat olive oil in baking pan, put in the quail, cook ¾ hour, basting frequently.

This recipe can be used with pigeons by larding birds with ½ lb. fresh pork fat and leaving in refrigerator 12 hours instead of 24.

CHESTNUT STUFFING

        3   lbs. peeled chestnuts
        1   qt. stale bread
        ¾   cup butter
        1   lemon, juice and grated rind
        1   tablespoon chopped parsley
            salt and pepper to taste
            a dash of nutmeg

Boil nuts in salted water, mash. Fry bread crumbs in butter which has first been slightly browned, mix with nuts. Add seasoning and enough stock until it is of the desired consistency. This is excellent for turkey or chicken or duck.

TURKEY STUFFING WITH WINE
Mrs. Albin Provosty

This recipe will stuff a ten pound bird

        8   slices bread, dry
        2   lbs. ground meat
        2   large onions, chopped
        1   medium sized can mushrooms
        1½   cups pecans
        1   piece celery
        1   bell pepper
        1   clove garlic
        1   cup sherry wine
        2   tablespoons butter

Cut pecans in small pieces, chop, celery, garlic and all seasonings. Brown the onions slightly in the butter, add the pepper, celery, garlic and ground meat. Cook slightly. Season to taste, add pecans and mushrooms, which have been cut in halves or quarters. Add the bread which has been slightly moistened with the wine. The juice from the mushrooms may be used also if it is too dry. Mix all

well, cook for five minutes. Remove from the fire and stuff the fowl. Roast as any fowl.

OYSTER STUFFING FOR TURKEY
Mrs. Albin Provosty

This dressing will stuff a ten pound turkey

             liver and gizzard of the fowl
        3   doz. oysters
        ½   loaf stale bread
        2   tablespoons butter
        3   large onions, chopped fine
        1   tablespoon each chopped parsley,
             thyme, bay leaf
             salt, pepper to taste

Drain oysters of their liquor and use it to moisten the stale bread, which should be squeezed afterwards until quite dry. Chop oysters, liver and gizzard of fowl. Put a tablespoon of bacon drippings, (or lard if the bacon is not at hand) in a frying pan with the onions. Fry these to a golden brown, add the liver and gizzards which have been boiled. When they begin to brown add the seasonings, salt and pepper and mix well. Then add the butter, blending all thoroughly and last of all the oysters. Stir and cook for five minutes, remove from the fire and stuff the fowl.

Variations on the above may be made by substituting corn bread for white bread, or, as some prefer, ½ corn bread and the other half white.

In place of the oysters ground artichokes may be used. There should be about two cups and they should be boiled and mashed

Mushrooms are an interesting substitute for the oysters.

Pecan meats are preferred by some households.

A small can of truffles with four hard boiled eggs, all cut up and used instead of oysters make a delicious dressing.

PRIME RIBS OF BEEF

    prime ribs of beef
1   onion
    salt, pepper
    suet drippings
    bacon fat

Brown the roast in the roasting pan under very hot flames, or on top of stove turning it to brown evenly.

Put an onion on top, and cover the meat with drippings (a little bacon fat may be used if the flavor is desired).

Place in the oven and reduce the heat (a quick oven will cook it unevenly). Bake 10 to 15 minutes to the pound if the roast is desired pink; more, if desired well done. Salt and pepper when done.

BEEF STEAK AND KIDNEY PIE
Mrs. Frank H. Lawton

2   pounds rump steak, free from fat
6   or 8 lamb kidneys, cut in halves
        and parboiled
4   large onions
1   bay leaf
2   teaspoons Worcestershire Sauce
        parsley, salt, pepper, butter

Cut steak into thick squares. Thoroughly cover each piece of meat and each piece of kidney with flour.

Put a layer of meat in bottom of a good sized casserole.

Add salt, pepper, chopped parsley, dot with bits of butter and add drops of Worcestershire Sauce. Then add a thick layer of onions sliced thin. Follow same procedure with floured, sliced kidney, salt, pepper, parsley, butter, Worcestershire Sauce and onions to top of casserole, onions last. Now cover completely with freshly boiling water, not merely hot. Put on cover of casserole and let stand 3 or 4 hours. With cover still on, cook slowly 4 hours in low heat. Do not hurry it. Just before wanted, take cover off and cover with rich pastry rolled very thin so it will cook and brown quickly. The onions should be entirely cooked away if heat is kept low for 4 hours.

VEAL AND SAUSAGE PIE
Mrs. J. L. Onorato

Put in a deep baking dish, first, a fine cutlet, then a layer of sausage, skinned and cut in layers (loose sausage is also very satisfactory with this). Continue layers until dish is full. Use no water as the veal supplies that. Cover pan, cook in oven 1 hour. Remove cover and replace with a good short pie crust. Make a couple of slits in it. Bake. This is also good cold.

STUFFED VEAL POCKET
Miss Ethel Forman

Toast 8 slices of bread and crumble them up.

Cut 2 onions fine and one green pepper, teaspoon of salt and little parsley. Make roux by browning one tablespoon flour in hot lard, stirring all the time. Put in other ingredients and cook for five minutes. Stuff the pocket well. Sew the pocket up, as you do chicken. Put in moderate oven, basting every once in a while.

VEAL CUTLETS MAINTENON

6   veal cutlets
1   cup of consommé
1   cup milk
½   pod garlic
1   teaspoon salt
1   egg yolk
1   wine glass Madeira
½   tablespoon mushrooms
2   tablespoons butter

Trim your boned cutlets, fry very quickly so they are brown but not fully cooked. Put them in the flat dish in which they are to be served, leaving plenty of room for the sauce. Make this sauce of equal quantities of rich clear consommé and milk, with seasoning and a mere suggestion of garlic.

Let the sauce reduce until it begins to thicken.

Take it from the fire and stir in beaten yolks of egg so that it will be thick enough to cover the cutlets well. Put the dish into a quick oven. The cutlets should be cooked by the time the sauce begins to brown. Sprinkle over them Madeira that has been slowly cooked with chopped mushrooms, and serve more of this in a sauce boat.

WIENER SCHNITZEL
Mr. Conrad Kolb

2½ pounds of veal from the leg
2   eggs
⅛   pound butter
½   lemon, the juice
6   eggs, fried
    flour
    salt, pepper

The veal is cut into six ¾ inch slices, pounded, salted, peppered. Beat the egg well, dip the meat into it and then into the flour. Heat the butter and fry the slices light brown on both sides. While they fry drip the lemon juice on.

When well done put them on a hot platter. Make the gravy with ½ cup of water poured into frying butter. Add salt if necessary, cook and pour over the cutlets. The eggs are fried and placed on each cutlet.

TRIPE
Mrs. J. L. Onorato
1½ lbs. young veal tripe
1 pt. cream sauce
    grated cheese

Boil tripe until tender from three to four hours. Then cut into strips like shoe-string potatoes. Make a rich cream sauce using much cream. Add the tripe. Season well and simmer fifteen minutes. Served with grated cheese, Roman or Parmisan.

TONGUE
Mrs. J. L. Onorato
Boil tongue until tender. Chop fine. Melt a glass of currant jelly and pour over it, and let simmer about two hours. Serve with it, red cabbage, cooked with raisins, and ground artichokes.

TONGUE IN CRANBERRY RAISIN SAUCE
Mrs. H. U. Hall
3½ to 4 lb. tongue, smoked
3 tablespoons butter
2 tablespoons minced onion
3 tablespoons flour
1½ cups bouillon
⅓ cup cranberries
½ cup sugar
½ cup water
¼ cup seedless raisins

Put tongue on in cold water in covered kettle. When water boils off, cover again with cold water and cook 3½ to 4 hours until tender. Cool in water in which cooked. Then remove skin and fat and place in covered baking dish. Meanwhile melt butter in top of double boiler, directly over heat. Add onion, cook until delicately browned. Remove from fire, add flour and blend thoroughly. Add bouillon, place over hot water and cook until thick, stirring frequently. Cook sugar and water until clear, add cranberries, and cook until they burst. Drain and add to the brown sauce with the raisins, pour over tongue and cover. Bake in a moderate oven for thirty minutes. Serves six liberally.

TONGUE IN BLACKBERRY SAUCE
Lt. Comdr. and Mrs. S. W. Wallace
1 tongue
1 to 2 bay leaves
1 to 2 celery tops
1 cup seedless raisins, stewed
1 cup water
1 lemon
    pickling spices
    cloves
    blackberry jelly

Boil tongue in salted water containing one tablespoon pickling spices, one or two bay leaves and a few celery tops. When tender, remove skin and roots and stick well with cloves.

Place in a buttered baking dish. Melt a glass of blackberry jelly nad pour over, add 1 cup seedless raisins stewed in one cup of water until soft, spread on top. Squeeze juice of one lemon over all. Bake twenty minutes basting frequently.

FILET MIGNON MARINÉ
Mrs. Walter Torian
3 pounds filet mignon
3 pods garlic
1 cup vinegar
2 onions, cut fine
2 cloves
1 tablespoon lard
1 tablespoon flour
1 can mushrooms
    minced parsley
    red pepper, salt
    bay leaf

Stick the filet with garlic and red pepper, put it into a crock, cover with the vinegar, and add the bay leaf, half the chopped onion and the cloves. Set in the ice-box for two days, turning the filet over night and morning. On the third day, drain it well.

Make a brown roux with the flour and lard, add the rest of the chopped onion and cook it. Now put the meat in, cover tightly and let it cook on a slow fire until tender. Next the mushrooms and chopped parsley and garlic. If there is not enough gravy, add water and let simmer ten minutes.

SAUER BRATEN
Mr. Conrad Kolb
4 lbs. meat
2 quarts vinegar
1 onion cut in slices
10 pepper corns
3 bay leaves
⅛ lb. bacon
3 cloves
2½ tablespoons flour
2 tablespoons drippings
½ glass red wine
    some salt

For the sour pot roast take the meat from rump, pound it, put into vinegar and spices and leave it for four days, turning it over once in a while. After this, take it out and lard it with bacon cut into pieces one third inch thick and 2½ inches long. Pierce the meat with a pointed knife and insert the bacon.

Heat the lard and fry meat light brown on both sides and place on platter. Brown the flour in the lard and pour on the vinegar with the spices, water and salt. Put in a piece of honeycake if on hand, and ½ tablespoon of sugar. Boil all and put the roasted meat into the gravy. The meat roast must be covered and baked in an oven for 2½ to 3 hours turning it and basting it with the gravy.

One-half hour before done pour in red wine.

When the roast is tender, finish the gravy. Put the roast on a platter, take all grease off the gravy and strain it.

If it is too thick add more water, if not sour enough add more vinegar.

HUNGARIAN GOULASH
Mr. Conrad Kolb

```
2   lbs. beef, shank meat
2   small onions, cut in cubes
1   tablespoon lard
1   tablespoon flour
1   teaspoon Hungarian paprika
1   cup bouillon, or water
2   bay leaves
```

Brown onions in lard and add meat cut in one and a half inch squares. Stew for about ten minutes until brown and add salt and paprika, pepper and bay leaf and flour and cook for ten minutes longer.

Then add bouillon until covered. Cover pot and cook for two to two and a half hours, stirring often.

If same becomes dry, add more bouillon. If desired a glass of red wine may be added when finished.

This is best served with noodles or mashed potatoes.

BOILED LAMB á L'ANGLAISE
Mrs. Walter Torian

```
1   small leg lamb
4   cups stock (water in which lamb
        boiled)
4   hard boiled eggs
2   raw eggs
1   clove garlic, minced
2   tablespoons melted butter
2   tablespoons flour, heaping
1   cup capers
    red pepper, salt, to taste
```

Wrap the leg of lamb in a piece of mosquito netting. Place it in tepid water enough to cover it, and let boil hard until done.

Mash up the yolks of hard-boiled eggs with 2 raw yolks, to paste, rub in the minced garlic, the minced parsley, red pepper, salt, then add the melted butter. Add the flour, stirring it into the stock slowly. When cool, add the hard-boiled egg mixture.

Cook until thick, then add the capers, and cook only one minute after that. Pour over the lamb and garnish with chopped white of hard-boiled eggs and minced parsley.

MUTTON CHOPS au DIABLE

```
6   mutton chops
1   egg
½   cup butter
½   teaspoon salt
1   tablespoon flour
½   cup water
1   tablespoon Worcestershire Sauce
½   cup capers
7   tablespoons mushroom sauce
    toasted bread crumbs
```

Take off the outer skin as this is the part of the mutton that gives the strong taste. Grate crackers or crust of bread, break an egg, stir and dip the chops in this. Then in the crumbs and broil them. Use ½ cup of butter, brown a tablespoon of flour in the heated butter, add ½ cup of water, Worcestershire Sauce, capers and mushrooms to pour over chops.

ROAST PORK

```
1   8 lb. pork leg
1   tablespoon olive oil
2   tablespoons vinegar
2   teaspoons ground sage
2   teaspoons cayenne pepper
2   teaspoons salt
```

Rub meat with vinegar and seasoning, wrap pork in a linen cloth that has been dipped in vinegar, repeating this when dry. Let stand 24 hours. When ready to cook, rub with olive oil and flour. Roast 25 minutes to the pound.

BAKED HAM
Miss Margot Samuel

```
12    lb. ham
1½    cups vinegar
1½    cups sherry
6     apples
      Seasonings: 1 bunch carrots, one
        large stalk celery (with the green
        leaves), 6 onions, 1 small bunch
        thyme, 1 small bunch bay leaves,
        a handful each of black pepper
        corns, cloves and allspice, 2 long
        hot peppers, 2 large sweet pep-
        pers, and the peelings of the ap-
        ples.
```

Soak the ham overnight and in the morning discard the water and cover with fresh cold water. Add all the seasonings and bring to a boil. Allow it to cook slowly about twenty minutes to each pound of ham. When done remove from the fire and allow the ham to stand in the liquor all night. Skin the ham and rub brown sugar well into the fat. Place in a baking pan and pour sherry over. Surround with the apples and bake for about a half an hour until piping hot all through. Then run under the flames to brown. Serve with the baked apples.

BAKED STUFFED HAM

```
5   lb. ham
    brown sugar
    cloves
Stuffing:
4   onions
2   bay leaves
1   teaspoon each celery seed, thyme,
        cloves, sage, allspice, paprika, red
        pepper, black pepper
½   teaspoon each mace and dry mustard
13  large soda crackers
1   cup Madeira wine
    parsley, few sprigs
    celery, 3 or 4 stalks
    sugar
```

Cover the ham with brown sugar and dot with cloves. Bake until nearly done.

With sharp knife, cut holes at intervals all about it. Fill with the stuffing and bake in a moderate oven until richly done.

For the stuffing—the herbs, spices, seasoning and soda-crackers are all ground together thoroughly, and moistened to a paste with the wine.

HAM au MARQUIS
Mrs. Walter Torian

slices of cooked ham
1 teaspoon Coleman's Mustard
1 tablespoon brown sugar
vinegar

Mix the mustard and brown sugar, with enough vinegar to make a paste. Spread this over the ham and broil it.

An aristocratic legacy, it is said—credibly.

BAKED STUFFED HAM PONTALBA

14 lb. ham.

If a dry smoked ham is used it must be soaked 12 hours, but with the modern cured hams this is unnecessary.

Remove the bone. This is difficult to do and small, very sharp knives are necessary. Your butcher will, however, perform this feat for you.

Take out about half a pound of meat from the cavity and grind it. Add it to the following stuffing:

3 lbs. pecans, shelled and ground, 1 onion, chopped fine, 1 small can truffles, cut up, 2 bay leaves, 2 sprigs thyme, 2 teaspoons sage, 1 teaspoon powdered cloves, ½ coffeespoon cayenne. 1 glass Madeira wine.

These are all mixed well with the ground ham and the whole stuffed firmly into the cavity of the ham and sewed in tightly. Then get a large cloth. Place the following seasonings in it:

1 onion, chopped, 2 bay leaves, 1 tablespoon sage, 1 teaspoon powdered cloves.

Sew the cloth firmly around the ham and put on to boil with about three gallons of water. Put all the same seasonings in the water that you put inside the cloth. Add also:

1 apple
1 cup cane syrup

Allow the ham to boil for six hours and then to cool in the same water in which it boiled. Remove the skin, dress with sugar and bread crumbs, bake until thoroughly heated through and browned.

While these directions are given for a large ham a picnic ham may be substituted which will serve for the ordinary family meal. One pound of pecans will be sufficient and seasonings reduced to taste.

BOULETTE de SAUCISSON
Mrs. Walter Torian

2 lbs. sausage meat, well seasoned
3 cloves garlic
red pepper, sage
flour
onion, parsley, minced

Marinate, the sausage meat with the garlic, red pepper, sage: let it stay in the ice-box with these seasonings at least all night.

Mould into balls, dredge in flour, and fry in piping hot lard.

Remove the sausage onto a warm platter, and make a roux, stirring into the grease a teaspoon of flour, the chopped onion and parsley.

Served with yellow hominy, they make one of those good old 'light' southern breakfasts, calculated to start a Sunday in the right direction.

PORK SAUSAGE
Mrs. David T. Merrick
Bel Air Plantation

8 lbs. pork, the lean
2 lbs. pork, the fat
3 tablespoons salt
1 tablespoon red pepper
1 tablespoon sage
1 tablespoon black pepper

Grind the pork very fine, and mix with seasonings.

CROQUETTE DE SAUCISSE MARINÉ

The sausage meat is left overnight to marinate with a little vinegar and spices, and garlic. The next morning it is seasoned highly and ½ cup of sherry is added. After that pleasant touch, it is shaped in croquette form and fried in sizzling hot lard.

PORK CHOPS á L'ANANA

4 pork chops
4 slices pineapple
1 tablespoon bacon fat
½ cup pineapple juice
salt, pepper

Add the pork chops to the hot bacon fat in frying pan, and let them stay until they turn a golden brown on both sides. Lay them in an earthenware casserole or glass baking dish, and season them with salt and pepper. Brown the slices of pineapple lightly in the same fat in which the chops are cooked, lay one on each chop, and pour the pineapple juice over all. Cover closely and let bake in a slow oven for 1¾ hours. If necessary add a little water during baking.

LIVER WITH SWEETBREADS
Mr. A. Ferrer

    2   lbs. fine calf's liver
    1   lb. sweetbreads
    ½   lb. chicken livers
    1   can mushrooms
    ¼   lb. butter

Parboil the sweetbreads, cut in small pieces, set aside.

Cook the liver in a very hot skillet with olive oil, 5 minutes. (Turn liver with spatula: it should never be pricked with a fork). Place on a silver platter and set in a warm oven.

Now put the chicken livers in the hot skillet, then the sweetbreads, then the mushrooms, a dash of Worcestershire Sauce, minced parsley, a tiny speck of minced garlic and ¼ lb. of butter.

Turn all of this out onto the liver and serve piping hot.

CALF'S LIVER PAYSAN

    1   lb. calf's liver
    3   onions, medium size
    3   tablespoons minced parsley
        cayenne pepper
        flour
        lard or olive oil

Cut the liver into small cubes. Wash and drain them. Slice the onions and put them in a bowl with parsley and the liver, and a sprinkling of cayenne over all.

Cover the bowl and let stand for an hour. Take out the pieces of liver, dredge them lightly in flour, and fry in deep fat, lard or olive oil.

LIVER au VINGT-CINQ PIASTRES

    1½ lbs. calf's liver
    1   tablespoon minced onions
    1   clove of minced garlic
    1   tablespoon minced green pepper
    4   tomatoes, or 1 small can
    1   tablespoon lard, heaping
    1   tablespoon flour
    1½ cups water
        thyme, bay leaf, salt, pepper

This is worth twelve hours expectancy at least. Buy a chunk of the finest calf's liver, uncut. Place on ice the night before serving, in a deep bowl, with a large piece of ice on top. Before cooking, remove all skin and fibres.

Have ready a large pot of boiling water, and at the same time, a roux, made of the flour stirred evenly into the lard; brown the onions slightly, and add the other seasonings and tomatoes.

Plunge the liver into the boiling water, remove at once, plunge it in again, and then put it immediately into the roux. Add the water, cover, and let simmer till tender, basting at intervals.

When done, and the sauce nicely thickened, slash the liver (not cutting completely through) in several places, baste well with the sauce, and serve piping hot.

This recipe was given as a token of great regard by the famous Mme. Begué to one of her most favored clients with the injunction that he must never give it away, but that he might sell it for twenty-five dollars. The gracious gentlewoman, his wife, parts with it now for the first time.

BEGUÉ'S FAMOUS LIVER
Mrs. Walter Torian

Secure a fine calf liver. Skin, and slice in thick slices. Have a quantity of lard in the frying pan, well heated. Place the liver in the lard and let it cook slowly after seasoning with salt and pepper for about ten minutes. The lard should cover the liver. Simmer on slow fire, and, when cooked, drain off grease and serve on hot plate.

BRUNSWICK STEW
Mr. James L. Crump

    3   lbs. pig jowl or pork
    3   lbs. beef
    2   lbs. pig liver, ground up

"Also a nice fat hen will do no harm."

Place in water about 4 or 5 times the above volume and boil vigorously for 1 hour. Then slow down and let remain at boiling point or just simmering for 3 hours or more. Now add the following vegetables.

    1   2 lb. can best peas
    1   2 lb. can best corn
    1   2 lb. can best tomatoes
    1   pint bottle catsup
    1   quart mashed potatoes
    1   lb. chopped onions

Add the following seasoning 1 hour before serving.

    4   tablespoons vinegar
    2   tablespoons Worcestershire Sauce
    ½   lemon rind, grated
        salt and black pepper to taste

Always keep stew boiling. This quantity is for a large crowd.

GRILLARDES TANTINE
Mrs. Walter Torian

    1   beef or veal round about one inch
        thick
    2   onions cut fine
    3   cloves garlic cut fine
    1   tablespoonful lard
    1   sweet pepper, minced
        salt and red pepper to taste

Place an iron skillet on the fire and put lard in it. Put the grillardes in the lard with onions, garlic, sweet pepper, red pepper and salt to taste. Cover the skillet and lower the burner and let the grillardes cook slowly with the seasoning turning frequently.

When the grillardes are well browned, also the onions, add ½ teacup of hot water and let them cook until very tender. Serve hot with hominy.

The 'grujean' (yellow hominy) is a favored companion for this dish.

GRILLARDES POINTE COUPÉE

2   veal rounds
1   green pepper
1   can tomatoes, or 6 soft fresh ones
1   medium onion
1   pod garlic
1½ tablespoons flour, heaping
1   tablespoon lard, heaping
    cup hot water
    salt, pepper, to taste

Cut the rounds to size appropriate for individual serving. Fry the rounds about five minutes in the hot lard, then remove them and set aside.

Brown the flour and green pepper in the same lard, add the onions and garlic chopped fine, then the other ingredients. Put back the meat, cover and let it cook about two hours. A deep iron skillet should be used. One-half tablespoon of tomato paste may be added if desired.

GRILLARDES PANNÉES

2   veal rounds
1   egg
    salt and pepper
    toasted bread crumbs

Cut rounds into pieces about 4 inches square. Make some toasted bread-crumbs which you have toasted a light color in a slow oven. Run these through the sifter to avoid lumps. Break egg, dip each piece of meat in the egg, then in the bread crumbs, seeing that both sides are covered. Fry each piece in deep hot fat, turning gently from side to side until a rich golden color. The Creoles always serve pickles with this dish, and place the meat on a platter with mashed potatoes in the center.

VIEUX CARRÉ DAUBE
Rémy Moran

3   lbs. heavy veal
2   tablespoons lard
4   onions, minced
1   pod red pepper or cayenne to taste
1   clove garlic, minced
1   sweet pepper, minced
½   can tomatoes, at least ½ lb.
1   teaspoon flour
    salt, green onions, and parsley to taste

Put lard in a deep iron pot and, when hot, put in the veal and brown well on both sides. Then add onions, garlic, red pepper cut fine, or cayenne to taste, and bell pepper. Put onions, garlic and pepper in with the daube and fry until brown. Add tomatoes to which has been added the flour. Cover the pot well and cook 15 minutes on a slow fire, then add one-half cup of water and cook until daube is tender. Add green onions and parsley, salt and pepper to taste. Serve hot with rice.

DAUBE GLACÉ
Mr. Valerian Allain
(Through Mrs. Felix J. Puig)

3   lbs. beef round with bone
4   calves feet
3   or 4 onions
3   or 4 pieces of garlic
3   or 4 sprigs of thyme
1   tablespoon salt
½   stalk of celery
1   tablespoon parsley
2   whole carrots
8   ozs. claret wine
    the tip of a teaspoon of red pepper or a fresh red pepper

Soak daube over night in refrigerator with all seasonings and wine. Next morning, place all in a large pot filled with cold water, let come to a quick boil for a short time then reduce heat and let simmer three or four hours, until bones can be removed from calves feet and beef. Skim the grease from top from time to time. Take from the fire. Skin meat, cut carrots in fancy slices, place around sides and bottom of mold, put beef in whole or chopped. Strain juice, taste to see if sufficiently seasoned. Pour over meat in mold and set aside to congeal, add a few drops of lemon juice.

DAUBE GLACÉ
Célimène Burns

1   large thick round steak
1   pint olive oil
2   pods garlic
2   pigs' feet
2   calves' feet
4   shallots, chopped
    chopped parsley, celery, sage, bay leaf
    sliced lemon
    red pepper, salt

Lard steak with fresh pork.

Into olive oil put the garlic, sage, sliced green peppers (seeded and veined) bay leaf, chopped celery.

Put the steak to soak in this overnight, adding a large quantity of red pepper and salt.

Next morning, fry it a little in the same olive oil.

Pour all together in a pot, adding the pigs' feet and the calves feet, cover plentifully with water, cover the pot and let it cook three hours or more, till thoroughly tender.

Take out the bones of the pigs' feet and the calves' feet, strain the liquid and put it back again over the meat. Add chopped parsley and shallots, both finely minced, let the pot come to a boil, then remove.

Fold daube into a deep rectangular pan preferably, or into a bowl, and pour the liquid over it. Set in the icebox for 24 hours. Put several thin slices of lemon on the top.

A delicious dish. Celery, chopped fine, and mayonnaise, make savory when serving.

BROIL CHOPS

To broil chops to nice crisp brown without any burnt edges, wrap the chops tightly in oiled paper. When broiled in this way the meat is puffed and tender from the confined steam of the juices. Chops should first be partly cooked in a hot frying pan, sprinkled with a few drops of onion juice, then placed on oiled paper, a few dots of butter added and papers tightly twisted. Place in a baking dish and finish cooking in the oven for 10 minutes.

SWEETBREADS AND HAM
Lt. Comdr. and Mrs. S. W. Wallace

    1   lb. sweetbreads
    6   slices of ham, boiled
    6   slices toast, sandwich bread
        preferred
    1   can Campbell's mushroom soup

Parboil sweetbreads according to directions in other receipes. Fry ham slightly on each side and place on toast, then cut sweetbreads into ½ inch slices, flour well and brown in butter, salt and pepper, then place on the slices of toast and ham. This can be kept in a warm oven until ready to serve. Heat the mushroom soup and thin with milk to desired consistency and pour over all.

SWEETBREADS SUPRÊME

    2   plump sweetbreads
    1   scant teaspoon salt
    1   cup soup stock
    2   carrots, minced
    1   turnip, minced
    1½   tablespoons of butter
    1½   tablespoons of flour
    ½   cup white stock
    4   drops lemon juice
    ½   cup cream
    ½   cup button mushrooms

Parboil the sweetbreads in boiling salted water. Trim well, and return to the fire with the soup stock, carrots and turnips. Allow the stock to boil and then simmer twenty min-

utes. Serve with the following sauce:

Stir the flour carefully into the melted butter, add white stock, lemon juice, and cream, then the mushrooms and let all cook together for ten minutes.

CHILE CON CARNE
Mrs. Petrie Hamilton

    5   good sized onions, cut fine
    1   pound ground round steak, fried
    1   two-pound can tomatoes
    1   two-pound can red kidney beans or
    ½   cup red kidney beans soaked over
         night and boiled until done
    1   chopped green pepper
    2   tablespoons chili powder
         salt

Mix all together and let simmer for at least an hour, adding a little water from time to time if necessary. Cook in a covered iron skillet.

BAKED HASH

    2   lbs. brisket
    1   onion
    2   tablespoons butter
    3   large potatoes

Use brisket which has made your pot of rich soup. For the baked hash grind this brisket through a meat grinder. Chop onion and fry lightly in butter. Mix with the ground meat, season highly with salt and pepper, put in a baking dish, covering with mashed potatoes. Dot with butter and bake until the potatoes are well browned.

Use the soup as a separate dish, which will supply family of four, for two days with nourishing soup.

CURRIED KIDNEYS
Mrs. Stanley Arthur

    3   sets kidneys, veal preferred
    1½   tablespoons butter
    1   tablespoon flour
    1   large onion, chopped
    ½   clove garlic, minced
    2   teaspoons curry powder
         salt and pepper

Wash and slice kidneys, removing gristle and hard parts. Season well with salt and pepper. Put butter in saucepan; when very hot add flour and stir constantly to prevent burning, then the onion and garlic and stir until brown. Put in sliced kidneys, cover and let cook not longer than five minutes. Longer cooking makes kidneys tough and indigestible. No water is necessary, as the kidneys make their own gravy which is rich and delicious. Stir in curry powder and serve with boiled rice.

This recipe can be used with pie crust dough for covered kidney pie.

HOW TO COOK A STEAK
By Roark Bradford

"If you are one of these people who are impatient, go to any good restaurant and order your steak. On the other hand, if you realize that it took time to build up civilization, and that even Cleopatra was not made in a day, it will be worth your while to undertake broiling your own steak in the following fashion:

THE STEAK

Go to a good butcher-shop, make him trot out that prime loin of corn-fed steer, and cut off your meat from the big end of the loin. The meat should be not less than two, nor more than four inches thick. Insist upon the cut being of uniform thickness; for no reason, a butcher will thin it down toward the tail of the steak if you don't watch him.

Once in possession of your prime cut of meat, you had, just for the sake of unexpected emergencies, better buy half a dozen, or even a dozen more such cuts. It will cost you money, but you said you wanted a steak, didn't you?

Take your cut steaks to a cold storage house and hang them separately, so that air can circulate all around them. Then forget about them for at least six months. A year will be better; longer than a year will do little, if any good. Some claim they are better after two years, but I doubt it. It sounds like intellectualism instead of ordinary healthy lust.

PREPARATION FOR BROILING

Get one of your steaks out of storage—one ought to be enough for half a dozen hungry people—and trim off the leathery outside edge. Also trim out and save about half the suet. Rub one teacup full of powdered sugar into each side of steak. This sounds pretty bad, I know, but it really is what makes your steak worth waiting for. Be certain that all the sugar has dissolved, and that the surface of the meat has a sticky glisten to it. Imbed one clove of garlic into the steak, next to the bone. Do not attempt other flavoring, such as salt, pepper and the like. That will come later.

BROILING

Your charcoal furnace should be fired well in advance of the time for cooking, so that only a bed of live embers are in the hod when actual cooking begins. Put your steak in a wire broiling rack and sear each side by holding it about six inches above your fire, allowing about one minute for each side. (This quick heat draws together and burns all the sugar into a thick black crust, which holds all the juices in the meat.)

After both sides are seared, hold your broiling rack about a foot above the coals so the cooking process will be slower than the searing, and turn frequently so the heat will be applied evenly to both sides. For blood-rare steak, ten minutes usually is long enough for the cooking. For well-done steak, 20 to 25 minutes will be needed.

SAUCE—IF YOU LIKE SAUCE

Take the suet from the steak, and render slowly in a deep iron skillet. As soon as the fat begins to run, put in two finely chopped cloves of garlic and one finely chopped small onion. As the garlic and onion begin to burn black, remove the burned bits, and at the same time, add an occasional tablespoon of red wine and a dash of Tabasco Sauce until a teacupful of wine and approximately a teaspoonful of Tabasco has been slowly worked into the sauce. Add salt to taste.

SERVING

After steak is done, scrape burnt sugar from surface, carve in suitable portions, arrange on platter and pour sauce over it."

CHESTNUTS RAFFINÉS

1　lb. chestnuts
¾　cup raisins
½　cup cream
　　salt

Scald the chestnuts, shell, and scrape them. Boil until tender, then add raisins.

Cook 20 minutes, then pour off any remaining liquid.

Steam a few seconds and add cream.

Serve very hot,—any kind of meat will be the gainer for this companionship.

CORN PUDDING à la EMMA

6　ears corn, grated
3　eggs
1　cup milk
2　tablespoons butter
1　teaspoon salt
½　green pepper
½　teaspoon baking powder
1　teaspoon flour

Mix butter well, then add the beaten yolks of eggs, then the grated corn and the other ingredients, lastly the whites of eggs, beaten stiffly. Bake slowly for thirty minutes. Green pepper may be omitted.

Grated American cheese may be added.

CORN SAUTÉ WITH PEPPERS

6　ears corn
2　large sweet peppers
2　cloves garlic, minced
2　white shallots, minced
2　tablespoons butter

Cut corn from the cobs. Remove seeds from peppers and cut fine. Melt butter, fry the minced onion and garlic in it for five minutes, then add corn and green pepper. Salt and pepper to taste. Fry five minutes more then add two tablespoons of hot water, cover closely, reduce heat and simmer for fifteen minutes. Just before serving stir in the other spoonful of butter.

EGG-PLANTS FARCIS
Mrs. M. C. Maury-Lyons

2　very large eggplants
4　onions, medium sized
1　can tomatoes
.3　dozen oysters
　　bread crumbs
　　cooked spaghetti

Cut off the stem part of each eggplant so that they may stand lengthwise. Cut off the other end more deeply and carefully scoop out the inside.

Brown the onions in butter, add the tomatoes and sauté the scraped out eggplant in this.

Mix in the boiled spaghetti, then the oysters, and let it cook a few minutes more. Stuff the egg-plants

with this, sprinkle the bread crumbs thickly on top. Dot with butter, and run them in the oven until the bread crumbs brown.

It is a pretty sight for the table, and a savoury taste for the palate. With a salad, and this, a luncheon or a Sunday night supper is complete.

EGGPLANT SOUFFLÉ
Mrs. S. A. Fortier

1　eggplant
2　tablespoons butter
2　teaspoons flour
1　cup milk
½　cup grated cheese
¾　cup soft bread crumbs
2　teaspoons onion, grated fine
1　tablespoon tomato catsup
2　eggs
1　teaspoon salt

Peel the eggplant, dice and cook until tender, then mash well. Melt the butter, in a saucepan, stir in the flour slowly till smooth, then add the milk, stirring till smooth and thick. Add the mashed eggplant, cheese, bread crumbs, onion, catsup, salt and the lightly beaten egg yolks. Lastly fold in the stiffly beaten whites. Bake in a greased baking-pan set in a pan of hot water in a moderate oven, about 30 minutes.

ONIONS FARCIS

6　large onions
1　bouillon cube, dissolved in ¾ cup
　　water
1½　cups shelled peas
6　tablespoons butter
　　salt, pepper to taste

Parboil onions about 15 minutes, adding salt to the boiling water.

Make a cavity in the center of each onion. Have the peas cooked for five minutes in boiling water, and drained. Fill each cavity with peas, placing over each a tablespoon of butter, and over that bits of the center parts of the onion. Add the dissolved boullion cube. Cook uncovered for half an hour or more, until onions brown.

FRENCH ARTICHOKES

1　tablespoon vinegar
1　teaspoon salt
　　Hollandaise sauce or drawn butter

Trim the sharp points of the leaves with scissors.

Wash well, place in cold water, adding vinegar to destroy possible insects.

Put the artichokes in a pot of boiling water seasoned with a teaspoon of salt. Let them boil gently, until you can draw out the leaves easily or until the outer leaves are tender.

Remove from the fire and drain upon a dish, placing them upside down, so that the water will run off. Serve hot, with drawn butter or with Hollandaise sauce. The time for boiling an artichoke varies with the vegetable, from 25 to 30 minutes.

Note: Before cooking artichokes, it is well always to soak them in cold water some two or three hours: it makes them more tender.

ARTICHOKE RING
Mrs. Frank H. Lawton

Artichokes, boil until tender. Scrape off tender part including the hearts.

Put through meat grinder with small piece of garlic.

    Add ½ pint cream
½ cup bread crumbs
4 eggs (whites beaten very stiff and
       folded in last)
    salt and pepper to taste

Bake ¾ hour in moderate oven with mold in pan of water.

Creamed sweetbreads and mushrooms go well with this, also crabs or oysters.

BANANAS IN JACKETS
Mrs. J. N. Roussel

    large, ripe bananas
    biscuit dough
    sugar

Peel the bananas. Roll the biscuit dough thin.

Cut off the ends of each banana, slantwise, and follow the slant in cutting each banana in two.

Roll each one in sugar, then cover with the dough, as in a jacket. Bake in a moderate oven, and serve as a vegetable.

BAKED BEANS
Mrs. James Mulvaney

1   qt. York state marrow fat beans
1   lb. fat salt pork
3   medium sized onions, sliced thin
1   tablespoon molasses
3   tablespoons sugar
¼   tablespoon dry mustard
    pinch of ginger, salt

Soak the beans overnight in cold water to cover. In the morning drain, cover with fresh water and cook very slowly, adding the mustard, ginger, onions, salt and about ¼ of the pork. Cook very slowly testing from time to time by removing a few beans in a spoon and blowing on them. When the skins burst they are done. Scald the rind of the remaining pork and cut a ¼ inch slice from it. Lay it in the bottom of a "Boston Bean" pot. A deep earthenware casserole will do. Cut through rind of remaining pork every half inch making the cuts about one inch deep. Drain off any remaining water in which the beans have boiled and pour them in the pot. Bury the pork in the top, leaving the rind exposed. Mix, in a cup or bowl, the molasses, sugar, and 1 tablespoon of salt, with a cup of boiling water. Stir well and pour over the beans.

Cover the pot and allow to cook very slowly for six to eight hours adding more water from time to time as needed. Uncover for the last hour to brown and crisp the pork rind. The secret of success with baked beans is in the long slow cooking, which is most easily attained by using the very heavy earthenware pots which are made for this purpose.

FRENCH FRIED BANANAS
Mrs. Grace Stevenson

    bananas
    corn flakes
    eggs

Cut bananas in desired sizes, dip in egg, then in crushed cornflakes Fry at 380° until golden brown.

Serve with broiled lamb, veal, or pork chops.

FRIED PLANTAINS

Select very ripe plantains, peel and slice lengthwise. Fry them slowly in butter or other fat until nicely browned. Remove them to a hot platter and dust with sugar. Add a few tablespoons of sugar to the fat left in the pan and just a little water, about half a cup. Pour the resulting syrup over the plantains.

STUFFED CABBAGE
Mrs. J. N. Roussel

1   green cabbage
½   lb. boiled ham
2   tablespoons butter
1   onion
1   tablespoon salt

Select a loose leafed green cabbage. For stuffing use boiled ham chopped. Lightly broil ham in butter with chopped onion, salt and pepper. Carefully pull open the outer leaves of the cabbage and insert the stuffing. Tie in a clean cloth and boil.

CUCUMBER RING

2   cups grated cucumber
3   eggs
1   teaspoon sugar
1   teaspoon baking powder
¾   teaspoon salt
1½   tablespoons flour
1½   cups milk
½   teaspoon black pepper

Beat egg yolks until light. Add milk, cucumber and seasoning. Sift in flour and baking powder. Sift add stiffly beaten whites. Turn into a well buttered baking dish and place in moderate oven and cook until firm Serve hot as soon as done.

CARROT RING
Mrs. Edward Rightor
2 cups boiled carrots
6 eggs, beaten separately
1 cup grated bread crumbs
1 teaspoon onion juice
1 teaspoon mustard
½ teaspoon paprika
1 pint thin cream or top milk

Mash the carrots, add bread crumbs and seasoning, beat in the egg yolks and then fold in the stiffly beaten whites. Turn into a buttered ring mold, place in a pan of hot water. Cook thirty minutes.

Serve as a vegetable, or fill with crab or shrimp with mushroom sauce. The lowly carrot is glorified!

FRENCH FRIED ONIONS
Mrs. Hunter Leake
1 large Bermuda onion
1 pint milk
thin batter

Slice onion, soak an hour in milk. Drain and dry. Dip in thin batter as for batter cakes and fry a light brown. Very delicious with steaks or any kind of meat. This will serve 5 or 6 people.

NEW PEAS
Mrs. Afred T. Pattison
1 tablespoon sugar
1 quart shelled peas
1 cup diced raw ham, with fat
10 hearts of shallots
1 cup cold water

Put all the ingredients together in a pot and allow them to simmer very slowly three quarters of an hour or an hour. Shake from time to time to prevent burning.

FRIED APPLES
One of the nicest of all dishes is fried apples, cooked in plenty of butter, with a few drops of water and a sprinkling of sugar added. Slice the apples thinly, leaving the skins on; lay them in the hot butter in the open frying pan and turn occasionally until perfectly tender and somewhat candied around the edges. Serve with French toast and bacon; fried oatmeal or mush; or plain buttered toast and an omelet for breakfast.

IRISH POTATOES IN POKE
Irish potatoes
bacon

Boil large Irish potatoes in jackets, peel. Fold three pieces of strips of bacon around each one, holding the strips in place with tooth-picks. Set them in an uncovered baking-pan in the top part of the oven, and let them stay until the bacon becomes crisp.

DUCHESSE POTATOES
Mrs. J. N. Roussel
3 cups mashed potatoes
1 egg
1 teaspoon baking powder
lard

The potatoes should be well seasoned with salt and pepper. Add to them the beaten egg and the baking powder. Drop a heaping teaspoonful at a time, in deep boiling fat. A small crisp fluffy bouché results.

SOUFFLÉS POTATOES au CORDON BLEU de PARIS
Mrs. J. N. Roussel
Take large firm potatoes. Wipe them off and peel them. Wipe them again, to keep them dry. Slice them evenly, about ⅛ inch thick. Dry each slice in a towel. Have two large pots of kidney beef lard, the deeper pot very hot, but not boiling. Drop one slice in this; if the lard does not bubble, it is not hot enough. When it is hotter, put in potatoes, moving them about constantly for about four minutes. Then drop a cupful at a time into boiling fat in the second pot. Leave them in till they are puffed (soufflés), which occurs very soon. Remove from the fire and set aside, to keep warm while others cook. Add salt.

SWEET POTATOES EN CASSEROLE· WITH PINEAPPLE
3 large sweet potatoes
24 marshmallows
brown sugar
sliced canned pineapple

Select large sweet potatoes of uniform size, the diameters of which correspond to that of pineapple. Wash potatoes thoroughly and boil until tender in boiling salted water (½ teaspoon salt to 1 pint of water). Remove, cool and peel potatoes. Slice in half-inch slices and place a layer in a buttered casserole. Then place over them alternate layers of pineapple, brown sugar and potato until all ingredients are used up. Add ½ cup of pineapple juice. Bake in a moderate oven, until the whole is flavored throughout and candied. Top with marshmallows and run in the oven to brown.

SWEET POTATOES ROYAL
Boil the potatoes, peel, and cream with butter and sugar, then add cinnamon. Sprinkle grated orange peel on top, and if desired, finely chopped pecans. Put in baking dish. Cover with marshmallows and set in the oven till marshmallows melt and brown.

ORANGE SWEET POTATO
Mrs. C. E. Griggs

3 oranges
4 medium sized sweet potatoes, boiled and used while hot
2 tablespoons grated orange rind
½ teaspoon nutmeg
½ cup melted butter
1 teaspoon salt

Cut oranges in half crosswise and remove pulp without breaking the skins. Flute edges of the orange cups with a sharp knife. Remove boiled sweet potato from skins. Mash and beat until fluffy with half grated orange rind, the nutmeg, one third cup melted butter, salt, and one third cup of the orange pulp, chopped. Pile mixture into the orange cups and pour remaining butter over the top. Sprinkle with the remaining orange rind. Place the filled cups on a baking sheet and brown under the broiler ing sheet and brown under the broiler. Serve immediately. Serves six.

CARROTS au SUCRE
Mrs. Alfred Pattison

4 bunches young carrots
1½ to 2 tablespoons butter
1 cup sugar or according to taste
1 saltspoon salt

Scrape carrots, cut into thin rounds. Put butter, carrots, sugar, and salt in heavy iron frying pan. Cover tightly and cook over slow fire until carrots are very tender, shaking pan every three or four minutes to prevent sticking to bottom. Serve hot. The time for cooking varies. It should take at least ¾ of an hour. Try to uncover pan as little as possible as the carrots are cooked by steam only. This is excellent.

SPINACH "AU BAIN MARIE"
Pudding with Mushrooms

3 bunches spinach
1 teaspoon salt
1 kitchen spoon butter
½ lemon
2 egg yolks
½ lb. mushrooms

Mash boiled spinach in an earthenware bowl with melted butter and lemon juice. When cool add well beaten egg yolks and pour into a buttered mold. Place in another pan containing water and cook for thirty minutes in a moderate oven. Turn out on a hot platter and fill the center with broiled mushrooms.

SPINACH au GRATIN à la MINNIE
Miss Hélène Villeré

6 bunches spinach
   cream sauce
½ lb. cheese
   hard-boiled eggs

Pluck the veins and stems thoroughly from the spinach, boil it in a minimum of water, then press it through a colander and whip it well. Dissolve the cheese in the cream sauce. In a baking-dish, put a layer of spinach, then a layer of the sliced hard boiled eggs then a layer of sauce. Repeat until the dish is filled. Top with bread crumbs, dotted with butter, and bake.

SPINACH SOUFFLÉ

1 tablespoon butter
1 tablespoon chopped onions
1½ tablespoons flour
1 cup milk
2 cups chopped cooked spinach
¾ teaspoon salt
2 tablespoons grated cheese
4 egg yolks
4 egg whites, beaten
   small onion, chopped
   pepper to taste

Brown onions in shortening, stir in flour, add milk slowly. Add spinach, cheese, seasoning. Heat, remove from fire and mix in unbeaten yolks. Cool, fold in whites. Pour into greased baking dish, and set dish in pan of water in a slow oven. Bake until mixture rises and sets.

SPINACH CRÉOLE
Mrs. William Westerfield

Put the spinach in boiling water (just a little!) containing a little salt and sugar. Boil it only two minutes, then drain it and put it in cold water to preserve its color. Then chop it up.

Put it in the frying pan with a little butter and a little cream, and let it cook 5 minutes. Then add a dash of garlic and nutmeg. If it is too thin, add just a little flour. A boon, the health food gone palatable!

STUFFED SUMMER SQUASH
Lt. Comdr. and Mrs. S. W. Wallace

   squash
   pineapple
   cheese sauce

Boil medium sized summer squash until tender, not too soft. Remove centers and chop fine. Combine with well drained crushed pineapple, season. Fill the shells, place in a Pyrex serving dish and cover with cheese sauce. (Make sauce by cream-sauce recipe and add cup of grated cheese). Put in the oven to brown.

BOILED RICE, CREOLE STYLE

Boiled rice makes its daily appearance on southern tables with as great regularity as the boiled Irish potato appears in other parts of the country. Perfectly dry, every grain separate and thoroughly cooked with its delicious nutty flavor, it is entirely different from the sticky glutinous mass which horrifies the wanderer north of the Mason and Dixon line. The proper preparation is very simple and two methods are here described;

1½ cups rice (will serve six)
½ teaspoon salt

Have a large pot full of briskly boiling water. Add the rice slowly so as not to arrest the boiling. Stir as little as possible. When the water begins to thicken and the grains to soften remove from the fire, drain water off through a colander and pour cold water over it, then place the colander over another pot containing boiling water. Allow to steam thus for an hour or so. Then place the colander in the oven for a few minutes just before serving.

OR

1 cup rice to each cup cold water
½ teaspoon salt
1 level teaspoon lard

Put all on to cook in a double boiler for an hour or longer. Every bit of water will be absorbed and none of the nourishment lost as it is in the previous method.

GRUJEAN CREOLE
Mrs. Walter Torian

2 cups yellow hominy (Grujean)
1 cup sweet cream
1 tablespoon butter

Cook the hominy as usual—that is wash it, and boil with salt until done, stirring to prevent lumping. Put into a double boiler, add the cream and butter and cook until thick. Delicious with grillardes.

TOMATOES à la CRÉOLE
Mrs. W. J. Bentley

1 large green pepper, chopped
1 small onion, chopped
3 large tomatoes
   salt, pepper, butter
Sauce:
¼ cup milk
¼ cup cream
1 tablespoon flour
1 tablespoon butter
   rounds of toast
   salt, pepper

Pare the tomatoes and cut them in two. Put them in baking tin, covering each one with a layer of chopped onions and peppers. Dot liberally with bits of butter, salt, and pepper. Bake about ½ hour, in a hot oven. Remove from the fire and keep hot.

The sauce. To the liquor in the pan, add the milk and cream. Rub the flour and butter together, and stir them in with the other ingredients, and add the salt and pepper. When the mixture thickens, remove it from the fire. Put the tomatoes on the rounds of buttered toast, and pour the cream sauce over all.

TOMATOES L'AIGRE-DOUCES
Mrs. Wm. J. Nolan

4 large, ripe, firm tomatoes
1 teaspoon sugar
1 clove garlic, minced
1 teaspoon lard
1 teaspoon parsley, minced
1 tablespoon vinegar
2 tablespoons olive oil
½ teaspoon salt

Cut the tomatoes through the center. Place the cut centers flat into a skillet in which the lard is already hot. Let fry a few minutes until light brown. Then turn them over to have the centers up. Add seasoning, and allow to simmer on the back of the stove until tender. If any are left over, they may be set away to reappear in a Spanish omelet the next day.

ASPARAGUS MOUSSE
Mrs. Harry A. Thompson

2 large cans asparagus
4 eggs
1 tablespoon flour
⅛ lb. butter
½ cup milk

Beat yolks and whites of eggs separately. Make custard in double boiler with flour, butter, milk and yolks of eggs with added juice of asparagus. When cooled, add whites of eggs and asparagus tips, put in greased mold and bake slowly with mold set in water.

CANDIED CUSHAW
Mrs. Leonard M. Levy

1 cushaw
¼ lb. butter
1½ cups sugar

Cut the neck of the cushaw into small rounds about ¼ inch thick (about eight rounds). Peel off the rind, place in a large long biscuit pan, cover with water, add butter and sugar, cook on top of the stove, carefully turning once with the pancake turner, until the syrup has thickened and they look crystallized. Serve as you would candied yams.

COLD SLAW
Mrs. William McClean

    3   cups cabbage, shredded
    1½ cups crisp celery, chopped
    1   small can grated pineapple
    1   small green pepper, chopped
    ½   cup blanched almonds, cut in thin
          slivers

Cabbage should be put in a bowl of ice water five or six hours before using and kept on ice. It should then be well drained and placed in a bowl which has been rubbed with garlic. The chopped celery, pepper, and almonds are then added and the pineapple which has been drained of its juice. The whole must be well mixed and dressed with boiled dressing.

MIRLETON

Pick the vegetable pears when they are about the size of a duck egg or a trifle larger. Wash and boil until tender. Cool, pare and take out seed. Marinate a few moments in French dressing.

On a bed of shredded lettuce put two halves for each serving. In the seed cavity put a filling of Neufchatel or cream cheese, moistened with a little cream if necessary, and with salt and pepper to taste. Garnish with mayonnaise and sprinkle with paprika.

MELANGE

Cook and cut into thin straw-like strips, carrots, beets, tender celery and hard-boiled eggs. Cut cold ham and cold tongue in the same size strips. Place these in mounds on a bed of shredded lettuce, alternating the meats and vegetables. In the center, place bell pepper cup filled with thousand island dressing.

AVOCADO MOUSSE

    1   tablespoon gelatine
    ¼   cup cold water
    ½   cup boiling water or stock
    1   teaspoon salt
    1   teaspoon onion juice
    2   cups avocado
    2   teaspoons Worcestershire Sauce
    ¼   cup whipped cream
    ½   cup mayonnaise

Cream avocado, add salt, Worcestershire Sauce and onion juice. Soak gelatine in cold water. Add boiling water. When cool pour it into cream and mayonnaise, that have been well mixed. Now combine this with the avocado and turn into a mold. Serve with tomatoes, hearts of lettuce and mayonnaise.

AVOCADO
(Alligator Pears)

Take ripe avocados, cut in halves, remove seed, scoop out the meat with a teaspoon, mix with pieces of tomato, and marinate with a sharp mayonnaise seasoned with Worcestershire Sauce and grated onion. Put back in shell. Chill. This makes a good beginning for a summer luncheon.

GROUND ARTICHOKE MOUSSE

    1   lb. ground artichokes, boiled and
          mashed through a colander
    1   heaping tablespoon gelatine softened
          in ½ cup cold water
    ½   cup boiling water
    1   teaspoon salt
    1   teaspoon onion juice
    2   teaspoons Worcestershire Sauce
    ½   cup whipped cream
    ½   cup mayonnaise

Add salt, Worcestershire, and onion juice, to the mashed artichokes. Dissolve the soaked gelatine in the boiling hot water and add. When cool fold in the cream and mayonnaise which have been well mixed. Mold and chill and serve with tomatoes, hearts of lettuce and mayonnaise.

PEGASUS SALAD
Mrs. Joel Harris Lawrence

    2   boiled potatoes
    2   hard boiled eggs
    1   small onion, chopped fine
    1   teaspoon dry mustard
    4   tablespoons olive oil
    2   tablespoons vinegar
    1   teaspoon anchovy sauce or paste
          salt and pepper, pinch garlic

Press potatoes through ricer, mash eggs, mix potatoes, eggs and onions. Make a dressing of other ingredients using rotary egg beater. Stir this into mixture. Serve on bed of lettuce. Garlic may be left out if flavor is not desired.

TOMATOES ST. MARTIN

    1   teaspoon lemon juice
    3   tablespoons olive oil
    3   tablespoons tomato catsup
    1   tablespoon Worcestershire Sauce
          peeled tomatoes
          Philadelphia cream cheese

Mix well the ingredients of the dressing and beat with rotary egg-beater until thick. Dig out slightly the tomatoes, put 1 teaspoonful of minced onions in each an hour before serving and chill. Then fill the hollow in each with cream cheese pushed through the ricer just before serving, and pour dressing over all.

ONION SALAD BEGUÉ
Mrs. Walter Torian

Pare and boil whole six large onions. When tender, remove from the water, drain, and set to cool. Season with salt, pepper, vinegar, and oil, add a chopped hard-boiled egg and serve.

LEEK SALAD

Boil and chill leeks. Serve with either French dressing or a mayonnaise. It is supposed to be one of the most tasty salads in the world.

ARTICHOKES IN TOMATO ASPIC

```
6   artichokes
1   qt. can tomatoes
1   bay leaf
2   cloves
½   cup boiling water
½   cup cold water
1   tablespoon gelatine, heaping
    grated onion, a little
```

Cook the tomatoes and the seasoning 15 minutes. Dissolve the gelatine in ½ cup of cold water and add the boiling water to it. Strain the tomatoes and add the gelatine. When cool, put a little in the mold to set. Next, add the boiled artichoke hearts, cut up, and the tender part of the leaves that have been scraped off with a silver knife, into the tomato juice. Pour all into the mold to set. A dish that never fails to delight; serve it on hearts of lettuce, with mayonnaise.

SOUR SWEET SALAD
Mrs. Emile Godchaux

```
6   cucumbers, sliced thin
2   cups celery, cut in small pieces
½   cup vinegar
½   cup sugar
½   cup water
```

Let vinegar, sugar and water come to a boil. Drop in the celery, cook 5 minutes, then add cucumbers and cook both 15 minutes.

2 cups stringbeans, cooked in plain water, 2½ cups shredded cabbage, may be used with the same salad dressing, putting in stringbeans first, then adding cabbage, to cook 10 to 15 minutes.

FRUIT SALAD aux AMANDES

```
1   tablespoon sugar
1   tablespoon flour
1   lb. blanched almonds
1   can pineapple
1   tablespoon mustard
1   can white cherries
1   pint whipped cream
1   pint milk
2   tablespoons gelatine
```

Heat the milk to the boiling point in a double boiler, and with it blend sugar, mustard and flour. Soften the gelatine in cold water and pour the above mixture over it. Beat briskly and when beginning to cool, add fruit and nuts cut small. Fold in the whipped cream, pour into molds. Serve on lettuce with mayonnaise, or with a boiled dressing fluffed up with whipped cream. The proportions given are for a large party, 8 to 10, but if one is willing to be so lavish as to provide this delicacy for a small family, amount of ingredients may be reduced.

One of its virtues is, that it can well play the dual role of salad and dessert.

FROZEN SALAD TENERIFFE
Mrs. Hugh deLacey Vincent

```
1   cup mayonnaise
1   cup whipped cream
1   cake Philadelphia cream cheese
1   cup canned pineapple
3   tablespoons sugar
1   small bottle Maraschino cherries
```

Mash the cherries, add them gradually to the whipped cream, keeping the mixture smooth. Add the mayonnaise. Drain all the juice from the fruit, and fold lightly into the mixture. Blend the cream cheese with the mayonnaise, and add to the other mixture, blending well.

Place in a melon mould or freezer, cover with waxed paper, and pack in ice and salt for 3 hours (2 parts of ice to 1 part salt).

JELLIED ORANGE
Mrs. Edward Rightor

```
1   envelope Knox Gelatine
½   cup water
1   cup orange juice
1   cup sugar
1   tablespoon lemon juice
1   cup pineapple, shredded
2   large carrots, grated
```

Soak gelatine in ¼ cup cold water and add ¼ cup boiling water, when cool add orange juice, sugar, pineapple and carrots.

Put in mold and place in refrigerator.

Serve with mayonnaise, that has had a cup of whipped cream added.

GRAPE SALAD

```
1½  lbs. mixed grapes, seeded and halved
1   tablespoon, level, gelatine in ½ cup
    water
1   pt. grape juice
```

Mold and serve on lettuce with mayonnaise or cooked dressing with whipped cream added.

PINEAPPLE SALAD
Mrs. John Barry

1	large can sliced pineapple
½	lb. marshmallows
½	lb. blanched whole almonds
½	teaspoon salt
½	teaspoon mustard
3	teaspoons flour
2½	tablespoons vinegar
½	tablespoon sugar
½	tablespoon butter
½	pt. whipped cream
½	cup thick cream
3	egg yolks

Drain pineapple overnight, or several hours before using. Mix sugar, salt, flour, mustard and vinegar in double boiler. Cook until it begins to thicken. Add the beaten egg yolks and butter, stirring all the while. Let cool, then thin with the cream. Cut the pineapple in small pieces and quarter the marshmallows. Pour the dressing over the pineapple and marshmallows, mix thoroughly and place in refrigerator to get very cold.

Before serving add almonds and the stiffly whipped cream. Serve on hearts of lettuce. Cheese biscuits or cheese straws make an excellent accompaniment for this dish.

CHICKEN SALAD
Mrs. Grace Stevenson

Stew one chicken slowly with one quart of water to which one tablespoon of tarragon vinegar and three cloves of garlic have been added, also salt and pepper. When tender cut from bones and cube. Add one cup mushrooms, ¼ cup diced green and red peppers—return to stock and season highly.

Core and pare eight medium sized apples leaving one inch band of peel around the centers. Fill each apple with the chicken mixture and place them in a roasting pan with some of the chicken stock. Bake until the apples are tender but not falling apart. Baste several times. When done, chill. Serve on nest of endive with mayonnaise.

EGGS GÊLÉS AU CAVIAR

½	box gelatine
2	cans bouillon
2	cans water
½	lemon
6	eggs, hard-boiled
	caviar
	mayonnaise
	celery, onions, parsley

Boil the bouillon and the water with the celery, onions, parsley and half a lemon. Let it all boil down and strain it over the gelatine that has been dissolved in water.

Halve the eggs, take out the yolks, cream them with mayonnaise and mix caviar with them. Then put the two halves together to resemble a whole egg. Lay the eggs at intervals in a ring mold and strain the mixture over them.

Serve with shrimp or crabmeat with mayonnaise in the center.

TURKEY SALAD
Miss Charlotte E. Mitchell

1	15-lb. turkey
12	hard-boiled eggs
6	stalks good celery
1½	green peppers
1	red pepper pod
1	tablespoon minced parsley
12	bay leaves and some stems
2	sprigs thyme
½	teaspoon minced shallots
1	lemon, sliced
	salt to taste
	well seasoned mayonnaise—without sugar
1	bottle, small, capers

Boil turkey until legs pull off easily in water to which has been added salt, bay leaves, thyme, celery leaves, green pepper, red pepper and lemon. Remove skin and fat while hot. When thoroughly cooled, remove meat from bones and cut into large cubes. Add to meat finely chopped celery and some tender leaves, chopped green peppers, parsley. Mix thoroughly with just enough mayonnaise to moisten the meat. Let stand 2 hours in ice box, if possible. Before serving add eggs (not too finely chopped), shallots, parsley and Tabasco to taste. Never stir or mash the salad, lift it from the bottom with a pan cake turner. Serve in lettuce cup with a heaping spoonful of stiff mayonnaise on top with three or four capers. Garnish with tomatoes if desired. Serve with a large kitchen spoon—never mold. This is a service for 25 people.

A fine addition to this salad is to make an aspic of the turkey soup and serve with mayonnaise on side.

Chicken salad may be made in the same way.

EGG MOUSSE

1	dozen eggs, hard boiled, chopped
1	cup warm milk
1¼	tablespoons of gelatine
1	cup mayonnaise
	salt and pepper

Mix cut eggs and mayonnaise. Soak gelatine in ½ cup cold milk, then add ½ cup hot milk. When cool, pour over eggs. Season with salt and pepper. Pour in ring mold. When jellied, turn out on platter and in the center put cut beets. Garnish with lettuce and mayonnaise.

CRAB MEAT WITH ROQUEFORT DRESSING

1   doz. hard crabs
6   tomatoes
3   hard-boiled eggs
    Roquefort cheese dressing
    salt
    pepper
    bay-leaf, thyme

Boil the crabs with salt, pepper, bay leaf and thyme. Pick crab meat and season. Slice the hard-boiled eggs and the tomatoes. Pour French dressing over them and set aside. Later, put the sliced hard-boiled eggs and tomatoes around the crab meat and pour the French dressing over it, and pour over all Roquefort cheese dressing.

LOBSTER MOUSSE
Mrs. Sterling Parkerson

1   can tomato soup
3   cakes Philadelphia cream cheese
2   tablespoons gelatine
¾   cup finely chopped celery
¾   cup finely chopped green peppers
2   tablespoons grated onion
1   large can lobster
1   cup mayonnaise

Mash the cream cheese in the tomato soup, and heat in a double-boiler until the cheese is melted and very hot. Soak the gelatine for five minutes in a cup of water and add to the soup mixture. As soon as this begins to congeal, add the celery, green pepper, and onions, and the lobster, which has been broken into small pieces. Add the mayonnaise and season highly with salt, Tabasco, and Worcestershire Sauce.

Place in a wet mold and when set, serve on a bed of lettuce leaves, garnished with mayonnaise.

Note: This is a rich and filling salad. It should not be served at dinner or when other heavy food is served. But it is a thing of perfect grace for a Sunday night supper, or for a light luncheon. Shrimp can be used instead of lobster.

LOBSTER MOUSSE
Mrs. Seth Miller

Chop meat of two lobsters weighing about 1½ pounds each (or 1 pound of shrimp). Melt 1 tablespoon of gelatine in ½ cup of tomato sauce. When cool, mix with ½ pint of whipped cream and ½ cup of mayonnaise. Pepper and salt to taste. Mix together and fill round mold. Chill. Serve with center filled with lettuce and mayonnaise.

SHRIMP SUPRÈME

1   cup boiled shrimp
¾   cup chopped celery
1   pimento, chopped
1½   teaspoons grated onion
1   small bottle stuffed olives, sliced
1   heaping tablespoon gelatine
¾   cup mayonnaise
2   hard boiled eggs, chopped
1   lemon, juice
     salt to taste

Soak gelatine in 2 tablespoons cold water, melt over hot water and add lemon juice. Let cool, add mayonnaise, salt and pour this mixture over the other ingredients. Mix well and pour into molds. Place in ice box to congeal, and serve on lettuce with mayonnaise; canned tuna fish may be substituted for shrimp.

FISH ASPIC
Mrs. May Westerfield Born

½ lb. fish for each person served

Clean and skin fish. Put the head, skin and bones in enough water to cover. Place pot on fire. To this add salt, cayenne pepper, thyme, four or five bay leaves, a few cloves, a few allspice, juice and rind of one lemon and ½ glass of vinegar. Boil ten minutes and strain through thin cloth. Now boil the tenderloin (firm part) of the fish in the same fish broth. When fish is done, take out and let cool. Beat up the whites of four eggs, add to fish broth and let boil four or five minutes. Strain this through cloth. Add ½ ounce of gelatine to each pound of fish and sufficient fish broth to make right consistency for the gelatine. Place in ring mold in ice box.

PATÈ DE FOIE GRAS ASPIC
Mrs. Alfred T. Pattison

2   to 3 calves feet
    (some chicken feet and heads add
    to the flavor)
1   qt. water
1   lb. piece shin bone
½   soup bunch
1   small clove garlic
2   eggs, the whites
1   can bouillon
    salt, pepper to taste

Boil all of this except the egg whites and the bouillon until calves feet boil to pieces, at least 2 hours cooking. Strain and let cool, then clarify with white of eggs. When clear, add bouillon and 1 pint water. Season to taste and set in molds to harden. This amount makes about 3 pints of jelly. It can be kept in the ice box, and used for several days. The paté can be put in individual moulds of this jelly or in a large ring of it. It is delicious served with hearts of lettuce salad and French dressing.

Note: The calves' feet may be put to use, instead of wasting them, the meat picked from the bone and made into a stew with brown gravy; or served "en poulette" with a cream sauce thickened with the yolks of an egg, it makes a delicious dish.

SWEETBREAD SALAD

    1   set sweetbreads
    1   stalk celery
        salt, pepper, onion juice

Boil the sweetbread until thoroughly done, about twenty to thirty minutes. Cool, clean and cut into dice. Cut the celery, very fine. Season with salt, pepper, and onion juice and chill. When ready to serve place on crisp white lettuce leaves and dress with mayonnaise.

LETTUCE AUX CRÊPES

    1   cup raisins
    ½   cup cottage cheese
    ½   cup American cheese, grated
    ½   cup mayonnaise, highly seasoned
        large lettuce leaves

Make a paste of the mayonnaise and the cheeses. Add the raisins. Spread thickly on large lettuce leaves and roll like French pancakes. Serve on a bed of lettuce leaves. Instead of the raisins sliced stuffed olives may be used.

COCKTAIL SAUCE
Mrs. Lucien E. Lyons, Sr.

1 cup stiff, unsalted mayonnaise
2 tablespoons Chili sauce
2 tablespoons Tarragon vinegar
2 tablespoons anchovy sauce
4 tablespoons tomato catsup
1 tablespoon olive oil

Mix anchovy sauce in olive oil, add other ingredients and stir until creamy. Lemon juice and more pepper may be added if mayonnaise does not carry sufficent seasoning.

This is to be used with lobster, crab meat or shrimp.

COCKTAIL SAUCE BONFOUCA
Mrs. Homer Dupuy

1 cup Chili Sauce
1 lemon, juice
1 tablespoon vinegar
1 onion, chopped fine
1 teaspoon Worcestershire Sauce
few drops Tabasco

Strain, let stand for several hours in refrigerator before serving.

AVOYELLES COCKTAIL SAUCE

½ lemon, juice
1 cup tomato sauce
2 tablespoons Worcestershire Sauce
1 tablespoon pepper sauce
½ cup celery, finely chopped

Mix thoroughly and place over shrimp in cocktail glasses. Serve with crisp crackers and lettuce salad if desired.

LETTUCE CHAPON DRESSING

½ teaspoon fine salt
½ teaspoon ground white pepper
melt same in 2 tablespoons good vinegar
add 6 tablespoons fine olive oil
stir same and pour over lettuce
mix whole thing and let soak for 5 minutes before serving

Have head of lettuce loose in bowl. Cut pieces of crust of stale bread. Take 1 clove of garlic, dip same in coarse salt and rub the bread with it and pour the dressing over lettuce and bread.

SALAD DRESSING ST. DENIS

3 eggs, the yolks
2 teaspoons salt
1 teaspoon pepper
1 teaspoon made mustard
1 large lemon, the juice
celery tops, radishes
olive oil

Mayonnaise dressing: rub the yolks of the eggs with a few drops of olive oil at a time, by slow stirring. When well mixed and thick like jelly, put in the salt, pepper, made mustard, and the lemon juice. Pour over the salad and garnish with celery tops and round radishes.

MAYONNAISE

5 tablespoons Wesson Oil
2 tablespoons lemon juice
½ teaspoon sugar
½ teaspoon salt
1 raw egg
½ pt. Wesson, Mazola or Penick Oil

Beat the first 4 of these ingredients well together with a rotary egg beater. Then add the whole egg. Beat well, add the ½ pint of Wesson oil and beat again until very stiff.

SALAD DRESSING ROXANE
Mrs. Walter Torian

1 tablespoon vinegar
1 tablespoon olive oil
1 whole pickled sweet pepper
1 hard-boiled egg
salt, pepper
chopped onion
minced parsley
pod of garlic

Mix together well the oil, vinegar, salt, pepper, chopped onion, sweet pepper and garlic. Put it in the ice box to chill thoroughly.

Just before serving add a chopped hard-boiled egg.

SALAD DRESSING PASTORAL
Mrs. Walter Torian

2 hard boiled eggs
2 cloves garlic, minced
3 tablespoons olive oil
3 tablespoons Tarragon vinegar
1 teaspoon powdered sugar
sprig of celery, minced
salt, red pepper
lettuce
paprika

Mash the egg yolks fine with the minced garlic. Add the olive oil drop by drop, then the minced celery, salt and red pepper. Thin with the Tarragon vinegar. Have the salad bowl ready, chilled. Shred the lettuce with scissors, and toss the salad dressing into it. Chop the white of eggs very fine and sprinkle over this, following with the powdered sugar and a little paprika. Serve very cold.

Note: The breath of the Arctic must blow on the ingredients, everything thoroughly chilled. This dressing is an adjunct equally to be valued with broiled ham.

SAUCE REMOULADE

3 hard-boiled eggs, chopped
1 raw yolk of egg
1 tablespoon Tarragon vinegar
3 tablespoons olive oil
½ clove garlic, minced very fine
½ teaspoon prepared mustard
½ lemon, the juice
salt, cayenne to taste

SAUCE ARNAUD

To be served with cold boiled shrimp. Peel the shrimp and set them in a bowl. In another bowl, have a good French dressing, and to it add minced shallots, Creole mustard, paprika, salt and pepper, and horse radish. Pour this over the shrimp, and turn them about in it repeatedly. Set in the ice-box half an hour before serving.

SAUCE RAVIGOTE
Arnaud
mayonnaise
cream
finely minced shallots
bay leaf

Stir all the ingredients well together.

SALAD DRESSING ROYAL
½ cup oil
5 tablespoons vinegar
1 teaspoon powdered sugar
½ small Bermuda onion, chopped fine
2 tablespoons minced parsley
½ teaspoon red pepper
1 tablespoon minced green pepper
1 teaspoon salt
1 teaspoon dry mustard

Mix all these ingredients well together, and set them aside for an hour or two.

Then shake hard for 5 minutes.

SALAD DRESSING á l'ITALIEN
1½ cups Italian oil
½ cup vinegar
¼ cup sugar
¾ teaspoon salt
½ cup tomato catsup
pepper to taste
clove of garlic
paprika

Mix the ingredients all together in a bowl well rubbed with the garlic and beat well with an egg beater. Keep the dressing in a glass jar in the ice box until ready to serve.

It is better that it remain a day or two, as the flavoring becomes better blended.

DRESSING FOR FRUIT SALAD
Mrs. W. J. Bentley
¼ cup vinegar
1 teaspoon sugar
½ teaspoon salt
¼ teaspoon cornstarch
¼ teaspoon flour
½ teaspoon mustard
½ pt. whipped cream

Cook all the ingredients, except the whipped cream in a double boiler. It makes about two tablespoons of dressing. Mix the resulting mixture when cooled with the whipped cream.

ROQUEFORT CHEESE DRESSING
⅛ lb. Roquefort cheese
2 tablespoons Tarragon vinegar
1 tablespoon lemon juice
8 tablespoons olive oil

Mix the Roquefort cheese with the olive oil, then thin with the vinegar and lemon juice, mashing and mixing well.

ROQUEFORT CHEESE DRESSING
Mrs. Petrie Hamilton
¼ cup Roquefort cheese
4 tablespoons olive oil
1 hard-boiled egg, the yolk only
2 tablespoons whipping cream
2 tablespoons vinegar
salt, pepper, cayenne

Rub the cheese with the olive oil to a cream. Add slowly the sifted yolk of the egg, beating constantly. Add the cream and the vinegar, drop by drop, beating constantly, or it will curdle. Season with salt, pepper, and cayenne.

RUSSIAN DRESSING
2 egg yolks
¼ teaspoon sugar
1 tablespoon Tarragon vinegar
1 teaspoon prepared mustard
1 cup olive oil, mixed by spoonful
salt and pepper to taste

Assemble the above and beat with Dover egg beater. Then add
1 large pimento, chopped
3 or 4 large olives, chopped
3 tablespoons catsup

BOILED DRESSING
1 teaspoon flour
4 tablespoons sugar
1 teaspoon mustard
½ lemon, the juice
1 teaspoon Tarragon vinegar
2 egg yolks
2½ tablespoons olive oil
1 cup cream, whipped
salt and cayenne pepper to taste

Mix the dry ingredients, add juices and vinegar. Cook in a double boiler until thick. Stir in the lightly beaten egg yolks, cook three minutes more, stirring constantly. Let cool, add olive oil and whipped cream.

COOKED SALAD DRESSING
Mrs. Petrie Hamilton
5 egg yolks
1 tablespoon mustard
1 teaspoon salt
2 tablespoons sugar
3 tablespoons melted butter
¼ teaspoon cayenne pepper
1 cup vinegar
¼ teaspoon celery seed

Put in double boiler and cook until it thickens, stirring constantly. When done, add the juice of one onion. Particularly good to make potato salad.

"MIGNON" SALAD DRESSING
Mrs. Charles M. Peaslee

½ cup granulated sugar
⅓ cup Heinz catsup
¼ cup cider vinegar
1 cup Mazola, Wesson or Penick Oil
¼ teaspoon salt
1 teaspoon Worcestershire Sauce
1 medium size onion
1 small clove garlic
6 cloves
dash of Tabasco Sauce

Rub bowl with garlic and salt. Grate garlic, and onions, add all other ingredients. Strain into quart bottle. Shake well. Make day before using. Keeps indefinitely.

WHITE CREAM SAUCE

1 tablespoon butter
1 tablespoon flour
1 cup milk (or milk and cream)
¼ teaspoon salt, pepper to taste
paprika if desired

Melt the butter in a double-boiler, stir in the flour slowly, and add the seasonings. Cook about a minute, stirring constantly, and not allowing the flour to brown. Then add the milk very slowly, stirring continually, and bring to the boiling point. Let boil two of three minutes, never cease stirring.

Keep warm over hot water until ready for use. If a MEDIUM THICK sauce is desired, use 2 tablespoons of butter and two of flour. If a THICK sauce is the object, then use 2 tablespoons of butter and 4 of flour.

NEWBERG SAUCE

½ lb. butter
1 tablespoon flour
4 egg yolks
½ pt. cream or rich milk
1 glass sherry wine
salt, pepper to taste

Melt the butter. Add flour gradually blending well together. Add yolks of eggs then cream or milk slowly.

Season to taste.

Cook until thick.

EGG SAUCE

Chopped hard boiled eggs added to a cream sauce.

CAPER SAUCE

Make a white sauce and add ½ cup of finely cut French capers and chopped hard boiled eggs, whites chopped and yolks mashed, before serving. This sauce is served with boiled mutton.

BROWN ROUX

2 tablespoons of flour to one of shortening. (Lard is cheaper and often preferable and leaves no characteristic taste if properly blended).

The flour must be stirred in very slowly, to the shortening when it bubbles. Salt, pepper, and other seasonings to taste. This roux is the basis for most Creole cooking, and is adapted in various ways, serving as a base for grillardes, gumbos, stews and so forth.

When so used, the flour must be allowed to brown only slightly, as it must continue to brown in the further processes of cooking.

TOMATO SAUCE

1 No. 2 can tomatoes
2 tablespoons butter
2 tablespoons flour
1 blade mace
1 bay leaf
1 small onion
¼ tablespoon Worcestershire Sauce

Cook the tomatoes with the mace, bay leaf and onion for twenty minutes. Strain and add the Worcestershire. In a separate pot melt the butter and add the flour to it stirring till smooth. Add the strained tomato gradually, stirring so that it will not lump. Cook for a few minutes until thick.

TOMATO SAUCE FOR SPAGHETTI

1 tablespoon butter
1 tablespoon flour
1 cup tomato, juice and pulp
1 cup meat stock
1 carrot, 1 onion
2 cloves
1 clove garlic, a little thyme
¼ lb. raw ham

Mince the carrot, onion, and ham, and cook in the butter for ten or fifteen minutes, with the thyme, cloves, and garlic, which has also been minced. Rub the flour to a smooth paste with a little of the stock and add to the first mixture, and also add the tomatoes. Season with salt and pepper and cook for ten or twenty minutes. It may be strained of desired, but is best used with all the ingredients left in. It should be mixed with the spaghetti before serving.

SPANISH SAUCE

Spanish sauce is made exactly like the Tomato Sauce for Spaghetti but every bit of grease is removed and it is served after being strained. A glass of Madeira wine added to a pint of this sauce transforms it to **Madeira Sauce**.

MUSHROOM SAUCE
Hilda Phelps Hammond

    1   tablespoon butter
    1   tablespoon flour
    1½ cups boiling water or bouillon
    2   teaspoons lemon juice
    ½   teaspoon Worcestershire Sauce
    1   cup mushrooms, chopped
    1   tablespoon sherry

Melt the butter in a saucepan. Stir in the flour till smooth. Add the boiling water gradually, stirring constantly, then the pepper, salt, lemon juice and Worcestershire. Then add the mushrooms and simmer. If canned mushrooms are used ten minutes is long enough, if fresh, then a half hour or until tender. Remove from the fire, add sherry, and serve with steak or chicken. The sherry may be omitted.

SAUCE MARCHAND de VIN

    6   green onions, chopped fine
    3   tablespoons olive oil
    1   tablespoon flour
    1   cup mushrooms, cut fine
    3   cloves garlic, minced
    1   glass red or white wine
        marrow from a large beef bone

Cook the onions in the olive oil until lightly browned, rub in the flour until smooth. Add the mushrooms and garlic and continue cooking for ten minutes. Remove the marrow from the bone, cut in slices and add to the sauce, then the wine. Cook five minutes or more and serve hot on steak or chops. If sauce is too thick add a little stock or juice from the meat.

BLACK BUTTER SAUCE

Warm an ounce of good butter in a frying pan until it turns brown, add some parsley, heat again for one minute, then drop in carefully five drops of vinegar.

ANCHOVY SAUCE

To one pint of drawn butter add one heaping tablespoon of anchovy essence, stir well together and serve.

BARBECUE SAUCE

    2   tablespoons butter
    2   tablespoons vinegar
    1   teaspoon mustard
    1   teaspoon Worcestershire Sauce
    1   teaspoon sugar
    ¼   teaspoon salt
        a strong dash Tabasco and black
        pepper

Blend all together, heat to a boil, and pour over broiled chicken or any other meat desired. Let stand a few minutes before serving.

BARBECUE SAUCE
Mr. James L. Crump

    1   quart water
    1   quart vinegar
    1   pint catsup
    1   bottle Worcestershire Sauce
    ½   lb. butter
    1   cup black pepper
    1   cup red pepper
    ¼   cup flour diluted in cold water for
        thickening

Put on stove and bring to boil. This will make three quarts of sauce.

HORSERADISH SAUCE

    1   teaspoonful mustard
    1   tablespoon vinegar
    1   good sized root horseradish, grated
    ½   pint cream
        salt to taste

Mix the mustard and vinegar and add the horseradish; let stand for an hour, then add the cream. Excellent with roast beef.

AVOCADO SAUCE

Peel and remove seed of two avocados. Mash to a smooth paste, add the juice of a lemon or two limes, salt, pepper to taste, tablespoon mayonnaise and one teaspoon grated onion. Mix well and stir in a cup of French dressing. This is delicious served on lettuce or tomatoes. If tomatoes cut in small pieces are used, it is an excellent relish to use with meat or pancakes filled with creamed chicken.

HOLLANDAISE SAUCE No. 1
FOR FISH

Take the yolks of 2 eggs and beat. Drip ½ lb. of melted butter like mayonnaise in a double-boiler or on a slow fire until thick.

Add the juice of 1 lemon, 12 lake shrimp, ½ can mushrooms, 2 truffles cut in slices and a little water from the fish.

Take off the fire and serve over fish.

HOLLANDAISE SAUCE NO. 2

    2   tablespoons butter
    1   tablespoon flour
    ½   lemon
    ½   teaspoon salt
    2   yolks of egg

Blend butter with flour, cook over hot water until slightly thickened. To this add the juice of lemon and salt. Remove from fire and beat in the yolks of eggs. Beat a minute and serve.

HOLLANDAISE SAUCE No. 3

    6   tablespoons melted butter
    4   eggs, the yolks
    2   lemons, the juice

Melt the buter in a double boiler, add gradually the egg yolks, slightly beaten, and the lemon juice, stirring constantly until thick. Add seasonings.

MOCK HOLLANDAISE SAUCE
Mrs. W. P. Bentley

    1   pt. milk
    2   tablespoons flour
    ½   stick butter
    2   eggs, the yolks
    ½   lemon, the juice

Put the milk, the flour, and the butter in a double-boiler, and let them simmer gently until thick. Turn off the fire, and, with the milk, flour, and butter mixture still over the boiling water, beat in the beaten egg yolks. Take from the fire and squeeze in the lemon juice.

FISH SAUCE DELERY

    6   yolks of hard-boiled eggs
    1½ teaspoons Coleman's mustard
    1½ cups mayonnaise
    6   shallots
    1½ teaspoons garlic oil
    7   drops Tabasco Sauce
    6   whites of hard-boiled eggs
        capers

Mix yolks of eggs with mustard, then mix in mayonnaise. Chop shallots very fine, then blend together; put in garlic, oil, and a few drops of Tabasco. Mix in chopped whites of egg. Add a few capers, stir well and serve..

SAUCE BÉARNAISE CREOLE
Mrs. M. C. Maury-Lyons

    4   eggs, the yolks
    2   tablespoons grated onions
    2   tablespoons Tarragon vinegar
    ½   teaspoon salt
    ½   teaspoon pepper
    1   stick butter
    ½   cup water
    ½   teaspoon beef extract

Beat the yolks carefully, put into a double-boiler and add the other ingredients, stirring gently but steadily. This sauce you will find has more character than its pure French prototype.

SAUCE COTE D'OR

    4   egg yolks
    2   tablespoons Tarragon vinegar
    2   tablespoons water
    ½   lb. butter
    1   coffeespoon salt
        pepper to taste
        a few drops lemon juice

Put vinegar and well beaten egg yolks, lemon juice, salt and pepper in a double boiler over hot water, not boiling, beat constantly until thick (ten or twelve minutes). Now add melted butter that is lukewarm by melting over hot water. Add water, a teaspoonful at a time. When butter and water are added, remove from fire, beat well and add more salt, pepper, and lemon juice if necessary for taste.

SAUCE FOR FISH

    1   small jar sour gherkins
    1   small jar capers
    ½   bunch parsley
    ½   bunch shallots
    ¾   cup olive oil
    ½   cup Wesson or Penick Oil

Chop the gherkins, capers, parsley, shallots very, very fine. Heat the oils, add the chopped ingredients, continue to heat a few moments; then serve with boiled fish.

STEAK SAUCE

    ½   cup vinegar
    4   ozs. butter
    1   cup tomato catsup
    ¼   tablespoon salt
    ¼   tablespoon white pepper
    ½   lemon, sliced
    1   small clove garlic, minced
    1   medium onion, chopped fine
    ½   cup olive oil
    1   tablespoon prepared mustard
        few drops Tabasco

Mix all ingredients together, boil for fifteen minutes on a slow fire and strain. The advantage of this sauce is not only in its tang, but in the fact that it will keep indefinitely in the ice box.

TARTAR SAUCE
Mrs. D. D. Curran

    2   eggs
    ½   cup pure olive oil
    3   tablespoons vinegar
    1   tablespoon mild mustard
    1   teaspoon sugar
    ¼   teaspoon pepper
    1   teaspoon salt
    1   teaspoon onion juice
    1   tablespoon chopped capers
    1   cucumber pickle, chopped

The first step is the same as for making mayonnaise. Then the other ingredients chopped fine, are added.

"EPICUREAN SAUCE"
Lt. Comdr. and Mrs. S. W. Wallace

    3   tablespoons mayonnaise
    ½   cup cream, whipped
    1   teaspoon Worcestershire Sauce
    1   tablespoon prepared mustard
    3   tablespoons horseradish

Mix all ingredients well.

MINT SAUCE FOR LAMB
Mrs. Walter Torian

1 cup vinegar
2 tablespoons water
4 tablespoons minced mint leaves
2 tablespoons sugar

Soak 3 hours and serve with lamb.

CURRY SAUCE
Lt. Comdr. and Mrs. S. W. Wallace

2 tablespoons shortening
2 tablespoons flour
½ teaspoon salt
1 lemon
2 teaspoons curry powder
1 can apricots

Use the buffet size can apricots. Blend shortening, flour, curry and salt. Add syrup from apricots and enough water to make desired consistency. Add lemon juice to suit taste. Add any meat, fish or eggs as may be desired. Serve with chutney, Bombay Duck, onions sliced, and fried crisp in deep fat, currants dried, chopped hard-boiled egg, crisp bacon, chopped fine, chopped peanuts, chopped green pepers, shredded cocoanut.

SAUCE FOR BAKED HAM
Mrs. John May

2 tablespoons tomato catsup
2 tablespoons sherry
2 tablespoons Tarragon vinegar
2 tablespoons butter
1 tablespoon Worcestershire Sauce
1 teaspoon mustard

Mix vinegar with mustard, add other ingredients. Heat.

SAUCE MARGUERITE

4 tablespoons butter
2 tablespoons flour
2 cups fish stock, strained
2 egg yolks
¾ cup sherry wine
2 tablespoons chopped parsley
1 teaspoonful lemon juice

Blend butter with flour in top of double boiler, slowly add the fish stock and stir until smooth. Lower flame and add the slightly beaten egg yolks always stirring slowly, then add lemon juice. When sauce becomes quite thick, remove from fire and add the sherry and parsley. Pour over the fish and serve at once. This will serve ten people.

TANTE MATHILDE'S CORNBREAD
Mrs. Walter Torian
2 cups sifted yellow cornmeal
3 eggs
2 teaspoons baking powder
½ teaspoon salt
1 cup flour
2 cups milk
1 coffeespoon sugar
2 tablespoons lard

Beat the eggs, yolks and whites separately. To the cornmeal add the baking powder, salt, flour, and milk, then the beaten yolks, and the sugar and fold in whites.

Put the lard into a black stove-pan and set it into the oven, until very, very hot. Pour the bread mixture into this. The pan should be small enough so that the bread mixture may be fairly deep. Cook until thoroughly done.

SOUTHERN EGG BREAD
2 cups white cornmeal
3 eggs
1 level teaspoon salt
1 tablespoon melted shortening
3 level teaspoons baking powder
1½ cups milk
1 cup cold boiled rice

Sift the cornmeal, salt, and baking powder together; add the well-beaten eggs, then the shortening, milk and rice. Beat well. Pour into a shallow, well-greased pan and bake half an hour in a hot oven. For cornmeal sticks, use the same mixture pouring it into greased iron cornbread stick pan.

ACADIAN "COUSH-COUSH"
Mrs. Walter Torian
2 cups corn meal (Aunt Jemima)
2 teaspoons baking powder
½ teaspoon salt
1½ cups boiling water
3 eggs, beaten together
1 teaspoon lard

Scald meal and salt. When cool, add baking powder and beaten eggs. Have iron skillet piping hot, put lard in it, pour meal mixture in and allow it to cook 5 minutes. Scrape lightly from the bottom with spatula, reduce heat and place another hot iron skillet on top and steam 10 minutes longer. A rare treat served with bacon or hash and coffee for breakfast.

CORN DODGERS
2 eggs
1 tablespoon milk
1 tablespoon lard, level
1 teaspoon salt
2 cups cornmeal
hot water

Mix salt, lard, and meal, and pour boiling water over all, sufficient to wet dough. Beat the yolks of the egg well, add milk, and pour into meal that has been cooled. Fold in well beaten whites of egg.

Drop by the teaspoonful on a well-greased baking sheet, two inches apart. Bake in a hot oven 15 or 20 minutes.

SPOON BREAD
Mrs. Petrie Hamilton
3 eggs
1¼ pints milk
½ cup cornmeal
½ teaspoon baking powder
1 teaspoon salt
1 heaping tablespoon butter

Heat 1 pint of milk to the boiling point. Stir in cornmeal gradually, and cook until the consistency of mush. Then add the cold milk, butter, salt, baking powder and the well beaten egg yolks. Fold in the egg whites beaten stiff. Pour into a buttered baking dish and bake one-half hour. Serve at once.

BATTER BREAD
1 qt. sweet milk
1 cup cornmeal
3 eggs
1 teaspoon baking powder
1 teaspoon salt
1 tablespoon Crisco, rounded

Heat a pint of the milk with meal, stirring all the time until it thickens to consistency of mush. Then take off the fire, and add salt, Crisco, and the rest of the milk. Add the beaten yolks and then fold in the whites of the eggs. Blend well and pour into hot earthenware or glass baking dish, greased with Crisco. Bake about half an hour. Serve at once.

PLANTATION CORN MUFFINS
2 cups cornmeal
1 cup cooked grits or rice
2 or 3 eggs
1 teaspoon salt
1 cup milk
1 teaspoon each lard and butter
½ teaspoon baking powder

Scald the meal by pouring over it about 1½ cups of boiling water, add salt and beat until it is very smooth. Add the butter and lard, rice and milk, and continue beating. Then the baking powder, beat again. Have well greased rings smoking hot and pour in the batter. Bake in a very hot oven.

OWENDAW
Tezcuco Plantation
2 cups cooked hominy
1 heaping tablespoon butter or lard
4 eggs
1 pint milk
½ pint cornmeal

Have the cooked hominy hot and mix into it the butter (or lard). Beat the eggs very light and stir them into the hominy. Next the milk, stirring in very gradually. Lastly the cornmeal. The batter should be the consistency of thick boiled custard. If thicker, add a little more milk.

Bake with a good deal of heat at the bottom of the oven, not too much at the top, for that would prevent its rising. Bake in a deep pan and enjoy a treasured plantation legacy.

GRIDDLE CAKES aux MIETTES
Mrs. M. C. Maury Lyons

1½	cups fine stale bread crumbs
1½	cups scalded milk
2	tablespoons butter
½	cup flour
½	teaspoon salt
2	teaspoons baking powder

Mix the milk and butter with the crumbs and blend well.

Now add the eggs, well beaten, to the flour with the salt and baking powder sifted with it. Finally mix all together, stir well, and the batter is ready for the skillet. Use a minimum of lard in the latter.

CORNMEAL BATTER CAKES

2	cups sifted flour
½	cup cornmeal
1½	cups milk
1	egg
2½	teaspoons baking powder
1	teaspoon salt
2	tablespoons lard, level

It is more convenient to make this in a large pitcher, so that it may be poured out onto the griddle.

POP OVERS

3	eggs, well beaten
2	cups sifted flour
1	teaspoon salt
2	cups milk, more or less

Make this batter smooth and press through a sieve, and bake in hot iron muffin rings in a very slow oven for 25 minutes—increase heat, and continue baking 15 minutes longer.

CAKES au BAYOU TECHE
Mrs. Walter Torian

2	cups buttermilk or clabber
1	coffeespoon soda, scant
1⅓	cups sifted flour, pinch of salt
2	tablespoons melted butter
1	tablespoon cane syrup

Sift the soda, with the flour. Stir in the buttermilk or clabber, the butter and cane syrup. The batter must be very thick. Drop one tablespoon at a time on a very lightly buttered griddle. Serve with home made sausage and good coffee for a perfect breakfast.

SOUR MILK WAFFLES
Mrs. W. E. Winship

3	eggs
2	cups thick sour milk
2	cups flour
2	teaspoons baking powder
¾	teaspoon soda
6	tablespoons melted butter
¼	teaspoon salt

Separate eggs. Beat yolks. Add one cup sour milk. Sift dry ingredients, add to yolks. Add other cup sour milk, then butter and stiffly beaten whites. Bake in hot greased waffle iron, unless an electric waffle iron is used, when no grease is necessary. Serve with butter and hot maple syrup.

WAFFLES

1	cup milk
1	cup flour
1	tablespoon cornmeal
1	teaspoon salt, level
2	teaspoons melted lard
2	tablespoons melted butter
2	eggs
1	teaspoon baking powder

Beat the yolks of the eggs and the milk together and add the shortening. Sift the flour, salt, and baking powder; add it to the milk and eggs. Just before cooking, add the well beaten whites.

ROLLS
Mrs. Paul Saunders

6	cups flour
2	yeast cakes
2	eggs
2	cups sweet milk, scalded and cooled
1	tablespoon sugar
4	kitchen spoons lard, measured after melting
2	teaspoons salt

Mix the dry ingredients and sift. Add lard. When milk is tepid add yeast cake and whole egg. Pour into flour and mix well. Place in a covered vessel, and let rise 2 hours. Pour onto a bread board which has been floured, roll and cut into rings and let rise another hour. Keep covered. Brush tops with butter and bake in a rather quick oven about 20 minutes.

BISCUITS—ST. JAMES

2	cups sifted flour
1	tablespoon lard
2	heaping teaspoons baking powder
½	teaspoon salt
1	tablespoon butter
¾	cup milk, more or less

Mix the flour, salt and baking powder together and sift once again, then add one tablespoonful of lard. Rub well together the lard and flour, then add enough cold milk to make a soft dough. Sift some flour on a biscuit board, and roll the biscuit dough about one-half inch thick. Melt the butter, spread over the surface of the biscuit dough, then fold the dough over once. Cut out with a biscuit cutter and put the biscuits in a pan. Brush a little cold milk on the top of each biscuit and set to rise for fifteen minutes. Then put in a hot oven and bake until done.

ROLLS

2   cups flour
4   teaspoons baking powder
½   teaspoon salt
2   tablespoons lard
2   eggs
½   cup milk
2   tablespoons butter

Sift together flour, salt and baking powder, then add the lard and butter, mixing in well with the tips of fingers. Beat one whole egg and one egg yolk in milk and work into other ingredients. Mix well and roll out thin on a well floured board, cut the dough as for biscuits and fold like Parker House rolls. Place on a greased baking sheet and brush top with melted butter and egg white. Bake in hot oven.

LUNCHEON BISCUITS
Mrs. L. Symington Goode

2   cups flour
2   teaspoons baking powder
1   teaspoon salt, level
2   tablespoons lard
     cold water

Sift the salt and baking powder with the flour, work in the lard lightly with a silver knife until well mixed. Add enough cold water to make a soft dough, roll out thin and bake immediately in a very hot oven.

BEATEN BISCUITS
Mrs. David T. Merrick

1   quart sifted flour
1   teaspoon salt
⅓   cup hog lard
⅓   cup butter
1   cup ice water
1   teaspoon sugar, heaping

Mix the dry ingredients. Add the water, sweetened with the sugar and work until there is life in the dough, about 15 minutes (not too long as that takes the life out of the dough). Then beat with rolling pin or use a machine until the dough blisters. Roll, cut with a biscuit cutter and stick in the centers with a fork. Bake in a moderate oven. If the stove is too hot, the biscuits will begin to blister.

FOUR O'CLOCK BISCUITS

2   cups flour
4   teaspoons baking powder
½   teaspoon salt
4   tablespoons shortening
⅔   cup milk

Mix and sift the dry ingredients. Work in the shortening with the finger tips till it looks like a coarse meal. Make a well in the center, and pour in the milk all at once. Stir until well mixed. Dough should be soft. Turn on a well floured board Knead it quickly and lightly for a few minutes. Pat or roll to ½ inch

thickness and cut with a small biscuit cutter. Bake in a very hot oven about twelve minutes. Instead of rolling out one may drop them from a spoon avoiding the kneading process. They are toothsome morsels for tea.

CHEESE BISCUITS

½   lb. grated American cheese
½   cup butter
½   cup lard
1   to 2 tablespoons ice water
1½   cups flour
½   teaspoon salt, cayenne pepper to
     taste
     halved pecans

Work up on marble slab without handling much. Roll out thin, cut with biscuit cutter. Place a pecan half on each biscuit. Bake in a slow oven.

CHEESE PERFECTIONS

1   lb. sharp cheese
1   stick butter or ¼ lb.
1½   cups flour
1½   teaspoons baking soda
1   teaspoon salt and cayenne to taste

Put the cheese through meat grinder and set aside with butter to get soft. To this add dry ingredients sifted and work well with your hands. Put into pastry tube and press in strips on tins. Bake.

CHEESE STRAWS

1   cup grated cheese
1   cup sifted flour
½   cup butter
1   to 2 tablespoons ice water
     cayenne, small pinch salt

Put ingredients together as for pastry, with knife. Roll thin and cut in narrow strips. Set on buttered paper in pans and cook in a very hot stove.

CHEESE STRAWS
Mrs. Randolph Griswold

1   stick butter
2   cups grated sharp cheese
1½   cups sifted flour
1   teaspoon baking powder
½   teaspoon salt
¼   teaspoon pepper

Cream the butter, add grated cheese. Cream well together and mix in dry ingredients. Roll out to one-eighth of an inch thick, cut in strips one-half inch wide and bake in a moderate oven until delicately browned.

CHEESE STRAWS DE LUXE
Mrs. Paul King Rand

4   cups grated cheese
¼   lb. butter
3   cups sifted flour
3   teaspoons baking powder, level
3   good dashes cayenne pepper
1½   teaspoons salt

Knead the ingredients lightly into a dough. Run them through a cookie grinder, place on a baking sheet and bake in a very slow oven.

POLK MUFFINS

3 eggs
1 pint milk
3 tablespoons flour
1 tablespoon melted butter or lard

Beat the eggs and blend the ingredients well together. The batter should be about as thick as thick cream.

Bake in patty pans in a quick oven. Really a treat!

PAIN PERDU
Mrs. Walter Torian

sliced bread
orange flour water
milk
egg
grated nutmeg
½ tablespoon lard
½ teaspoon milk
1 tablespoon butter

Soak the slices of bread a few minutes in milk to which a few drops of orange flower water and a very little sugar have been added. Remove, press lightly and set aside for a few moments. Beat the yolks and whites separately. Add the yolks to the whites and put in a little grated nutmeg. Dip the slices of bread in this, then fry in the mixed lard and butter. Take out, sprinkle powdered sugar and cinnamon over them and serve hot.

NUT STICKS
Mrs. O. LeR. Goforth

2 cups flour
2 teaspoons baking powder
1 teaspoon salt
4 tablespoons shortening
¾ cup nuts, chopped fine
butter
milk

Sift dry ingredients, cut in shortening, add enough milk to make a soft dough. Roll out dough to ½ inch thickness or less, brush with melted butter. Spread half dough with nuts. Fold other half over it. Cut into strips 1 inch by 3 inches. Brush with melted butter. Bake 20 minutes at 400°. Twice during baking brush with melted butter.

SALLIE LUNN
Agnes Thompson

2 eggs, separated
1 tablespoon butter
¼ teaspoon salt
3 cups flour
2 teaspoons baking powder
2 tablespoons melted butter

Beat the sugar and the egg yolks together well, add milk alternately with the flour, which has been sifted with the salt and baking powder. Beat till smooth and free from lumps. Add the melted butter, and fold in the whites of the eggs which have been beaten till very stiff. Pour into a well greased stem pan and bake in a moderate oven for about ½ hour. As it begins to brown brush with melted butter. After removal from the oven brush again lightly with butter and sprinkle liberally with sugar and cinnamon. Run in oven a second, serve hot.

SCOTCH SHORT BREAD
Mrs. L. Symington Goode

1 cup butter
½ cup sugar
2 cups flour
½ teaspoon baking powder
¼ teaspoon salt

Cream the butter with the sugar, add flour, baking powder and salt sifted together. Work in gradually. Roll about ¼ inch thick. Sprinkle with sugar and bake in a slow oven about ¾ hour.

ENGLISH NUT BREAD
Mrs. Petrie Hamilton

2 eggs
½ cup sugar
2 cups milk
3¾ cups flour
1 cup chopped pecans
3 teaspoons baking powder, heaping

Pour into buttered bread pans and set in a warm place to rise for ½ hour. Bake in a moderate oven 30 to 40 minutes.

COFFEE CAKE

2 tablespoons butter
⅔ cup sugar
⅔ cup milk
1 egg, well beaten
2 cups flour
1 teaspoon baking powder, heaping
½ cup nuts, chopped fine
1 cup raisins

Bake in slow oven 20 minutes. Spread butter, sugar and cinnamon on top. Run under flame for a few seconds.

BRIOCHES
Mrs. Armand Legendre

1 pound flour
4 ozs. butter
½ oz. compressed yeast
2 eggs
¼ gill milk
1 tablespoon sugar
salt

Mix the yeast with a little luke warm water, stiffen with enough flour to make a stiff batter and leave to rise in a warm place for 1 hour. Put what remains of the flour into a basin, add a good pinch of salt and the beaten egg. Melt the butter, warm the milk, add gradually to the yeast, then mix the contents of the two bowls together and knead well for at least 15 minutes. Cover and leave in a moderately warm place for 2 or 3 hours, then shape and bake in a brisk oven. They may be baked in fluted tins, or in little cottage loaves. The perfect accompaniment for morning coffee—not the Deux Magots nor the Café de Paris could improve on them.

BANANA BREAD

2   eggs, well beaten
1   cup sugar
1   teaspoon salt
2   tablespoons sour milk
½   cup butter
3   ripe bananas
2   cups flour
1   teaspoon soda

Sift flour and measure. Add level teaspoon soda and sift 3 times. Cream sugar and butter, mash bananas and add. Beat eggs well and add to mixture. Add flour and sour milk and bake in loaf pan ¾ to 1 hour in slow oven (325 F.)

MITTIE'S WHOLE WHEAT BREAD

2   cups sweet milk
1   Fleishman's yeast cake
4   rounded tablespoons lard
3   level tablespoons sugar
1   tablespoon salt
4   cups white flour
3   cups whole wheat flour

Heat the milk luke warm. Dissolve yeast in it then the lard and sugar. Add 3 cups white flour and place in a warm place to rise twice its size. Then add the whole wheat flour, salt and the other cup of white flour. Knead well, set it to rise again until twice its size, then roll out and cut. This quantity makes one loaf and 21 rolls.

RICE FRITTERS
Mrs. Albin Provosty

1   cup cooked rice
3   eggs
½   cup flour
1   teaspoon baking powder
     sugar to taste

Mash the rice. Mix all ingredients together and beat to a light thin batter. Drop by tablespoonfuls into hot boiling lard. Fry to a nice brown, drain on brown paper and dust with powdered sugar. This is a sweet entremet and also a nice breakfast dish.

QUICK DELIVERY HOT BREAD
Mrs. Cleveland Sessums

1   Pullman loaf or square bread
½   lb. butter

Use a sharp knife and cut the crust off the two sides and ends of the Pullman loaf. Be sure to leave the top and bottom crust. Next cut the bread in two, lengthwise. You now have two halves.

Divide each half into squares, cutting into sixths or eighths, according to the number of your guests. In cutting your squares, be sure not to cut through the bottom crust which serves as a foundation (the little squares must be held together by it.) Run one of these halves in the oven until very hot and toasted on top. Have the butter melting and pour generously on the bread, so that the butter runs down the sides of the squares. Serve one-half loaf of squares with early part of the meal and toast the other half for the latter part.

CALAS TOUT CHAUD
Mrs. Albin Provosty

½   cup rice
3   cups boiling water
3   eggs
¼   cup sugar
½   cake compressed yeast
½   teaspoon grated nutmeg
3   tablespoons flour

Boil rice until soft in the water. When soft set aside to cool. Mash and mix with the yeast which has been dissolved in a half a cup of luke warm water. Set to rise for twelve hours. Then beat three eggs thoroughly and add to the rice, beating well. Add the sugar the flour and nutmeg, beat to a thick batter. Have ready a deep frying pan with sufficient boiling hot lard for the cakes to swim in. Drop the batter by spoonfuls into the lard and fry to a nice brown. Drain on brown paper, keep in a warm place. Pile on a hot dish and sprinkle liberally with powdered sugar.

The musical cry of portly mammies in "tignon" and guinea blue gown, "Calas! Calas, tout chaud!", as they peddled these danties through the streets of the town was one of the distinctive street songs of old New Orleans. It is still heard on fete days.

CALAS CHIFFON
Mrs. S. A. Fortier

¼   cup cooked salted rice
1   cup rice water
½   cake yeast
2   cups flour
2   teaspoons sugar
2   eggs
½   teaspoon salt

Mash the rice. Add the yeast which has been dissolved in the luke-warm rice water and 1 cup flour. Let set twelve hours. Then add the eggs, well beaten, and the other cup of flour. Drop by tablespoonfuls into deep hot fat and fry till a golden brown. Drain and dust liberally with powdered sugar. This fritter may be served for breakfast as a hot bread, or for tea, made somewhat smaller, and is also a delicious dessert with coffee.

CHAMBLISS PUDDING
Mrs. Amedée Bringier

1 light cup chopped butter
1 cup pulverized sugar
2 cups sifted flour, measured after sifting
3 eggs beaten separately
1 teaspoon baking powder, heaping
3 tablespoons cream

Cream the butter and the sugar together. Add the well beaten yolks, then the whites, the flour with the baking powder sifted in, and lastly the cream. Beat well, and flavor to taste. Bake. Serve with liquid sauce. Currants will add further grace to this delicious pudding, an old-time favorite that has not lost its prestige.

MERINGUE PUDDING
Mrs. Geo. Boutcher

6 egg whites
6 tablespoons sugar, level
½ cup raisins, large
½ glass sherry
1 cup pecans, chopped
    whipped cream

Seed the raisins and soak them in sherry overnight. Beat the whites of eggs very stiff, add sifted sugar, beat vigorously, add raisins and nuts. Turn into a pyrex bowl and bake for 15 minutes. Serve with whipped cream.

DATE PUDDING

1 teaspoon vanilla
4 eggs
1 cup pecans
2 cups dates
2 cups sugar
2 teaspoons baking powder, rounded
½ pt. cream
4 tablespoons flour, level

Cream the egg yolks and sugar very light. Add flour, and beat well. Then add the baking powder, nuts and dates. Fold in the stiffly beaten whites. Put in a square pan in hot water and bake in a moderate oven about 1 hour. When cold serve with whipped cream.

WALNUT DATE PUDDING

2 cups stoned dates, cut or chopped
1 cup English walnuts
3 tablespoons flour, heaping
½ cup sugar
1 teaspoon baking powder, heaping
2 eggs
1 cup whipped cream

Break up the nuts. Sprinkle the dates with flour. Beat the eggs together. Mix well all the ingredients except the cream, pour into a baking dish and set in a pan of boiling water. Bake half an hour.

When done, remove, and pour in the cream while the pudding is still warm. Chill and serve with whipped cream.

SPONGE PUDDING
Mrs. Petrie Hamilton

¼ cup sugar
½ cup flour, measured before sifting
1 pt. milk
¼ cup butter
5 eggs
1 teaspoon vanilla

Mix the sugar, milk, and flour together, and cook in a double boiler until it becomes a clear, smooth paste. Then add the butter. When well mixed, stir in the well beaten egg yolks, the flavoring, and the well beaten egg whites. Pour into a baking pan, set in a pan of hot water, and bake about 30 minutes. Serve at once with cabinet sauce.

Mrs. H. Waller Fowler blends two and one-half squares of Baker's unsweetened chocolate to the above mixture and presto!—a delicious chocolate soufflé. Whipped cream goes with it.

TART ANGÉLIQUE

8 egg whites
2 cupfuls sugar
1 teaspoonful vinegar
1 teaspoonful vanilla
½ pt. whipping cream

Flavor whipped cream highly with sherry or whiskey.

Add 2 tablespoons of sugar.

Beat whites of eggs for ten minutes, then add sugar gradually by sifting a little in at a time, beating it for ten minutes. Add vinegar and vanilla. Put in large deep cake pan with loose bottom lightly buttered. Bake in a very, very slow oven for one hour. When cold, pile flavored whipped cream on top. Sprinkle with nuts and cherries.

MARSHMALLOW PUDDING

24 to 30 marshmallows
1 egg
¾ cup sugar
2 cups sweet milk
    cracker crumbs

Butter a baking dish and cover the bottom with a layer of cracker crumbs, broken fine. Cut marshmallows in half and spread over cracker crumbs. Continue with a layer of cracker crumbs and a layer of marshmallows until the dish is full. Beat the egg until very light and combine with the sugar and milk. Flavor with sherry, or almond if preferred. The substitution of crumbled macaroons for the plain cracker crumbs makes a very delicious pudding. In this case the sugar is omitted.

OMELET SOUFFLÉ
Mrs. Curran Perkins

3   eggs
3   tablespoons powdered sugar
½   lemon

Beat the yolks and whites of the eggs separately, the whites until they are stiff enough to cut with a knife. Add the sugar gradually to the yolks, beating until the mixture is thick and smooth. Add the juice of the lemon and a little of the grated peel. Stir the yolks and whites lightly together, pour into a warmed and buttered dish and bake in a quick oven a few minutes.

CUP CUSTARD

1   qt. milk
5   eggs
5   ozs. granulated sugar
2   teaspoons vanilla

Let milk come to a boil. Break eggs into sugar, beat and add milk gradually, not too hot, stir until the sugar is melted. Put a spoonful of caramel sauce in each cup, fill with the custard and cook in a pan of water in oven. Do not cook them too long for they will curdle.

To serve turn cups over in a saucer and brown color of caramel will be on top of custard.

TECHE CUSTARD
Mrs. Walter Torian

5   eggs
1   qt. milk
5   tablespoons granulated sugar
1   teaspoon bitter almond extract
    few drops cochineal
    pinch of citric acid

Scald the milk. Set aside 3 whites of eggs and beat rest of egg yolks and whites together. Add sugar and beat in well. Now pour scalding milk over the eggs slowly, beating all the while. Put in the bitter almond. Pour into custard cups or a small casserole, filling about ¾ full. Put the cups, or casserole, in a pan with hot water in it (note, not enough so that it may boil up into the custard) consign to the oven and cook slowly until firm. Remove from the pan and allow to cool. Beat the three whites until very light. Put in the three tablespoons of sugar, slowly, beating all the time until very stiff. Add the citric acid then the cochineal, one drop at a time until it is a light pink color. Top the custard with this and serve with thin sweet cream.

RUSSIAN CUSTARD
Mrs. S. A. Fortier

2½ dozen lady fingers
1   qt. cream
    candied cherries
    pecans
Custard:
1   qt. milk
3   eggs
4   tablespoons sugar
2   teaspoons vanilla

Break the lady fingers in two and line the bottom of a deep dish with them. Cover with whipped cream, sprinkled over with chopped nuts and cherries. Another layer over this, and repeat until the dish is filled, letting the top layer be lady fingers. Take a knife and make many holes and fill them with the custard. Then place in the ice box overnight, or for several hours.

For the custard: Cream the eggs and sugar. Add to the boiling milk in a double boiler, stirring constantly until thick. Cool, flavor before adding to pudding.

PEACHES AU CHATEAU BLANC

4   large freestone peaches
6   macaroons, rolled fine
2   eggs
1   peach kernel, crushed to a paste

Cut the peaches round and remove the stones. Take out 3 or 4 tablespoons of the pulp, mash very fine; add the powdered macaroons, mix well with the two stiffly beaten yolks and sweeten to taste. Add the peach kernel and blend with the mixture.

Stuff the peaches with this, place them in a pan, and bake until done. Remove from the oven, and top with méringue made with the sweetened whites of the eggs. Run into the oven and brown slowly. A delicious sweet after a heavy dinner, or luncheon.

BREAD PUDDING au CHOCOLAT

2   eggs
2   squares chocolate
4   cups scalded milk
2   cups stale bread crumbs
⅔   cup sugar
1   teaspoon vanilla
¼   teaspoon salt

Soak the bread about a half hour, melt the chocolate in a saucepan over hot water, add half the sugar and enough milk taken from the bread and milk to make a consistency to pour. Add this to the mixture and the remaining sugar. Bake.

CHOCOLATE ROLL

1 teaspoon cornstarch
5 eggs, beaten separately
1 tablespoon cocoa, scant
½ cup powdered sugar
1 pt. cream, whipped

Beat yolk and sugar, add cocoa, and gently fold in the whites. Bake in a slow oven. Roll while warm with whipped cream sweetened with confectioner's sugar. Serve with chocolate sauce.

SPONGE CAKE au CHOCOLAT
Mrs. J. N. Roussel

1 pt. milk
1 cup sugar
4 heaping tablespoons Baker's cocoa
1 tablespoon flour, heaping
sponge cake
whipped cream

Blend the dry ingredients. Add a little warm milk, stirring constantly; then the rest of the milk which is now boiling. Set on the fire in a double boiler and stir constantly, letting it remain until it is thick as the filling in a cream puff.

Cut around the top of the sponge cake 1 inch from the outer rim and about 2 inches down, and lift out the center piece, thus separating it. Into the cavity put the chocolate filling. Replace a thin part of the piece of cake removed, as a top and cover with stiff whipped cream.

INDIAN PUDDING

3 tablespoons cornmeal
3 cups milk
⅓ cup molasses
½ cup sugar
1 egg
½ teaspoon ginger
½ teaspoon cinnamon
¼ teaspoon salt
1 cup milk
butter the size of a walnut

Scald the milk and pour it over the meal stirring constantly to prevent lumps. Add the molasses and cook until the mixture thickens, stirring all the time or it will burn. Remove from fire and add the sugar, butter, spices, and salt, and the egg well beaten. Turn into a buttered making dish and bake a half hour at 300 degrees. After the first half hour pour a cup of milk over it and continue baking until firm. Serve with cream.

CREAMY RICE PUDDING

2 tablespoons rice
1 quart milk
6 tablespoons sugar
¼ teaspoon salt
⅛ teaspoon nutmeg
½ cup seedless raisins

Turn into a buttered baking dish.

Dot top with 2 teaspoons butter. Put into a slow oven (300 Fahrenheit) and keep the flame low. Stir occasionally, the first hour to keep rice from sticking. Bake another hour without stirring. Then mix ½ cup seedless raisins. Bake another hour (three hours in all) without stirring. Serve hot or cold with cream.

BLACKBERRY ROLY-POLY

2 cups flour
2 teaspoons baking powder
½ teaspoon salt
4 tablespoons butter
¾ cup milk
1½ cups fresh blackberries
6 tablespoons sugar

Sift flour once, measure, add baking powder and salt, and sift again. Cut in shortening, add milk gradually until soft dough is formed, turn out immediately on slightly floured board and roll ¼ inch thick. Brush with melted butter, cover with blackberries and sprinkle with sugar. Roll as for jelly rolls. Place in greased loaf pan with edge of roll on under side. Brush with melted butter, bake in hot oven (400 degrees F) twenty to twenty-five minutes. Serve hot with cream or Blackberry Sauce, page 96.

PINEAPPLE TORTE

½ lb. butter
2 cups flour
½ cup sugar
1 egg yolk
1 large can pineapple, crushed
Custard:
2 egg yolks
1 cup milk
1 teaspoon cornstarch
Méringue:
3 egg whites
2 tablespoons sugar

Mix like a pie crust and press into form (the dough cannot be rolled, as it is springy and spongy). Bake in biscuit pan. Thicken the crushed pineapple with a scant teaspoon of cornstarch and place on the baked torte.

Pour the custard over all, and top with meringue. Run in the oven and cook slowly, so that the meringue will set.

TARTE â l'APRICOT
Mrs. Rafferty

Pie pastry:
2 cups milk
2 egg yolks, beaten
2 tablespoons sugar
2 tablespoons flour
1 teaspoon vanilla
1 can sliced apricots
1 tablespoon tapioca
red coloring

Line a layer cake tin with pastry, bringing it well up the sides and bake till a delicate brown. Make a custard of the milk, the egg yolks with the sugar and flour mixed together, cooking until thick when the vanilla is added. Cool and pour into pastry.

Drain the apricots, saving the juice, remove the skins carefully, so as not to break the flesh. Lay them close together, round side up on the custard. Cook the tapioca in the apricot juice, add a little red color and pour it over the tart to glaze.

This recent importation by the inveterate traveler who gives it, is already taking a foremost place among our cherished French culinary inheritances.

WALDORF STEAMED PUDDING
Mrs. J. B. Barnard

```
    1   cup molasses
    1   cup suet, chopped
    1   cup milk
 2 ½   cups flour
    1   cup large raisins
    1   lb. English walnuts, chopped
   ¼   lb. figs, chopped
    1   teaspoon soda
```

Mix well and steam two to three hours.

SAUCE

```
   ½   cup butter
    1   cup powdered sugar
    1   cup whipped cream
```

Cream butter and sugar as for hard sauce, add whipped cream and heat to scalding over hot water.

LEMON PUDDING

```
    4   eggs
 1 ½   cups sugar
 1 ½   cups flour
   ¾   cup butter
    2   lemons, grated rind and juice
    2   teaspoons baking powder
    1   cup milk
        dash of salt
Sauce:
    2   tablespoons water
    1   cup sugar
    1   pint milk
    1   teaspoon cornstarch
    2   tablespoon sherry
        butter size of egg
```

Cream the butter and sugar, add the well beaten yolks, and rind and juice of the lemons, and milk. Stir in the dry ingredients, fold in whites, pour into well greased pan with lid, filling it to about ¾ fullness, and place over boiling water. Boil until done. Serve with sauce.

For the sauce, two tablespoons of water are put in a saucepan; to this add the butter, which has been creamed with the sugar, the milk thickened with 1 teaspoon of cornstarch, and the sherry.

ENGLISH PLUM PUDDING

```
   ½   lb. finely crumbled suet or
   ½   lb. butter
    2   lbs. raisins
    1   lb. currents
   ½   lb. brown sugar
   ½   lb. citron
    1   lb. flour
    1   cup milk
    1   cup black molasses
    2   cups pecans
    8   eggs
    2   teaspoons baking powder
    1   teaspoon salt
    1   tablespoon each allspice, nutmeg
        and cinnamon
```

Mix as you would for fruit cake. Dredge fruit and pecans well with flour and add to cake mixture. Pour into a well-floured cloth, tie tight but allow room for pudding to expand. Drop into a kettle of boiling water and cook three hours. Serve with hard sauce. This recipe makes two large puddings.

APPLES INGENUES

```
apples
cinnamon
sugar
butter
bread
```

Peel core and chop the apples. Season with cinnamon and sugar, liberally. Dip thin slices of bread in melted butter and line moulds with them, filling with the apples. Sprinkle very lightly with toasted bread crumbs, mixed with sugar and cinnamon, dot with small bits of butter and bake. Even the grown people will enjoy them.

CABINET PUDDING
Mrs. Petrie Hamilton

```
    6   eggs
    6   tablespoons sugar
    1   pt. sherry wine
    2   tablespoons gelatine
    1   cup broken pecan meats
    1   doz. macaroons, broken to bits
   ¼   lb. crystallized cherries
   ¼   lb. crystallized pineapple
```

Beat the yolks of the eggs until light and add sugar gradually. Soak the gelatine in ¼ cup of cold water for 5 minutes. Let the wine come to a boil and pour it over the gelatine. Pour this mixture while hot over the egg and sugar. Place in a double boiler and cook until thickened, stirring constantly. Allow this to cool, then stir in the well beaten egg whites. Add the macaroons, cherries, pineapple and nuts. Mold, and serve with whipped cream.

STRAWBERRY SHORTBREAD

A short biscuit dough is rolled very thin and circles cut the exact size of the bottom of the pan to be used. The unbaked layers are placed one on top of the other with a generous spreading of softened butter between each one and baked in a slow oven until nicely browned. In the meantime the strawberries have been mashed and sweetened. On removal of the shortbread from the oven the layers 're separated and the berries spread between. The whole is topped with whipped cream and served at once. If a crisper torte is desired each layer is baked separately, whereas, for the New England Strawberry Shortcake only one thick cake is baked. It is split and buttered while hot and the strawberries added as before.

BUTTERSCOTCH PUDDING
Mrs. Wm. J. Mitchell

      1 lb. brown sugar
      ¼ lb. butter
      1 qt. milk
      2 eggs
      1 package gelatine

Melt the butter and sugar slowly in an iron skillet. Have ready the milk, scalded. Pour part of it into the melted butter and sugar, the remainder over gelatine which has been soaked in cold water. Mix with the beaten yolks of egs and add to the first mixture, which has been left over a very slow fire. Mix well. Remove from the fire and add the beaten whites of eggs. Put into a melon mold. When ready to serve, surround it on the platter with whipped cream.

CZARINA PUDDING

     36 almonds
      1 pt. milk
      4 eggs
      1 pt. cream
      1 teaspoon vanilla
      1 cup chopped raisins
         sugar

Blanch and chop the almonds, and put with the milk in a double boiler to boil 20 minutes. Beat the eggs very light and add to them the cream, vanilla, and the milk and almonds. Sweeten to taste. Beat for 5 minutes and put into a freezer. When partly frozen, add the raisins, then set to freeze hard.

CHOCOLATE WHIP

      1 cup scalded milk
      4 eggs
      4 tablespoons sugar
      7 teaspoons Baker's cocoa

Mix the sugar and cocoa with milk and add the egg yolks well beaten. Cook until thick, in a double boiler. Cool and fold in the stiffly beaten whites. You can add a dozen marshmallows to advantage, or if you prefer the whip to be firmer, you may add 2 teaspoons of gelatine.

CHOCOLATE PUDDING
Miss Ethel Forman

      1 qt. milk
      5 tablespoons cornstarch
      2 egg yolks
      1 cake German sweet chocolate
      7 tablespoons sugar

Put three cups of the milk on the fire in a double boiler. Heat and remove some of it in a cup to dissolve the grated chocolate. Add this to the hot milk. Dissolve the cornstarch in the remaining cup of cold milk and add it to the hot milk slowly, stirring until thick. Mix the slightly beaten egg with the sugar and add to the mixture, stirring constantly for five minutes. Pour into a mold or serving bowl. Chill and serve with whipped cream.

PEACH DUMPLING

      ½ cup milk
      6 large soft peaches
      1 cup flour
      2 level teaspoons baking powder
      ½ teaspoon salt
         butter size of an egg

Sift together dry ingredients. With the fingers mix in butter thoroughly and add milk.

Roll out and cut in pieces to cover fruit. Have dough just moist enough to be able to handle it.

Sauce: 1 cup sugar, butter, the size of a large egg, 2 cups water. Boil, and while boiling, drop in dumplings.

Then place in oven about ½ hour, or longer, if necessary.

Serve hot, with cream—or, they are also good cold.

STRAWBERRY DUMPLINGS

    2½ cups strawberries
      1 cup sugar
      1 tablespoon butter
      1 cup hot water
   Dumplings:
      1 cup flour
      2 teaspoons baking powder
      ¾ cup milk
      1 tablespoon lard
         pinch of salt

Let the various ingredients simmer together about 10 minutes. Then drop in the dumplings by spoonfuls and let cook 20 minutes.

Dumplings: Blend the ingredients into dough.

CRÊPES BRULÉES

¼   lb. flour
4   eggs
½   pt. cold milk
4   ozs. powdered sugar
1   teaspoon orange flower water

Sift flour into pan or bowl. Break the eggs, beat well, and add 1 oz. of powdered sugar. Mix thoroughly with the flour and then add the cold milk, pouring it in gradually. Mix well, add the orange flower water.

Have ready a pan, buttered slightly and when hot, drop 1 large tablespoon of batter in it. Turn pan around to spread the batter as thin as possible

Cook until brown and turn cake to cook other side. Lay the pan cake on a dish, butter well, sprinkle with powdered sugar and roll.

Place in baking dish peeling of 3 oranges grated, 12 lumps of sugar, 4 ozs. of good brandy, 4 ozs. of Kirchwasser.

Light fire and when burning well dip pan cakes in one by one for 1 minute and serve.

CRÊPES SUZETTE

1   cup powdered sugar
1   coffeespoon absinthe
1   egg yolk
2   cups flour
2   cups milk
4   tablespoons melted butter
8   eggs, beaten together

Mash the powdered sugar well into the absinthe, then add to it the well-beaten egg yolk to make a paste, beating it until it is like mayonnaise or thicker. Set aside. Stir the milk into the flour, with melted butter, and add the eggs beaten together. Mix all this and beat again, and fry.

Put a generous spoonful of the mixture just off the center of each and fold the crêpes over it at the sides and ends, pocketbook shaped. Run these into a brisk oven until brown. They puff up like an omelet soufflé and melt exquisitely in the mouth. To serve this style crêpes, sprinkle them with a little powdered sugar, pour curacao over them, and let the alcohol burn a few moments.

PANCAKE ANATOLE

2½   cups flour
½   cup breadcrumbs, fine
1   tablespoon baking powder
1   teaspoon salt
2   tablespoons melted butter
¼   cup sugar
2   cups milk
2   eggs

Mix and sift dry ingredients, beat eggs, add milk and pour on first mixture. Beat thoroughly and add butter. Drop by spoonfuls on greased hot griddle, letting mixture spread thinly. Turn when firm, and brown on other side. When all are done, roll each one, and serve very hot with hot melted orange marmalade.

CREOLE PUFFS

1   pint water
1   tablespoon each butter and sugar
1   lemon, the rind thinly peeled
4   eggs
    flour

Boil sugar, water, and lemon rind, five minutes. Remove rind. Take flour a handful at a time and sprinkle into the boiling syrup which has been kept on the fire. Stir vigorously every minute until it is so thick it is difficult to stir. Continue stirring and cooking until it leaves the side of the pan (the longer the better). Remove from the fire. Beat in four eggs, one at a time, stirring vigorously between each egg. Success depends on the vigor of the stirring. Drop bits of the paste the size of an egg into deep hot fat. Fry to a beautiful brown. Sprinkle with sugar.

CREOLE PANCAKES

1   lb. flour
3   eggs
½   tablespoon lard, or lard and butter
1   teaspoonful sugar
    milk to make a thin batter, or milk
    and water

This will serve eight or ten people. Crumble the shortening into the flour. Beat the eggs without separating, add the sugar and stir into the flour. Then add sufficient milk to make a thin batter. Use a heavy aluminum skillet so that no grease is necessary to fry them in. Heat the skillet but keep the fire low, and pour in enough batter to cover the skillet with a very thin coating. Turn like pancakes and when both sides are browned roll into cylinders. Keep hot until all are prepared and serve with melted butter and sugar or with syrup. To turn them into a simplified version of crepes suzette flavor the dough with grated orange rind. They may be served with a sauce made of ½ curacoa and ½ brandy. This is lighted just as they are taken to the table. If no curacoa is available be more liberal with the grated orange peel in the dough and add a few drops of orange juice to the brandy sauce before lighting it.

"ZABAYON"
Mrs. Wm. T. Nolan

    8   egg yolks
    6   level tablespoons sugar
    9   tablespoons Marsala wine

Cream yolks with sugar until very
light, stir in wine very slowly. Put in
a double boiler and cook to the consistency of a thick cream, stirring all
the time to prevent curdling. When
cool, pour into parfait glasses and put
in the refrigerator until ready to
serve. Plain rice wafers or sponge
cakes are a happy combination to
serve on the side.

This is an old Creole derivative of
Italian Zabaglione, which begins in
the same way, but goes on to add half
of the stiffly beaten whites to the
original mixture. And it is served hot
as often as cold.

CRÊME au CHOCOLAT

    ½   pt. whipped cream
    6   eggs
    ½   cup water
    ¼   lb. sweet chocolate
    1   teaspoon vanilla
    1   pinch salt
        brandy or sherry

Melt the chocolate over hot water.
Beat egg yolks very light, add
chocolate and fold in the stiffly beat-
en whites, and vanilla. Stir in gelatine
that was soaked in cold water and
melted in hot water.

Place in a bowl and chill thoroughly. Serve with whipped cream, flavor with brandy or sherry.

CHOCOLATE SPONGE VIENNOIS

    4   eggs, beaten separately
    ½   cup sugar
    ¾   tablespoon gelatine
    ¼   cup cold water to soak gelatine in
    ½   cup boiling water
    ⅛   lb. unsweetened chocolate
    1·½   teaspoons vanilla

Beat sugar into yolks. Add gelatine
to chocolate that has been melted in
hot water over hot water and stir all
into yolks. Fold mixture into whites,
flavor. Turn into mold and place in
the refrigerator. Serve with whipped
cream. A cold chocolate sauce poured
over the pudding before decorating
with cream adds to the deliciousness
of this dessert.

STRAWBERRY CÉLESTE

    1   qt. strawberries, dusted with
            powdered sugar
    1   pt. cream
    3   tablespoons brandy

Have berries very cold, put powdered sugar over them, add brandy
and then have cream stiffly beaten
and pour over them, dipping up and
down to mix well.

STRAWBERRY CREAM
Mrs. Pauline Curran Perkins

    1   qt. berries
    1   cup sugar
    ½   box gelatine
    ½   cup cold water
    ½   cup boiling water
    1   pt. whipping cream

Mash the berries with sugar and
let them stand until the sugar is well
dissolved. Strain them through a
sieve fine enough to keep back the
seeds. Soak the gelatine in the cold
water. Then dissolve in boiling water.
Strain it into the berry juice. Cool
and beat until slightly thickened, add
the whipped cream and place in a
plain mold.

CRÊME BRULÉE

    4   egg yolks, well beaten
    1   pt. cream
        brown or maple sugar

Beat the egg yolks very stiff. Heat
the cream to the boiling point and
pour it over the beaten egg yolks. Return to the fire in a double boiler.
Cook five minutes stirring constantly.
Remove and pour it into a buttered
baking dish. Cover the top with sugar,
then run in the oven and let it remain
until a crust is formed. Take out and
allow to cool. Place in refrigerator
until time to serve. Have it very cold.
Excellent with baked pears or any
other cooked fruit.

EGGNOG RING

    8   eggs, beaten separately
    1   cup granulated sugar
    1   envelope gelatine soaked in ½ cup
            of cold water
    ½   cup boiling water
    ¾   cup whiskey
    2   teaspoons vanilla
        whipped cream
        chopped almonds
        macaroons

To the yolks add whiskey, to the
whites add a cup of sifted granulated
sugar. Then mix. Dissolve the gelatine
in boiling water and fold it onto the
mixture.

Line a ring mold with lady fingers
and pour in the above mixture.

When ready to serve, turn onto a
platter and fill the center with stiff
whipped cream, in which are mixed
the almonds and macaroons, rolled
and sifted.

This beautiful and delicious dish
may be garnished, if desired, with
strawberries, cherries or raspberries.

CRÈME à l'AMANDE

1 pt. cream, whipped
1 lb. marshmallows
1 cup blanched almonds or pecans
1 teaspoon gelatine
½ cup water
Sauce:
 4 eggs
 1 cup powdered sugar
 ½ pt. cream, whipped
  vanilla

Dissolve the gelatine in water. Cut up the marshmallows. Mix gelatine, whipped cream and marshmallows thoroughly. Add nuts and mix them in well. Set in ice box to cool.

For the sauce:

Beat the eggs, yolks and whites separately. Cream the sugar with the yolks, stir the beaten whites into the whipped cream, combine, and add vanilla.

RUM PUDDING
Mrs. George Frierson

2 eggs
½ cup sugar
4 tablespoons whiskey or rum
1 pt. whipped cream

Beat the yolks and whites separately. To the yolks, add the sugar, then the whiskey, then the whipped cream. Lastly, the well beaten whites. Line a mold with lady fingers, and fill it with the above mixture. Pack, or set in frigidaire for 3 hours, and turn out on a platter, and decorate it with whipped cream.

This recipe is delicious if you soak a package of gelatine in ¼ cup cold milk and add to ¼ cup hot milk. When dissolved and cool, beat in mixture and proceed as above. This can be made the day before.

CHARLOTTE RUSSE
Mrs. Pauline Curran Perkins

6 egg yolks
6 teaspoons sugar
½ scant tablespoon gelatine
1 pt. sweet milk
1 pt. whipping cream
3 doz. lady fingers
1 tablespoon vanilla

Beat the yolks of eggs lightly, and add to them gradually the sugar. Put the gelatine in the sweet milk and set in a double boiler. When it comes to the boiling point pour it over the eggs, stirring constantly until well mixed. Place the mixture back on the fire to thicken. Do not allow it to boil. When thickened, take it off, strain it through a sieve and set aside. Line the bottom and the sides of a mold solidly with lady fingers. Mix the whipped cream and the cooled custard well together, add the vanilla and set in the frigidaire or pack with ice.

PARISIAN CHARLOTTE RUSSE

2 cups milk
4 eggs
½ pt. whipping cream
½ cup sugar
1 tablespoon vanilla
1 doz. lady fingers
½ doz. macaroons
2 tablespoons gelatine
½ cup water

Let milk come to a boil. Add well beaten egg yolks with the sugar. Cook until thick. Soak gelatine in advance in water, then put it in the custard and mix well. Crush the macaroons and put in the custard. When the mixture is slightly cool, fold in the whites and last of all the whipped cream. Line mold with lady fingers before pouring in mixture. Chill 3 hours before turning it out to serve.

CHARLOTTE RUSSE

1 qt whipping cream
5 tablespoons sugar
1 package gelatine
1 cup cold water or milk
1 cup hot milk
¼ cup whiskey
¾ cup sherry wine
2 teaspoons vanilla

Soak the gelatine in cold milk, or water and add it to the hot milk. When it is melted, allow it to cool. Whip the cream, add sugar, wine, whiskey and vanilla. Now pour in the gelatine and whip until it begins to jell. Place in the refrigerator until ready to serve.

MARSHMALLOW MOCHA
Mrs. Walter Torian

1 10c box marshmallows
1 cup strong black coffee
1 teaspoon vanilla
2 tablespoons sugar
2 cups cream, whipped

Put the marshmallows in with the coffee and the vanilla and let them stand overnight (not in the ice box). Next morning mash the marshmallows with a fork. Beat the cream and sugar well together and stir the marshmallow mixture into them. Put in parfait glasses, set in the ice box and serve cold.

CHOCOLATE PECAN PUFF
Lt. Comdr. and Mrs. S. W. Wallace

1 teaspoon gelatine
¼ cup hot coffee
1¾ cups milk
¼ teaspoon salt
1 cup sugar
½ cup ground pecans
1 tablespoon cold water
2 sqs. Bakers Chocolate
4 egg yolks
½ teaspoon vanilla
1 cup cream, whipped

Soak gelatine 5 minutes in cold

water, dissolve in hot coffee. Dissolve chocolate in hot milk and add sugar. Pour over egg yolks and cook until thick.

Add vanilla and nuts. Cool, fold in cream, put in mold.

MARSHMALLOW LOAF
Lt. Comdr. and Mrs. S. W. Wallace

    ½ lb. marshmallows, cut in quarters
    ½ cup top milk
    ½ lb. dates, cut in pieces
    ½ cup ground pecans
    ½ lb. graham crackers

Drop marshmallows in the milk. Grind the crackers with the dates and nuts. Work all together and form into a roll in wax paper. It is better after a day in the ice box. Slice and serve with whipped cream.

SHERRY MACAROONS

    6 eggs
    6 macaroons, crumbled
    6 tablespoons sugar
    2 tablespoons gelatine
    1 cup sherry
    1 small bottle Maraschino cherries
       whipped cream

Cream the sugar with the well beaten yolks of eggs, add the sherry and boil gently until thick, stirring constantly. Set aside to cool. Dissolve the gelatine in a cup of cold water, beating until thoroughly dissolved. Beat the whites very stiff and add to the cooled egg sugar-sherry mixture, alternately with the gelatine. Into this stir gently the macaroons and some of the cherries. Pour into a mold to set. Serve on a platter, with whipped cream, garnished with cherries.

ORANGE DELIGHT

Peel four or five oranges carefully, divide in sections, remove the seeds taking care to keep the sections whole. Place in deep kitchen bowl.

Boil ½ lb. sugar in 1 pint of water for five minutes. Pour over the orange and allow to stand for two hours. Drain out the orange pieces and place in a glass bowl. Put the syrup back on the stove and boil hard for five minutes. Allow it to cool so that the glass bowl will not crack and then pour the syrup over the fruit again. Place in the icebox to become t h o r o u g h l y chilled. Serve with whipped cream piled on top.

PEACHES IN BRANDY
Mrs. Bruton Dawkins

Take a good quality of canned peaches and drain the syrup from them. Take an equal amount of the syrup and brandy or whiskey and pour back over the peaches and allow to stand for two hours. Serve with whipped cream or with ice cream.

SUPER MELBA

    vanilla ice cream
    peaches, brandied, fresh, or tinned
    currant jelly
    apple jelly

The jellies are melted. Over each serving of ice cream one or two peach halves are placed, cut side down, and the melted jellies are poured over all.

FROZEN MARRON PUDDING

      6 or more macaroons, crushed
      ½ cup sugar
      1 pint milk
      3 eggs, beaten yolks and whites sep-
         arately
      ½ pint bottle marrons
      ¾ pint cream
         Flavor with brandy, sherry or
         vanilla

Make a custard with milk, egg yolks, and sugar and freeze to a thick mush. Line mold with macaroons and cover them with the custard. Whip cream, add chopped marrons, whites of eggs and flavoring. Fill center of mold with this mixture. Pack in the usual manner.

FROZEN RICE PUDDING

      ½ cup rice
      1 quart water
      1 quart milk
      2 small cups sugar
      1 pint whipping cream
      1 teaspoon rum

Bring the rice to a boil in the quart of cold water, pour off the water, add the milk and let cook one hour in a double boiler, add the sugar and cook half an hour longer, then add a pinch of salt, and cool. When cool, flavor with vanilla, add the whipped cream and freeze. Serve with melted current jelly or any fruit sauce.

PRALINE ICE CREAM

      ½ cup sugar
      ⅔ cup chopped pecan meats
      2 cups milk
      3 egg yolks
      ½ cup sugar
      1 cup cream, whipped
         vanilla
         salt, a few grains

Caramelize the sugar and add to it the pecan meats. Turn into a slightly buttered pan. Cool and pound, then sift.

Scald the milk, add the egg yolks, the other sugar, and the salt, and cook in a double boiler, stirring constantly until thick. Add to this the sifted caramel and nut mixture. Cool. Add the whipped cream and the vanilla, and freeze.

ICE CREAM au CARAMEL

      8 egg yolks
    1½ cups sugar
      ⅓ cup hot water
      2 cups milk
      ¼ teaspoon salt
    2¾ cups light cream

Heat the sugar in a saucepan until it is melted and amber colored. Now add the hot water and cook until the mixture is blended thoroughly.

Put the milk in a double boiler, scald it well, and add it slowly to the well beaten egg yolks. Add the caramel syrup, sugar and salt, and cook over hot water until the mixture thickens, stirring constantly to avoid lumps. When done, it should be of the consistency of custard.

Cool, add the cream, strain and freeze. Toasted pecan bits springled over it are good, or a chocolate sauce; but it is delicious per se and more reminiscent of the famous old Mannassier's, where it was a choice offering.

CARAMEL ICE CREAM
Mrs. Chas. Crawford

      1 pt. whipping cream
      1 pt. milk
      1 cup sugar, caramelled
      2 tablespoons plain sugar
      1 tablespoon gelatine
      1 teaspoon vanilla

Dissolve gelatine in one cup of the sweet milk, caramel 1 cup sugar and dissolve in the rest of the sweet milk after it has been scalded. Add milk with the dissolved gelatine and the plain sugar. When ready to freeze add pint of cream whipped stiff and vanilla. This makes about 1½ quarts of ice cream when frozen.

FROZEN BUTTERMILK

      1 quart buttermilk
      1 can condensed milk
      1 pinch soda
      1 pint cream
      2 teaspoons vanilla
      3 egg whites, well beaten

Add soda to buttermilk, then milk, cream and vanilla. Mix well. Fold in whites and freeze. A healthful refreshing summer dessert.

FROZEN CREAM CHEESE
Mrs. Walter Torian

      4 cream cheeses with their cream
      1 pint sweet cream
      1 can condensed milk
         vanilla to taste
         sugar to taste
      2 egg whites, beaten
      1 pinch soda

Mash the cream cheese alternately with the pint of cream, through a wire sieve. Add a pinch of soda and condensed milk and sweeten to taste. Add vanilla and the stiffly beaten whites of eggs. Freeze and pack.

ORANGE SHERBET

    1½ quarts orange juice
      ½ cup lemon juice
      1 cup sugar
      1 cup water
         grated rind of one orange

Boil sugar and water, add grated rind. Strain into fruit juice and freeze. Serve in candied orange cups.

FROZEN CHOCOLATE ROLL

    1   qt. milk
    3   tablespoons water
    1   cup sugar
    2   squares Baker's chocolate
    1½   teaspoons vanilla
    1   pt. whipping cream
    1½   tablespoons sugar

Melt the chocolate in water. Add the sugar and the milk, and let come to a boil. When cool, add vanilla and a tiny pinch of salt. Freeze.

When hard, take out the dasher, spread the cream around the sides of the freezer, leaving a hole in the center, into which pour the whipped cream, which has been sweetened and flavored. Cover freezer and pack to stand for two to three hours. Turn out on a platter by holding a hot cloth around the freezer. Cut in rounds.

FRUIT CREAM

    1   qt. cream
    ⅓   box gelatine
    6   tablespoons sherry
    ⅓   cup cold water
    ⅓   cup hot water
    ½   lb. crystallized fruit
    1   cup sugar

Dissolve gelatine in cold water, then in the hot. Whip the cream and mix with it sugar, sherry, and gelatine. Let it cool until it commences to set, then place in a mold, first a layer of cream, then fruit, and so on alternately until the mold is filled. Then set in the frigidaire, or pack in salt and ice for several hours.

PISTACHIO ICE CREAM

    ½   cup chopped pistachio nuts
    ½   cup chopped almonds
    1   tablespoon almond extract
    ¼   teaspoon salt
    1   cup sugar
    4   cups cream
         few drops green coloring

Mix all the ingredients and freeze.

For a yet more stupendous effect, press the cream around the sides of the freezer, and fill with grated French chocolate. Pack for 2 hours.

ORANGE MOUSSE

    1   pt. whipping cream
    ½   cup sugar
    1   teaspoon gelatine
    ¼   cup water
    ¾   cup orange juice
    1½   oranges
    2   egg whites, stiffly beaten

Whip cream, add sugar, flavor with orange and juice. Melt gelatine that has soaked in ¼ cup water. When cool add to cream. Add the egg whites well beaten. Line mold with orange that has been separated into sections. Pour in cream. Pack in ice and salt for 3 hours. Serve with Orange Sauce or without it. Refer to Sauces.

CARAMEL MOUSSE au ST. AUBIN

    1   milk
    1   tablespoon cornstarch or flour
    1   cup sugar
    2   eggs
    1   teaspoon vanilla
    1   pt. heavy cream

Put the sugar in a saucepan and brown it. Make a custard with milk, eggs, and cornstarch and add the caramel sugar. Stir until melted. Freeze.

Line a melon mold with this caramel mixture, fill the center with whipped cream flavored with whiskey, sherry, or vanilla. Cover with greased waxed paper before putting on the lid. Pack with two parts of ice to one of salt and let freeze 3 hours.

STRAWBERRY MOUSSE

    1   cup sugar
    1   pt. strawberries
    2   tablespoons gelatine
    ½   cup water
    1   qt. cream, whipped

Let the berries stand with the sugar for a while (about an hour). Crush the berries through a sieve. Soak the gelatine in the water, then dissolve over hot water, and mix with the strained berries. Put into the icebox until it becomes slightly hard, then fold in the whipped cream. Pack in salt and ice for several hours.

LEMON ICE
Mrs. Wm. J. Mitchell

    1   cup sugar
    2   cups water
    3   lemons (grated rind of 1)
    4   egg whites

Put the sugar and water into a saucepan and allow to boil for 8 minutes. Remove the saucepan from the fire and beat the contents until cold. Add the stiffly beaten whites of eggs, the strained juice of lemon and the grated rind. Freeze. Refreshing, cooling and delicious.

WATERMELON ICE
Mrs. Harry Thompson

    ½   large melon
    4   oranges, the juice
    3   lemons, the juice
    1   cup sugar
    1   egg, the white

Scoop meat from melon, extract juice. Add lemon and orange juice and sugar. Stir thoroughly and freeze. When slightly frozen add stiffly beaten white of egg and finish freezing. Serve in melon rind that has been neatly trimmed at top edge. Scoop out holes with potato scooper, one or two inches all around the top and fill with large cheeries or grapes. Decorate generously with fresh mint. This makes a tempting and delicious summer dessert.

PIE CRUST INFALLIBLE
    2   cups flour
    5   tablespoons lard
    ½   teaspoon baking-powder
        ice water
    1   tablespoon butter

Mix well, very lightly, with just enough ice water to make a stiff dough. Use silver knives for mixing and manipulate as little as possible. Roll out dough, butter half, fold over, butter again, until 1 tablespoon of butter has been used.

HOT WATER PASTRY
    ¼   lb. butter
    ¾   lb. flour
    1   gill hot water

Mix butter and flour in the usual manner. Moisten with the hot water, and roll.

PUMPKIN PIE
        fresh pumpkin
    1   pt. water
        salt
        butter
        brown sugar
        ground ginger
        milk
        cream
        eggs
        puff paste

Cut the pumpkin into small slices peeling and scraping off all of the shreds which hold the seeds. Add the water and cook until tender and nearly dry. Strain through a colander. When cold, add salt and butter. To every pint, half a salt spoon of salt and a piece of butter the size of a walnut.

For each 1½ cups of the strained pumpkin, add ⅔ cup brown sugar, 1 teaspoon of ground ginger, and 1½ cups milk, 1 cup cream, and 2 slightly beaten eggs.

Line a deep pie plate with puff paste, fill with the mixture, and bake in a moderately hot oven about ¾ of an hour.

ORANGE PIE
    2   tablespoons butter
    1   cup powdered sugar
    1   tablespoon cornstarch
    1   cup boiling water
    2   eggs
    2   large oranges
    2   tablespoons powdered sugar
        cold water

Beat to a cream the butter, the sugar. Mix the cornstarch with enough cold water to moisten it and stir it into a teacup of water, boiling hot, in the saucepan. Allow to cook only two minutes, stirring constantly. Add the butter and sugar and stir well. Remove from the fire and add the well beaten yolks of the eggs. Line the pie plate with pastry and bake. Add to the custard the juice of the two oranges and the grated rind

of one, place it in the baked crust and set back in the oven to brown slightly. Place on top méringue made of stiffly beaten whites, sweetened, set back in the oven for 2 or 3 minutes to brown. Serve cold.

QUADROON PIE
    1   cup brown sugar
    1   cup milk
    2   tablespoons butter
    1   teaspoon vanilla
    2   tablespoons flour
    1   teaspoon constarch
    2   eggs
    ½   teaspoon salt
        pie crust
        whipped cream

Cream the sugar and butter, add the milk, beat up well together, and put into a double boiler. Beat the eggs separately and well. To the yolks, add the flour, cornstarch, and salt. Add this to the mixture in the boiler and cook until it thickens, stirring all the while. Cool, and fold in the beaten whites, and add the vanilla. Put this into the pie-crust and top it with whipped cream.

LEMON PIE
Miss Ethel Forman
    3   lemons, rind and juice
    1   tablespoon flour
    4   eggs
    1   can condensed milk
    1½ cups water
    1   teaspoon butter
        sugar

Grate the lemon rinds and add to the flour. Rub to a thin cream with a little of the water. Add the rest of the water, the condensed milk and lemon juice, and last of all the egg yolks, well beaten. The pie shell should be partly baked before filling. When filled with the above mixture bake very slowly for a half hour or until set. Beat the egg whites very stiff with a little sugar. Cover the pie and run in the oven to brown slightly.

LEMON PIE
    1   tablespoon flour
    4   tablespoons sugar
    4   eggs
    1½ large lemons, grated rind and juice
    2   tablespoons boiling water

Cream egg yolks, sugar, and flour until very light, add lemon juice and grated rind. Put in a double-boiler and cook until the consistency of a thick cream. Remove from fire, add 2 tablespoons of boiling water. Have egg whites beaten very stiff wtih 2 tablespoons of sugar. Add half, folding in, to lemon cream, reserving the other half for the méringue. Put into a baked pie shell. Cover with méringue, and place in a very slow oven and brown.

MINCE MEAT
RECIPE OVER 100 YEARS OLD
Mrs. D. D. Curran

        4   lbs. apples, pared and chopped
        3   lbs. currants, washed and picked
        3   lbs. raisins, seeded and chopped
        ¾   lb. citron, shredded fine
        2   tablespoons cinnamon
        1   tablespoon powdered nutmeg
        2   tablespoons powdered mace
        1   tablespoon cloves
        1   tablespoon allspice
      2½   lbs. sugar
        1   tablespoon salt
        2   large glasses sherry
        2   large glasses whiskey or brandy
        2   cooked beef tongues, cold

Chop beef tongues fine and rub to a powder. Mix all ingredients in a crock. Cover closely and keep for at least three weeks before making into pies.

PECAN PIE

        4   eggs, beaten separately
        1   cup sugar
        1   cup white Karo syrup
        1   teaspoon vanilla
        2   tablespoons butter
        1   cup pecan nut meats

Cream egg yolks, add sugar, syrup, vanilla, and blend well. Fold in well beaten egg whites. Pour mixture into a rich uncooked pastry shell. Bake in moderate oven until of the consistency of custard pie, then cover top of pie thickly with halves of pecans and brown lightly.

CREAM CHEESE PIE

        1   cream cheese, with its cream
      1½   cups sugar
        3   eggs
        2   heaping tablespoons flour
            vanilla
            pinch of soda
            butter, cinnamon

Beat the eggs, yolks and whites separately. Mash the cream cheese into its cream, add the yolks, and heat in double boiler. Fold in the egg whites, stir in the flour, and add the vanilla. Place in a baking dish, sprinkle with sugar and cinnamon mixed, dot with butter, and bake in a hot oven about 20 minutes.

"JEFFERSON DAVIS" PIE

        ½   cup fresh butter
        2   cups brown sugar
        3   egg yolks
        1   glass tart jelly
            pastry

Line a pie shell with a flaky pastry. Cream the butter and sugar together, add the well beaten eggs. Mix thoroughly and add the jelly. This is a very rich pie and needs no méringue.

MOLASSES PIE
Mrs. Charles Farwell

        ½   cup butter
        1   cup white sugar
        4   eggs
        1   cup New Orleans molasses
        1   teaspoon nutmeg

Soften butter, add sugar, yolks of eggs, molasses, whites of eggs lightly beaten and nutmeg. Beat together well. Bake in pastry. This makes two pies.

PECAN PIE
Mrs. John Dent

        3   whole eggs, well beaten
        1   cup brown sugar
        1   cup red Karo
        1   cup pecans
        1   teaspoon vanilla

Mix in order given and bake in an uncooked pie crust very slowly. That is the secret of success.

CHESS PASTRY
Mrs. Fred Faust

    Pastry:
        ½   cup butter
        2   cups sugar
        4   eggs
        1   teaspoon vanilla

Melt the butter and sugar in a double boiler. Separate the eggs and beat thoroughly. Add the yolks to the sugar and butter mixture and stir till well mixed. They should hardly be cooked at all, simply well mixed over the fire. Then fold in the egg whites. Mix well and remove from the fire without further cooking. Add the vanilla. Have the pastry rolled out and fitted into a square pan. Pour in the egg mixture. Place in a very slow oven and cook for thirty minutes. It will be puffed up like a souffle. On removal from the oven it will settle and come away from the pastry a little. Before it is cool cover with the following icing, which being somewhat thin, and the pie being still warm, will spread of itself over the surface of the pie.

    Icing:
        1   lb. powdered sugar
        ¼   cup butter
        4   tablespoons cream
        ¼   teaspoon mapleine, or other desired
            flavoring

Cool and serve cut in squares.

MARSHMALLOW FUDGE CAKE

½   lb. chocolate
2   egg yolks
1   cup milk
½   cup butter
2   cups brown sugar
2   teaspoons vanilla
1   cup coffee
1½   teaspoons soda
3   cups bread flour
1½   boxes marshmallows

Melt the chocolate over hot water, and add egg yolks, then very, very slowly, the milk, stirring constantly. Cook it over hot water and stir until the mixture thickens. Set aside to cool.

Cream the butter and add sugar slowly. Add vanilla and coffee alternately with flour, mixed and sifted with soda. Add the chocolate mixture, beat thoroughly, and bake in three square pans lined with greased paper.

Remove the cake from the tins as soon as they are taken from the oven. Place the marshmallows immediately between the layers.

CHEESE CAKE
Mrs. Hinda E. Kleinfeldt

Filling:
2½   lbs. cottage cheese
½   lb. raisins (white preferred)
2   eggs
½   lb. butter
½   teaspoon cinnamon
1   lb. sugar

Mix together all ingredients until there are no lumps.

Dough:
1   cup milk
1   lb. butter
3   lbs. flour
2   lbs. sugar
3   eggs
2   level tablespoons baking powder
     a few grains of salt

Mix butter, sugar, eggs with the flour and baking powder, add milk. If the dough comes out a little stiff add a little more milk. Roll out on a floured board to a thickness of approximately ½ inch and place in a low baking pan lined with well buttered wax paper. Fill in with the cheese filling to a height of one inch and cover with a layer of dough the same thickness as the first layer. Puncture cake in scattered places with a pointed knife in order to prevent blistering. Paint top of cake with melted butter and place in a hot oven. Bake for approximately one-half hour. Then, without changing the position of the cake, reduce temperature to medium and bake for ½ hour or more until the cake becomes golden brown in color.

NUT CAKE

1   lb. butter
1   lb. sugar
1   lb. flour
1½   lbs. raisins
1½   lbs. pecans
8   eggs, beaten together
2   teaspoons baking powder
1   large glass wine
1   teaspoon nutmeg

Cream the sugar and butter well. Add the flour, into which you have sifted the baking powder, a little at a time, alternately with the milk. Beat the eggs without separating, and add. Next the wine in which the spices have been stirred, and last of all the fruit and nuts which have been dusted with flour. Bake in a moderate oven, in a loaf pan, for about 40 minutes.

JELLY ROLL

2   eggs
¼   cup milk
1   cup sifted sugar
1   cup sifted flour
1   teaspoon baking powder
½   teaspoon salt
     powdered sugar
     jelly

Beat the yolks until they are lemon color. Add gradually the sifted sugar and the milk. Sift the baking-powder, flour and salt together into the eggs and sugar, folding in, but not beating. Add the stiffly beaten whites.

Turn into a well greased shallow pan dusted with flour and bake ten minutes in a moderate oven. Turn out immediately on a slightly damp cloth sprinkled with powdered sugar. Spread with jelly and roll quickly.

ORANGE CAKE à la EVELYN

¼   lb. butter
1   orange, the juice and grated rind
1½   cups sugar
2   cups flour
3   eggs
½   teaspoon salt
2   teaspoons baking powder, heaping
Fillings:
1   cup sugar
1   orange, the juice
1   egg
2   tablespoons flour, heaping
½   cup water

Cream the butter and sugar together. Add one egg at a time until all have been well beaten. Add the juice of one orange, then the grated rind, and finally the flour with the baking powder. Bake in layers. For the filling, cook the orange juice and the sugar on a slow fire. Mix the flour well in the warm water and add it to the cooking sugar and orange juice, and let all cook until thick. Remove from fire and add the egg yolk. Beat well and place on the fire again for a few seconds.

UPSIDE DOWN CAKE

```
4    eggs, the whites
3    cups flour
1½   cups sugar
1    cup milk
½    cup butter
1    can sliced peaches
2    sliced bananas
4    slices canned pineapple
½    cup cherries
½    cup brown sugar
1    tablespoon butter, heaping
```

Cream the butter and the sugar. Add the beaten eggs, then the flour sifted with the baking-powder, and the milk, very gradually. Last of all, the vanilla. Put the butter in an iron skillet and add the brown sugar, letting it cook till it melts thoroughly. Then set the evenly cut fruits on the sugar, arranging them as close together as possible. Pour the cake batter over all. Bake in a medium hot oven.

Whipped cream makes a pleasant adjunct when serving.

GRAHAM CRACKER CAKE

```
2    eggs
1    cup sugar
2    teaspoons baking powder
1    cup milk
24   graham crackers
```

Beat the eggs, yolks and whites separately. Toast the crackers, break and sift them. Beat the sugar into the yolks well, then add crackers and milk alternately, and finally the beaten whites of the eggs. Bake in two layer pans, and serve with whipped cream between the layers and on top.

CHOCOLATE ALMOND CAKE
Mrs. M. C. Maury-Lyons

```
4    eggs
1    stick butter
1    cup chocolate
1    cup sugar
1    cup pounded almonds
```

Beat eggs separately. Cream the butter and sugar, and the beaten yolks, then the chocolate and pounded almonds.

Beat well, then add the beaten whites. Pour in a buttered mold and bake in a slow oven. Put in the ice box, and when cold, serve with whipped cream. Note that it requires no flour; note that it is easy to make. You will need no urging to note that it is delicious.

LAYER CAKE à L'ACAJOU

```
1½   cups sugar
½    cup butter
3    eggs
2    cups flour, sifted
1    teaspoon soda, scant
1    cup milk
⅓    cake Baker's chocolate
3    tablespoons hot water
```

Dissolve chocolate in hot water. Add half the milk to the chocolate.

Cream butter and sugar, and add the well beaten egg-yolks. Beat in the cooled chocolate and milk. Sift the flour and soda into the batter, then add the rest of the milk, fold in the whites, stiffly beaten. Add the vanilla.

Bake in two or three layers, and put the layers together with cooked white icing, or caramel. This cake is dark in color but light in consistency.

DEVIL'S FOOD CAKE
Miss Ethel Forman

```
4    tablespoons cocoa
1    cup sugar
1    cup butter
3    egg yolks
1    cup milk with a level teaspoon of
       soda dissolved
1    teaspoon vanilla
1⅓  cups flour, sifted 3 times
```

Mix cocoa and sugar together, add butter and cream. Then add egg yolks slightly beaten. Then add milk and flour alternately. Beat well and add vanilla. Bake in moderate oven.

EASY CHOCOLATE CAKE
(Can be mixed in one bowl)

```
2    squares Baker's chocolate
½    cup water
1    cup sugar
1    cup sour cream
2    eggs, slightly beaten
1½   cups cake flour
1    level teaspoon soda
       pinch of salt
```

Melt the chocolate in the water, over hot water. Remove from the fire and add sugar, sour cream and eggs. Sift flour once before measuring and twice afterwards with soda and salt. Beat hard for ten minutes and bake in a medium oven.

SPONGE CAKE

```
¾    lb. sugar
⅓    cup water
7    eggs, setting aside 2 whites for
       icing
1    lemon, the juice and grated rind
½    lb. sifted flour
```

Boil sugar and water. Beat yolks very light, then add the whites, stiffly beaten. Now pour the boiling sugar on the eggs, slowly beating all the while until cool. Add the lemon juice and grated rind. Have flour sifted 3 times and fold gently into the eggs and sugar. Then get it into a moderate oven as quickly as possible. The success of the cake lies in the mixing. Everything should be prepared before one beats the eggs. It is even better to have another beat the whites, so that the yolks need not stand one moment.

BANANA CAKE
Mrs. Albin Provosty

½ cup butter
1½ cups sugar
2 eggs
1¾ cups flour
4 tablespoons buttermilk with 1 teaspoon soda or 4 tablespoons sweet milk with 1 teaspoon baking powder
1 cup bananas, mashed and run through a sieve
1 teaspoon vanilla
pinch salt

Mix like any batter cake and add the banana pulp to the batter. Cook in layer cake pans and put together with sliced ripe bananas and with whipped cream on top.

PECAN CAKE
Mrs. Donald Maginnis

2½ cups pecans, ground
6½ tablespoons brown sugar
4 eggs, beaten separately
1 teaspoon vanilla

Add the sugar and pecans to the yolks, and beat vigorously. Now, add vanilla and the stiffly beaten whites.

Pour the mixture in three buttered layer cake tins and bake slowly.

Turn out when cold and put together with boiled white icing.

SPICE CAKE
Mrs. Thomas Jordan

¼ cup butter
½ cup sugar
1 egg
½ cup milk
1½ cups flour
2½ teaspoons baking powder
1 teaspoon cinnamon
½ teaspoon each, nutmeg, cloves, allspice
½ cup currants

Cream the butter, add sugar gradually, and egg well beaten. Mix and sift flour and baking powder, and add alternately with milk to first mixture. Then stir in spices and currants. Bake thirty minutes in a buttered shallow pan, or twenty minutes in muffin pans. Serve warm.

GINGER BREAD au VIEUX TEMPS
Mrs. M. C. Maury Lyons

2 cups molasses
½ cup butter
3 eggs
1 cup sugar
1 teaspoon cloves
1 tablespoon ginger
1 tablespoon allspice
1 tablespoon cinnamon
3 cups flour
1 cup hot water
2 teaspoons soda, dissolved in hot water

Warm the molasses with the butter.

Beat the eggs and sugar together, and pour into the warm molasses. Add the cloves, ginger, allspice, cinnamon, the flour, and the soda.

Bake in a very slow oven.

A hot sugar and butter sauce served with this makes a welcome combination.

SPONGE CAKE

6 eggs, beaten separately
1 cup sugar
1 cup flour, sifted three times
½ lemon, juice and rind grated

Beat yolks very light, add sugar, lemon juice, part of flour, rind. Fold in whites and remainder of flour. Bake in buttered pan in moderate oven. If eggs are large, four will be sufficient.

SPICED FRUIT LOAF
Mrs. Curran Perkins

⅔ cup butter
1¾ cups brown sugar
3 eggs
¾ cup orange juice
2 cups flour
2 teaspoons baking powder
1 teaspoon ground cloves
1 teaspoon cinnamon
1 teaspoon allspice
½ teaspoon salt
½ cup grated chocolate
1 teaspoon nutmeg
1 cup seedless raisins
1 cup hot mashed sweet potatoes
1 tablespoon grated orange peel

Cream the butter, add sugar gradually, then the well beaten eggs and orange juice, stir in the dry ingredients thoroughly sifted together, then the chocolate and the nuts and raisins, dredged with a little of the flour. Blend well. Mix in the sweet potatoes and orange peel and pour into an oiled loaf tin. Bake in a moderate oven for 1½ hours.

ORANGE BREAD
Miss Ethel Forman

2 cups whole wheat flour
2 cups white flour
3 teaspoons baking powder
1 teaspoon salt
¼ cup melted shortening
½ cup syrup, made by boiling the skins of two oranges in four cups of water with two cups of sugar until reduced to ½ cup
1 cup milk
3 eggs
1 cup orange peel, cut fine

Mix the dry ingredients including the orange peel. Add the syrup and the milk and shortening. Fold in the well beaten eggs and bake in a loaf pan slowly for a half hour or longer.

JAM CAKE
Mrs. Albin Provosty

1 cup butter
2 cups sugar
1 cup buttermilk
2 cups flour
4 eggs
1 cup blackberry jam
1 teaspoon each cinnamon, cloves, and nutmeg
1 teaspoon soda

Cream the butter and sugar together. Add the yolks of the eggs which have been beaten separately until thick and lemon colored. Add the blackberry jam and beat well. Stir the soda into the buttermilk and add it to the above mixture a little at a time alternately with the flour, into which you have already sifted the spices. Bake in layer cake pans and put together with the following filling:

½ cup milk
2 cups sugar
1 medium sized can of grated pineapples
 pinch of cream of tartar

Cook the milk, sugar and cream of tartar together until thick and creamy. Remove from the fire and beat thoroughly. When of the proper consistency to spread add the grated pineapple which has been drained and squeezed dry. Spread between layers.

FRUIT CAKE
Mrs. E. G. Simmons

12 eggs
¾ lb. butter
1 lb. sugar
1 glass tart jelly
2 glasses Bourbon whiskey, or brandy
1 lb. flour
2 level teaspoons baking powder
½ teaspoon soda
1 teaspoon each cinnamon, cloves, allspice
4 lbs raisins
1 lb. crystallized pineapple
½ lb. each orange peel, lemon peel
1 lb. each dried figs, dates, citron, pecan nut meats

Cut up all the fruits and nuts but not fine, and dredge well with flour using one half of the pound. Set aside. Beat the eggs, yolks and whites separately. Cream the butter and sugar together well and add the beaten yolks. Beat thoroughly. Then add the glass of jelly and the brandy or whiskey. Mix thoroughly. Sift the remaining flour with the soda and baking powder and powdered spices. Now mix in the floured fruits and nuts and last of all fold in the stiffly beaten egg whites. This will make about ten pounds of cake and may be cooked in several pans of whatever size desired. The oven must be very slow and they should bake from three to five hours according to the size of the cake.

WHITE FRUIT CAKE
Mrs. Petrie Hamilton

16 egg whites
¾ lb. butter
1 lb. sugar
1 wine glass brandy
2 teaspoons baking powder
2 lbs. blanched almonds
2 grated cocoanuts
1 lb. citron, cut fine
½ lb. crystallized cherries
½ lb. crystallized pineapple
1 nutmeg
2 teaspoons cinnamon
1 teaspoon vanilla
1 lb. flour

Use the directions for mixing above.

FRUIT CAKE
Mrs. J. Pettegrew Wright

1 lb. butter
1 lb. sugar
10 eggs
2 lbs. puffed raisins
1 lb. shelled pecans
1 lb. blanched almonds
1 lb. crystallized cherries
1 lb. crystallized pineapple
½ lb. citron
1 teaspoon ground allspice
1 teaspoon ground cinnamon
½ teaspoon cloves
1 lb. flour
1 glass brandy, wine or whiskey

Use directions for mixing above. Put in pecan meats whole and also cherries and almonds. For two five pound cakes steam for 2 hours and then bake thirty minutes in a slow oven.

WHITE CAKE
Miss Ethel Forman

6 eggs, whites only
10 ozs. sugar
5 ozs. butter
¾ lb. flour
1 cup milk
2 rounded teaspoons of yeast powder
1 teaspoon almond flavoring

Cream butter and sugar well, sift flour and baking powder together several times. Add to butter and sugar, alternating with milk. Add almond and stiffly beaten whites. Bake in moderate oven for loaf cake, or quick oven for layer cake.

DATE CAKE
Mrs. Richard Franklin White

3 eggs
1 cup pecans
1 package dates, cut fine
1 cup sugar
1 cup flour
1 teaspoon baking powder

Mix sugar, flour, and baking powder. Stir in the whole eggs one at a time and beat well. Now the pecans and dates. Bake very slowly in muffin tins and serve with the following sauce:

    1   cup boiling water
    1   cup brown sugar
    1   egg yolk

FLUFF CAKES

    6   egg whites
    1   cup sugar
    ½   pint cream
    1   teaspoon vanilla

Beat the egg-whites thirty minutes, add the sugar very gradually. Beat more. Drop the mixture from a spoon, about three inches apart, on well greased wax paper, placed on baking sheet. Light the oven as you place the cakes in. Bake very slowly, about 40 minutes. Serve with whipped cream, put the cream on top of cake, place another cake on top and put more cream on top of that.

CROQUIGNOLES
Mrs. Walter Torian

    3   eggs
    ½   cup sugar
    1   tablespoon butter
    1   teaspoon baking powder
    2   tablespoons ice water
    1   tablespoon vanilla
         flour (enough to make medium
             dough)
         nutmeg, a little

Beat the eggs together, mix in sugar, cream the butter into the mixture till light. Add flour (baking powder sifted with it), roll thin. Cut with cup and make 2 slashes in the centers of each piece and cook in deep fat. Sprinkle with powdered sugar and serve for tea.

DROP NUT COOKIES

    1   cup brown sugar
    1   tablespoon butter
    1   cup pecans
    1   egg
    ½   teaspoon vanilla
    7   level tablespoons flour

Cream butter and eggs together, add sugar, vanilla and nuts. Drop on well greased sheet and cook in modderate oven.

LES OREILLES DE COCHON

    2   teacups sifted flour
    1   teaspoonful baking powder
    2   eggs, beaten together
    1   tablespoonful mixed lard and butter
         pinch salt

Mix flour and baking powder, then rub in the butter and lard. Add the eggs beaten together. Roll very thin and cut in small pieces. Have a pot of deep fat very hot and drop the dough into it and give a twist with the fork. When a golden brown, place on a dish and sprinkle with powdered sugar and cinnamon while hot.

The secret of this famous, unique recipe is here released for the first time.

CHOCOLATE WAFFLES

    1¾   cups flour
    6   tablespoons sugar
    2   tablespoons melted butter
    3   teaspoons baking powder
    1   cup milk
    2   squares chocolate, melted
    ½   teaspoon salt
    2   eggs

Sift flour, baking powder, salt and add sugar, eggs, milk, butter and chocolate.

FRITTERS ALSACE

    4   tablespoons butter
    ⅓   cup flour
    ¼   teaspoon salt
    ⅔   cup milk
    2   eggs

Melt the butter. Add the flour and salt, and when well blended, add milk. Stir until boiling and cook until the mixture forms a paste leaving the sides of the pan. Then beat in the eggs, one at a time, beating very hard all the time. Drop a large teaspoonful into a pot of boiling lard and cook until brown on each side. Drain well and cover with sifted powdered sugar and serve with wine sauce.

OATMEAL COOKIES

    2   eggs
    1   cup flour
    3   cups oatmeal
    2½   cups sugar
    1¼   cups shortening (nucoa)
    1   teaspoon baking powder
    1   teaspoon salt

Mix dry ingredients then add beaten egg and shortening. Grease and flour biscuit pan and drop dough by scant teaspoonfuls. Bake in slow oven until a nice brown and remove from pan quickly.

If the cookies become cold and stick to the pan when being removed put back in oven for a minute.

THIN OATMEAL COOKIES
Mrs. J. B. Simmons

    2   eggs, well beaten
    2   cups sugar
    1   cup melted butter
    2   tablespoons sifted flour, heaping
    ½   teaspoon baking powder
    1   teaspoon vanilla
    2   cups rolled oats
         pinch salt

Beat the sugar into the beaten eggs, add the flour, with the baking-powder sifted with it, then the vanilla extract, and finally the rolled oats. The beating process is continuous!

Drop the mixture by teaspoons 4 inches apart on a well greased pan. Bake in moderate oven until a pretty golden brown. But be on your guard constantly, they love to burn!

Removing from the pan is a difficult process and trying to the temper of the cook. While very hot they refuse to stick together and as soon as cold they become so crisp they are apt to break at a touch. Keep them near the stove and work quickly—pressing the broken bits together into little heaps with the fingers. The pan must be well greased. When the knack of handling them is mastered they are more than worth the pains.

BABA au RUM MANASSIER
Mrs. Arthur Hammond

¼   lb. butter
8   ozs. flour
½   oz. compressed yeast
2   ozs. sugar
4   eggs
     a little milk
     cream
     rum

Sift 2 ozs. of flour into a small basin and make a well in the center. Dilute the yeast with luke warm milk, add this to the flour, to make a light dough. Set aside in a warm place to rise.

Next, sift the remainder of the flour into a large basin, and add the sugar, the warmed butter, a little milk, and the eggs, two at a time. Beat up well, for about 10 minutes, then add the prepared yeast, with 1 tablespoon of sweet cream. Work it again for a few minutes, and rather more than half fill the molds, which must be well buttered and sprinkled with fine sugar. Cover the molds and stand in a warm place to rise for about 1 hour. The contents should then have risen to fill the molds. Bake the mixture in a hot oven, then turn on to a pastry rack to cool.

Flavor and decorate as desired, with whipped cream squeezed through pastry tube.

LEBKUCHEN

1   lb. brown sugar
1   teaspoon cinnamon
½   nutmeg, grated
3   ozs. citron
4   eggs
1   teaspoon cloves
¼   lb. unblanched almonds
1½ cups sifted flour
Frosting:
     powdered sugar
     water
     white of egg, a little

Grind the almonds and the citron, not too fine. Mix all the ingredients well together and spread very thin in a shallow pan. Bake in a moderate oven, taking care that it does not brown.

Remove from the oven and cut into squares with a sharp knife, leaving them in the pan while spreading on the frosting (best use a paint brush for this).

Set back in the oven only long enough to dry—a few minutes. Keep in china jar or covered dish.

ALMOND CAKES

1   cup ground almonds
1   cup sugar
1   lemon, the grated rind
1   egg white

Put almonds, sugar and rind of lemon on board and mix with white of egg. Roll and cut in squares, and bake in slow oven. Watch carefully.

DANISH COOKIES
Mrs. Geo. Villeré

1¾ sticks butter
4   tablespoons confectioner's sugar
2   cups flour
2   teaspoons vanilla
1   teaspoon water
1   cup chopped nuts

Mix and shape with hand, break in small pieces and roll. Bake in moderate oven.

RUSSIAN ROCKS

1½ scant cups sugar
1   cup butter
3   cups flour
3   eggs
½   teaspoon soda, dissolved in ⅛ cup hot water
1   lb. raisins
1½ lbs. nuts
1   teaspoon cinnamon

Cream the sugar and the butter, beat in the eggs, then the flour, and add the soda; lastly the chopped raisins and nuts, with cinnamon. Mix well, and flavor to taste.

Drop from a teaspoon on buttered tins and bake.

BATONS des NOIX

1¾ sticks butter
5   tablespoons confectioner's sugar
2   cups flour
2   teaspoons vanilla
1   tablespoon water
1   cup nuts, ground or chopped fine

Cream the butter and sugar well, then add the sifted flour, vanilla, water, and nuts. Let chill in the icebox. Form with fingers into small rolls about the size of the thumb. Bake in oven at 450°. Sprinkle with powdered sugar.

CORN FLAKE KISSES

2   cups corn flakes
¾   cup sugar
2   eggs, beaten separately
1   cup chopped nuts
1   cup chopped raisins

Mix the dry ingredients, then add the eggs and mix well.

Bake in a moderate oven 15 to 20 minutes.

"S"
Mrs. Chas. H. Behre, Sr.

1½   lbs. flour
1   scant cup sugar
1   lb. butter
8   egg yolks

Wash the butter in two waters to remove the salt. Work into it the sugar, eggs, and flour, until you have a smooth paste. Take lumps of dough and roll out with the hand on a floured board into long rolls about the thickness of a finger. Cut rolls into three and a half inch pieces. Twist the pieces into S shapes. Brush with beaten egg white, sprinkle with sugar, and bake in a moderate oven to a delicate brown. Makes fifty to sixty cakes.

ALMOND CAKES

1   pound almonds
1   pound sugar
1   doz. eggs

Cream sugar and yolks of eggs thoroughly. Grind almonds in meat chopper, without removing skins. Add them to the yolks, then fold in the whites of eggs beaten to stiffness. Bake in a moderate oven in small muffin tins.

CHEESE TARTS

1   stick butter (¼ lb.)
1   cup flour
1   New York cream cheese
     jam or jelly

Work the first three ingredients well together, and place in the refrigerator until ready to use. Roll out thin, cut in squares, put jam on each, fold the edges together, and prick each tart lightly with a fork. Bake in rather quick oven. An excellent touch for tea or luncheon.

ICE BOX COOKIES
Mrs. Chas. Crawford

1   cup white sugar
1   cup brown sugar,
1   cup butter
2   eggs, slightly beaten
1   teaspoon vanilla
½   teaspoon salt
1   cup nut meats
1   teaspoon soda
3½   cups flour
     soda and flour sifted together

Make dough into smooth roll and divide into 3 parts. Put dough in covered dish and let stand at least over night in ice box before using. Cut thin across roll with very sharp knife and cook as needed. The dough will last indefinitely in ice-box.

CAUTION—cut very thin and bake in moderate oven taking great care not to burn.

SAND SHELLS

2   sticks butter (½ lb.)
2   cups flour
5   tablespoons powdered sugar
2   teaspoons vanilla
1½   cups chopped pecans

Cream the butter and the sugar, then add the flour, vanilla, and pecans. Work this and form it in crescents. Cook in a moderate oven ½ hour.

Roll the tarts in powdered sugar. Put them in paper lined tins and they will remain fresh and crisp a long time.

GINGER SNAPS
Miss Ethel Forman

1   egg
1   teaspoon salt
1   cup molasses
1   cup sugar
1   cup butter and lard mixed
1   level teaspoon soda
       (dissolve in ½ cup water)
1   tablespoon ginger

Work in enough flour to mold out rather soft. Roll thin and bake in quick oven. Crisp and delicious.

CREAM CAKES
Miss Ethel Forman

1   cup butter
4   eggs
½   teaspoon salt
1   cup boiling water
1   cup flour

Pour butter and water in saucepan and place on stove. As soon as boiling point is reached, add flour all at once, and stir vigorously. Remove from fire as soon as mixed and add unbeaten eggs one at a time, beating until thoroughly mixed between the addition of eggs. Drop by spoonfuls on a buttered sheet 2 inches apart, having mixture slightly piled in center. Bake 30 minutes in moderate oven. With a sharp knife make a cut in each large enough to admit of cream filling. This recipe makes 20 cream cakes.

POINT COUPÉE COOKIES
Mrs. E. T. Merrick

½   cup butter
2   cups sugar
3   eggs
½   cup sour heavy cream
1   teaspoon lemon juice
1   teaspoon nutmeg
1   teaspoon vanilla
3½   cups sifted flour
1   teaspoon soda
     pinch of salt

Cream together butter and sugar and eggs (eggs beaten lightly together). Then add flour, then the cream to which soda has been added and well stirred. Then the seasoning. Mix thoroughly and put in ice box until it stiffens (next day is best). Drop half teaspoonful on pan greased with butter, not too close together, bake in moderate oven. You can sprinkle a few nuts on top.

" 'TI'S GATEAUX"
Mrs. James Amédée Puech

1 cup flour
1 cup sugar
2 eggs
¼ lb. butter
1 teaspoon vanilla extract
⅓ cup milk
1 teaspoon baking powder

Cream sugar and butter. Add yolks of eggs, then put in flour sifted 3 times and beaten whites of eggs, alternately. Add ⅓ cup of milk, and then vanilla. Last add the baking powder. Drop batter in oblong cake pan with a small teaspoon. Do not allow to spread too much. Bake in a hot oven.

CHOCOLATE CAKES
Mrs. Charles E. Fenner

1 cup flour
1 teaspoon baking powder
½ teaspoon salt
½ cup butter or shortening
1 cup sugar
¾ cup nut meats
3 squares unsweetened chocolate
¾ cup raisins
½ cup milk
½ teaspoon vanilla

Sift all dry ingredients three times. Cream butter and sugar until fluffy. Add melted chocolate, then eggs, nuts and raisins. Add flour and milk, then vanilla. Bake in muffin rings or drop from a teaspoon. Bake in a rather slow oven.

DROP CAKES au PARISIEN

1 cup butter
1 cup currants
1 cup chopped walnuts
1 teaspoon cinnamon
1 teaspoon cloves
2½ cups flour
3 eggs
1½ cups brown sugar
1 cup raisins, cut in halves
1 teaspoon vanilla
1 teaspoon soda, dissolved in about
    ½ cup hot water

Mix well, and drop by the teaspoon on buttered tins, about ½ inch apart.

BAISERS CREOLES
Miss Ethel Forman

½ pound pulverized sugar
3 egg whites
1 teaspoon vanilla extract
½ cup chopped pecans

Sift sugar. Beat the whites of the eggs very stiff and add about a tablespoonful of the sugar at a time, beating very hard each time the sugar is added until it is all used. Stir in

quickly ½ cup of chopped pecans and vanilla. Drop on wrapping paper without greasing, ½ teaspoon, 2 inches apart. Bake in moderate oven. Watch closely.

KITTEN'S TONGUE

Take 2 eggs and not quite a cup of sugar. Whip them just a little, then add not quite a cupful of melted butter and a cup of flour. Stir the mixture, spread it on a tin in small quantities, bake them. Roll in nuts and sugar.

BROWNIES
Mrs. James Aldigé

1 cup sugar
2 eggs
½ cup butter
½ cup flour, sifted twice
1 teaspoon vanilla
1 cup pecans, cut in pieces
5 tablespoons sweet chocolate
    pinch of salt

Mix ingredients in the order given. Line square cake pan with paraffin paper. Bake in a slow oven (this is most important). Cut in squares.

BROWNIES
Mrs. Robt. Milling

½ cup (⅔ stick) butter
2 squares Baker's Chocolate
2 large tablespoons water
2 eggs
1 cup brown sugar
1 cup sifted flour
1 level teaspoon baking powder
1 teaspoon vanilla
1 large cup chopped pecans

Melt the chocolate with the water, cream the butter and sugar, add the melted chocolate. Beat the eggs without separating yolks and whites, and add to the above; then add flour, baking powder and nuts.

Butter a shallow 10 x 10 baking pan, pour the mixture in, and bake in slow oven about 25 minutes. Let cool in the pan a little while, cut in squares, sprinkle powdered sugar over them and serve. This quantity makes 24 squares.

COCOANUT KISSES
Mrs. Dave Hunter

1 can cocoanut
4 egg whites, beaten stiffly
1 cup sugar
4 cups corn flakes
1 cup nut meats

Add sugar to egg and then add cocoanut, nuts, and corn flakes. Bake in a slow oven on greased paper until delicately brown.

ANISE OR CARAWAY SEED CAKES

```
2   lbs. flour
1   lb. lard
½   lb. sugar
3   tablespoons anise or caraway seeds
1   cup water
1   teaspoon salt
```

Simmer the anise seeds five minutes in water. Sift the flour three times, the last time with the salt and sugar. Then mix the lard in lightly as for pie crust until it has a crumbly mealy appearance. Add the boiled seeds. Roll out thin and cut with a cookie cutter. Bake a light brown in a moderate oven, about twenty minutes.

BLACKBERRY SAUCE

```
1   cup fresh blackberries
1   cup water
1   tablespoon flour
½   cup sugar
2   teaspoons butter
¼   teaspoon salt
2   tablespoons lemon juice
    dash of cloves
```

Heat together blackberries and water. Let boil three minutes, strain. Combine flour and sugar. Add to hot fruit and cook until thickened, stirring frequently. Add butter, cloves, salt and lemon juice.

BAKED BANANAS IN CRANBERRY SAUCE

```
1    qt. cranberries
1    cup cold water
4    bananas
1½   cups sugar
1    lemon
```

Wash cranberries and cover with cold water. Cook quickly ten minutes and press through sieve. Peel and cut bananas lengthwise, place in baking dish and add the juice of one lemon. Put in oven and cook twenty minutes or more. Add sugar to hot cranberry juice, stir well and pour over bananas. Bake in a hot 400 degrees F. until bananas are done. This is delicious cold as a dessert or served with meats as you would cranberry sauce.

ORANGE SAUCE

```
6    oranges and grated rind of 4
¾    lb. sugar
3    cups boiling water
```

Wash oranges, grate rind. Take out pulp and juice of the six and set aside. Take the remainder of oranges, pour the boiling water over this and cook until tender, then press through ricer or sieve, now add sugar and grated rind and cook until thick. Serve with orange mousse. The juice and pulp are saved for the mousse.

HARD SAUCE

```
½   cup butter
1   cup powdered sugar
1   egg, the white
    sherry, brandy or vanilla
```

Cream butter and sugar thoroughly, add unbeaten white and beat again. Flavor with brandy, sherry or vanilla. The egg white can be omitted.

CABINET SAUCE
Mrs. Petrie Hamilton

```
¼   cup butter
¼   cup sugar
¼   cup whipping cream
⅛   cup whiskey
    nutmeg
```

Cream butter and sugar together, and slowly add the cream and whiskey. Place in a pan of hot water until hot and well blended. Then add nutmeg.

CHOCOLATE SAUCE

```
2   squares Baker's Chocolate
⅔   cup sugar
2   tablespoons butter
1   cup milk
1   teaspoon vanilla
```

Melt the butter and chocolate well together. Add the milk, stirring constantly, add sugar, bring to a boiling point and let boil ten minutes. Flavor.

SHERRY'S CHOCOLATE SAUCE

```
1½   cups powdered sugar
¼    lb. Baker's Chocolate
1    tablespoon butter
¼    cup sherry
1    teaspoon vanilla
½    cup cream
```

Beat the butter and sugar, add the chocolate, grated and melted, then the cream.

Boil for seven minutes, then add the sherry and vanilla.

YUM YUM CHOCOLATE SAUCE
Mrs. Irving Lyons

```
2    cups sugar
¼    cup cocoa
¾    cup corn starch
¾    cup milk
2    tablespoons butter
```

Boil all the ingredients except the butter together for four to five minutes. Add the butter and continue boiling until a soft ball forms when dropped into cold water. Serve warm with ice cream or a simple hot cake.

BRANDY SAUCE
Mrs. H. Waller Fowler

```
½   cup butter
1   teaspoonful flour, heaping
2   cups powdered sugar
1   cup rich milk
4   egg yolks
2   glasses wine or brandy, or to taste
```

Put the butter and flour in a saucepan and blend. Beat the egg yolks and combine with the milk, then add slowly to the flour stirring constantly to a smooth consistency. Cook in double boiler five minutes until thick as custard. Do not boil. Just before serving add the wine or brandy. This sauce is to be used hot on hot puddings.

LEMON CAKE FILLING
Mrs. Albin Provosty

2 eggs, the yolks only
1 cup sugar
1 lemon, the juice and rind
1 tablespoon cornstarch
1 cup water
2 tablespoons butter

Stir all ingredients except butter well together and cook in a double boiler until thick and smooth. Add the butter and when melted remove from the fire. Cool slightly and use between cake layers.

LEMON JELLY FILLING
Mrs. E. T. Merrick

2 eggs beaten thoroughly with ⅔ cup sugar, the rind and juice of 2 lemons

Mix together and let thicken in a vessel of hot water. It only needs to come to boiling point. Add a tiny piece of butter. Use between layers of cakes.

CREAM FILLING

Beat together the yolks of 2 eggs, 1 cup sugar, powdered, 2 tablespoons of cream and 1 tablespoon of vanilla. Beat and mix to a thick cream.

ICING à la Lucie

1½ cups milk
2 whole eggs
1 scant cup sugar
1 teaspoon cornstarch
1 cup grated chocolate

Heat the milk and add it to eggs and sugar. Dissolve cornstarch in a little water, and add chocolate. Boil all together until thick, then remove from stove, beat a little, and it is ready to spread on cake.

MOCHA ICING AND FILLING

1 tablespoon butter
1 cup confectioner's sugar
1 tablespoon cocoa
1 tablespoon strong coffee
½ teaspoon salt

Cream the butter and sugar together well. Add cocoa, coffee, and salt. Stir until smooth. If too dry, add coffee; if too moist, add sugar.

CHOCOLATE ICING

2 squares chocolate
1 cup sugar
1 tablespoon flour
⅓ cup milk
2 tablespoons butter
½ teaspoon vanilla

Melt the chocolate over hot water, add the sugar and flour mixed together. When smooth, add the milk slowly. Cook all this until it spins a thread 1 inch long. Add the butter and vanilla, cool, and beat until it is of such consistency that it will spread without running. If the frosting is too thick, set the pan over hot water and stir until it softens.

SEVEN MINUTE FROSTING

2 egg whites, unbeaten
1½ cups sugar
5 tablespoons cold water
1½ teaspoons light corn syrup
1 teaspoon vanilla

Put egg whites, sugar, water and corn syrup in upper part of double boiler. Beat with rotary egg beater until thoroughly mixed. Place over rapid boiling water, beat constantly and cook for 7 minutes, or until frosting will stand in peaks. Remove from fire, add vanilla, and beat until thick enough to spread. Makes enough frosting to cover two 9-inch layers.

PECAN PRALINES
Miss Ethel Forman

3   cups pecans
{ 2   cups brown sugar
{ 1   cup cream
{ 1   cup white sugar
{ 1   cup water

Cook separately until thick, pour together, and add 3 cups of pecans cut extra fine. Stir well. Drop on buttered sheet by spoonfuls.

PRALINE TOURNÉS
Mrs. Wm. J. de Treville

2   cups granulated sugar
2   cups shelled pecans
½   cup hot water
1   tablespoon vanilla

Boil sugar mixed with water until it threads. Add pecans and stir until sugar creams. Then add vanilla. Do not boil after pecans are added.

ORANGE SUGARED NUTS

Use the above recipe substituting brown sugar for white, and as you remove from the fire, add two tablespoons of grated orange rind. If a stronger flavor of orange is desired, add more of the grated rind.

SPICED PECANS
Pauline Griggs

1   cup sugar
½   cup water
1   to 2 tablespoons cinnamon
2¼ cups pecans

Make a syrup of the sugar, water and cinnamon, and boil until it begins to thread from the spoon. Drop in the pecans and cook until the syrup almost crystallizes in the pot. Pour out on a platter and separate the nuts with a fork.

CARAMEL PECANS
Mrs. Hunter Leake

3   cups granulated sugar
1   cup milk
2   tablespoons butter
2   cups pecans
1½ cups sugar

Boil the 3 cups of sugar with the milk. Melt the 1½ cups of sugar in an iron skillet to caramel. When the sugar and milk mixture makes a soft ball on being dropped into cold water, pour in the caramel, nuts and butter. Take off the fire and beat until creamy. Pour out and cut in squares.

SALTED PECANS
Mrs. Wm. J. De Treville

½   lb. shelled pecans
1   teaspoon butter
1   teaspoon salt

Break butter in bits over pecans, run in a quick oven and stir until brown. Turn out on brown paper, sprinkle salt over them and let cool.

TEZCUCO PLANTATION NOUGAT

1½ cups sugar
1   cup chopped pecans
    small lump butter

Put the sugar into a saucepan with the butter, and stir until it is melted to a syrup. Then throw in the pecans. Stir and then remove at once, pouring the candy into a buttered tin or onto a marble, and cut quickly, before it hardens.

MARZIPAN

½   pound sugar
½   pound shelled almonds
    rum (or water)
    powdered cocoa

Grind the sugar and almonds to a powder, pulverizing them thoroughly. Then work them together with either rum or water. Make into balls and dredge in uncooked cocoa. The balls should be the shape and size of small new potatoes.

DATE LOAF
Miss Ethel Forman

2   cups pecans
3   cups sugar
1   cup milk
1   pound dates

Mix all together and cook until it leaves the side of the pot. When you take it off fire stir in 2 cups of pecans. Put in wet napkin and roll. Cut in slices when cold.

STUFFED PRUNES

2   doz. large prunes
1   doz. pecans
1   doz. marshmallows
    granulated sugar
    brandy

Pit the prunes and place them in brandy for 2 hours. Stuff each prune with a nut and half a marshmallow. Roll in granulated sugar.

APRICOT GLAZE

One pound dried apricots soaked over night in one quart of water. In another pan soak ¼ ounce agar agar in one pint of water. The next day, press apricots through sieve, place on fire and bring to a good boil. Bring the agar agar mixture to a boil, stirring constantly until all agar is dissolved. To this hot mixture add two pounds sugar, stir until melted, and let it come to the boiling point again. Now, add the sieved apricots, and when this has boiled again for a moment, strain the entire mixture. This keeps indefinitely.

This sets like a gelatine mixture to use as a glaze over baked ham or fowl, tarts or pastry. Simply melt over low heat, and do not stir or it becomes cloudy.

CHOCOLATE ROLLS

½ lb. butter
¾ lb. confectioners sugar
½ lb. unsweetened chocolate, grated fine
2 ozs. sweet chocolate, grated fine
   almond flavoring, or coffee, essence

Rub all together and work into a smooth paste. Flavor as desired with the almond flavoring or coffee essence. Shape into small rolls to dry. Roll in grated sweet chocolate or vary in any number of ways with nuts, etc.

BRANDIED GRAPES

Clip tender grapes from cluster leaving a tiny stem. Put in jar, cover with brandy or whiskey. Serve after 24 hours with cocktails, however, they are good as long as you can keep them.

GRAPEFRUIT GLACÉ
Mrs. James Amedée Puech

1 grapefruit, the skin
1½ cups granulated sugar

Quarter skin of fruit and cut in long slices or dice. Boil skins seven times. When water boils, pour it off, each time using cold water for subsequent boiling, In 7th water, put in sugar, letting it come to a syrup. When cooked, take each strip with fork and roll piece by piece in granulated sugar. Sprinkle sugar on a large platter for convenience.

CRYSTALLIZED PUMPKIN
Mrs. E. M. Choppin

1 large yellow pumpkin
1 cup lime
6 to 8 pounds sugar
2 tablespoons vanilla

Cut the pumpkins in pieces 1 to 2 inches in size. Mix the lime in a large pan of water, mixing very well. When it settles, pour over the pumpkin. Soak over night. Mix the sugar in just enough water to make a thick syrup.

Wash the pumpkin and let it drain in the colander. When the syrup begins to cook, put in the pumpkin, stirring and basting it. When the sugar begins to crystallize, put in the vanilla. Take off the fire and stir until cool and crystallized.

Note: Be sure to let water run in your drain pipe after you have poured off the lime water. A most marvelous candy, one which defies the taste of pumpkin in a "guess-what?" contest.

MARRONS GLACÉ

Roast one lb. chestnuts. Peel and remove inner skins. Cool. Make a syrup in the proportions of ½ cup water to 1 cup sugar and boil to the cracking point. Place pan containing syrup in another pan of hot or boiling water. String the chestnuts onto a fine wire and make a ring. Hang the rings on the handle of a wooden spoon and place across the syrup pan so the chestnuts are immersed in the syrup. When they are thoroughly coated hang them up to dry.

CANDIED ORANGES TOULOUSE

Wash and cut oranges in halves. Pour boiling water over them and simmer until tender. Then, pour off the water and weigh, put a pound of sugar to the pound of fruit. Cook slowly fifteen minutes. Oranges may be filled with candied apples or cherries. Serve with meat course.

CANDIED APPLES

2 cups sugar
1½ cups water
   apples

Wash, pare, and core the apples. Put parings on to boil in the water. Cut the apples in balls with the potato cutter. Take the water from parings and make a syrup with the sugar. Cook the apple balls in syrup until candied. A drop and a half of vegetable coloring enhances their appearance.

MARMALADE
Mrs. A. G. Johnston

Select one grape fruit, one orange, and one lemon. Wash thoroughly. Cut in halves and remove seeds and tough center membranes. Slice very very thin.

Measure, and for every cup of fruit add three cups of cold water. Let stand twenty-four hours, place over a hot flame and boil for ten minutes. Remove cover, and let stand for another twenty-four hours.

Measure, and for each cup of fruit add one cup of granulated sugar. Mix until the sugar is melted, place over a hot fire, bring to a boil, and boil for an hour or longer. Then begin to test by a spoonful on a saucer. When it seems to jell it is done. Toward the latter part of the cooking place a stove lid or asbestos plate under the pot and use a low flame taking great care that it does not burn. You must use a large kettle to permit boiling.

Scouring the fruit rind prevents the necessity of skimming.

If you cannot get lemons, limes may be used in thes same proportion.

Sour oranges are better than sweet, yellow skins than russet.

Quick cooking is better than slow. Boil for an hour or longer.

The principal danger is burning Stir frequently with a wooden spoon, especially toward the end.

ECONOMICAL MARMALADE
Mrs. Irving Lyons

    8   carrots
    5   lemons
    6   cups sugar
    1   teaspoon salt

Put carrots and lemon rinds through the food grinder. Cover with water, add salt, sugar, and lemon juice. Cook until thick. Place in sterilized jars and seal with paraffin.

GINGER PEARS
Mrs. Irving Lyons

    4   lbs. cooking pears
    2   ozs. ginger root
    2   lemons
    2   to 2½ lbs. sugar

Scrape and cut ginger into tiny pieces and squeeze the juice of the lemon over it. Cover pears with sugar and allow to stand for several hours. Place over a slow fire with the ginger and the grated rind of the lemon. Continue cooking very slowly till the pears are tender and clear. Place in sterilized jars and seal while hot.

MINT PEARS

    1   large can pears
    1½   cups sugar
    ¾   cup water
    2   teaspoons essence of peppermint
    1½   teaspoons green food coloring

Drain the juice from the can of pears and add to it the water and sugar. Boil until it makes a medium thick syrup. Remove from the fire and add the green coloring. When cool add the essence of peppermint. Put the pears in the syrup and allow to stand for twenty-four hours. Fresh mint leaves may be used as a garnish. This is an interesting change from the mint sauce that usually accompanies roast lamb, and is very pretty served in a glass bowl with the syrup.

BRANDIED PEACHES

    9   pounds peaches
    5   pounds sugar
    1   quart alcohol
    1   pint water

Peel the peaches, or skin after plunging in boiling water. Then put them in cold water. Let the sugar cook with the water until it makes a thick syrup. Then put in peaches to float, cook until tender enough to be pierced with a straw. Next, put them in a colander to drain.

Continue in this way until all the peaches are cooked. Pour the syrup drained from the peaches back in with the other syrup and cook until it is thick. Put the peaches in jars, add 1 measure of syrup to ½ measure of alcohol, fill the jars and seal. Shake for several days.

These will keep indefinitely, if no one finds them!

CHEAP BRANDIED PEACHES
Mrs. Vera O'Leary

Plunge peaches in boiling water and then cold water to remove the skins. Fill mason jars with sugar and peaches in alternate layers and add 12 raisins to each jar. Put the covers on the jars and screw only half way. Place the jars in a cool place, or bury them in the ground, for six months until fermentation ceases. Then tighten the covers.

TOMATO CONSERVE

    7   pounds ripe tomatoes
    5   pounds sugar
    2   lemons, sliced very thin
    ½   doz. whole cloves
    2   sticks cinnamon
    ½   doz. allspice

Put all spices in cheese cloth and boil with tomatoes and lemons till latter are transparent, then add sugar and cook until thick. Delicious with meat or used on toast like a preserve.

PEACH CONSERVE
Mrs. J. T. Grace

14 large peaches
4   oranges
4   pints sugar
½   pound coarsely chopped pecans
2   slices crystalized pineapple cut in small pieces
¼   pound crystalized cherries, cut in small pieces

Peel the peaches and cut into small pieces. Add the sugar, pulp of oranges, and about ¾ of the grated orange peel. Cook together for 45 minutes. Add the nuts and the crystallized fruits and cook ten minutes longer.

This makes about 8 glases.

PEAR CONSERVE

5   pounds pears
3   oranges
1   lemon
1   pound raisins
4   pounds sugar

Use some of the rind of the oranges and all of that of the lemon. Mix all the ingredients, except the sugar, together and put the mixture through a meat grinder. Cover with the sugar and let stand all night.

The next morning, cook it over a slow fire two or three hours, until it is the right (fairly thick) consistency Stir often, as it scorches quickly.

PEACH PRESERVES
Mrs. E. T. Merrick

Peel, and halve peaches, let soak in water while preparing, to keep color. To each pound of peaches add 1 pound of sugar, drain fruit, cover with sugar and let stand over night. Next morning cook until syrup is thick. Seal in jars.

ORANGE DE LUXE
Mrs. Seth Miller

Take six or more oranges and with a sharp knife, pare off the oily part of the skin, taking care to keep the oranges smooth. Then make a small opening in the blossom end.

Put the oranges on the fire in cold water in which has been dissolved a teaspoonful of salt.

Bring to a boil, then place the oranges in more boiling water, without salt.

Boil until soft enough for a toothpick or a broom straw to be passed through the oranges.

Use a pound of sugar to a pound of fruit and 1 cup of water and boil to the consistency of a thin syrup. Place the hot boiled fruit in the hot syrup and boil it until well done and the syrup thick and honey colored.

PEACH AND PEAR PICKLE
Mrs. Carl Marshall

6   lbs. fruit—peaches whole and peeled pears peeled, halved and cored
3   lbs. sugar
1   pt. vinegar
1   tablespoon whole cloves
1   tablespoon whole cinnamon
½   tablespoon allspice

Put all in pot and cook until fruit assumes a transparent look. Put away in crock or preserve jars.

FIG PRESERVES
Mrs. E. T. Merrick

Clip the end of the stem of each fig, weigh fruit. To each pound use 1 pound of sugar. Add enough water to the sugar to make a good syrup. While boiling, slightly soak figs for a few minutes in lime water, 1 ounce of lime to a gallon of water. Then wash fruit well. Strain syrup, pour over figs, cook until well done and syrup is thick. When half done, add lemon if desired, or ginger.

QUICK CRANBERRY JELLY
Miss Ethel Forman

To every quart of berries, put 1 pint of water. Let berries cook for about 20 minutes, then strain through sieve. While still boiling, stir in sugar, 1 pint to every quart of berries. Do not continue to boil. Cool and put in glasses.

WATERMELON RIND OR RIPE CUCUMBER PICKLE
Mrs. Frank H. Lawton

1   gal. rind peeled and cut into strips
2   heaping teaspoons salt, water to cover

Soak rind in brine over night.

Boil in this same salt water until tender. Drain, press all water from rind, with a tea towel. Place rind in stone crock. Make the following syrup and pour over pickles:

3   pounds sugar
1   quart vinegar
1   oz. stick cinnamon
½   oz. whole cloves

Place spices in bag and boil in syrup 15 minutes. On each day for 9 days thereafter pour off syrup, boil up with spices and add a little sugar or vinegar as necessary so as to keep syrup the same consistency as on the first day. Add a small quantity of spice to the spice bag as seems desirable for flavor. These pickles may be kept in the crock. If they are to be sealed in jars, on last day put rind in syrup and boil for 10 minutes.

DELICIOUS SWEET PICKLE

Make quite a thick syrup by boiling the following ingredients:

    1 cup brown sugar
    ¾ cup vinegar
    1 cup water
       cinnamon bark
       a few whole cloves
    1 teaspoon allspice in bag

Cut 6 dill pickles in any shape you like and cook in this syrup for 20 minutes. The pickle is improved by standing in the syrup several days before using.

SWEET CUCUMBER PICKLES
Mrs. Geo. S. Frierson

    9 pounds large sour cucumber pickles
    4 pounds sugar
    1 tablespoon allspice
    1 tablespoon cloves
    6 buttons garlic
    1 cup tarragon vinegar

In porcelain or glass container, put cucumbers sliced in rounds, layer of cucumbers and layer of sugar. Add other ingredients. Stir once a day for three days, then they are ready to be used. Not necessary to put in sealed jar.

DILL PICKLES
Mrs. Geo. S. Frierson

Use above recipe and one cup of olive oil.

SWEET PEPPER RELISH
Mrs. Albin Provosty

    12 green peppers
    12 red peppers
    12 onions, medium sized
    6   tablespoons salt
    3   cups sugar
    3   cups vinegar
        cayenne pepper, celery salt, spices,
        to taste

Grind peppers and onions and allow them to drain well. Put on to boil with the vinegar, sugar and salt. Cook briskly about fifteen to twenty minutes. Add the hot pepper, celery salt and spices. Bottle while hot.

CHUTNEY
Lt. Comdr. and Mrs. S. W. Wallace

    ½   lb. onions, sliced
    2   lbs. quince, diced
    2   lbs. hard apples
    2   lbs. seedless raisins
    ½   teaspoon ground mace
    ½   teaspoon ground cinnamon
    ½   teaspoon ground cloves
    1½   teaspoons ground ginger
    1½   teaspoons ground paprika
    1¼   teaspoons ground cayenne
    2   ozs. garlic, chopped
    2   ozs. salt
    3½   lbs. sugar
    3   qts. cider vinegar
    2   lbs. candied dry ginger

Combine all ingredients and boil slowly 3 hours. This makes 12 pts.

CHUTNEY
Miss Frances Campbell

    1½   lbs. sour apples, chopped
    1½   lbs. raisins
    ¼   lb. salt
    2   ozs. ground ginger
    2   ozs. ground mustard
    ½   oz. cayenne pepper
    2   qts. vinegar
    5   lemons, grated rind, and juice
    1½   lbs. ripe tomatoes, chopped
    ½   lb. brown sugar
    ¼   lb. onions, chopped
    ¼   oz. white mustard seed
    2   ozs. chopped garlic
    ¼   oz. turmeric
    1   small tablespoon curry powder

Boil tomatoes, apples and vinegar together until soft and mash through a colander. Then put all together into kettle and boil one-half hour stirring all the time. Put up and seal.

GREEN ONION PICKLE
Mrs. Bruton Dawkins

    ½   gal. small Bermuda pickling onions
    2   lbs. sugar
    ½   gal. vinegar
    1   tablespoon mustard seed
    1   tablespoon celery seed
    1   teaspoon allspice

Make a brine strong enough to float an egg. Cover the onions, unpeeled, with this and allow to stand for twenty-four hours or longer (until the skins slip off easily.) Remove peel and cover the peeled onions with ice water (with ice floating in it) and let them stand for three hours.

Make a syrup of sugar and vinegar and place the spices in it in a bag. Let this simmer slowly for one half hour. Strain. Drain the onions from the ice water and pour the syrup over them and heat thoroughly but do not boil. Put in jars while hot and seal.

If desired one teaspoonful of olive oil may be added to each jar.

GREEN TOMATO PICKLES
Mrs. Bruton Dawkins

    1   peck green tomatoes, sliced
         thin
    6   large white onions, sliced very thin

Place them in a bag with a teacup of salt poured over them, and let them drain for twelve hours. Place in a preserving kettle with the following:

    1   lb. sugar (for moderate sweetness)
    1   tablespoon powdered mustard
    1   teaspoon black pepper
    1   tablespoon celery seed
    1   cup horseradish, freshly ground
    ½   cup mustard seed
    1   tablespoon allspice, 1 teaspoon
         cloves, put in a bag

Cook the above mixture on a slow fire until tender, about thirty minutes. Put in jars while hot and seal.

TOMATO CATSUP
Mrs. Bruton Dawkins

½ bushel very ripe tomatoes
1 qt. good cider vinegar
1 doz. small creole onions, the strong red ones
½ cup sugar
2 tablespoons cayenne pepper or six small hot red peppers or to taste
2 tablespoons black pepper
1 teaspoon allspice, ground
¼ teaspoon cloves, ground
2 tablespoons powdered mustard
4 tablespoons salt
4 cloves garlic
1 cup horseradish
4 tablespoons black mustard seed
4 tablespoons white mustard seed
1 package celery seed

Tie in a bag the following: black mustard seed, white mustard seed, and celery seed.

Clean tomatoes well, do not peel. Quarter them, sprinkle lightly with salt and allow to stand three hours. This will give water enough in which to boil them. Place on a slow fire and boil until they fall to pieces. There should be one gallon of the tomato pulp. Add finely chopped onions and garlic to this, and cook until soft enough to pass through a colander. When the mass has been passed through the colander, add remaining ingredients except the horseradish. Cook down on a very slow fire for three or four hours until it thickens (It burns easily!) Add now a cup of grated horseradish. Bottle while hot. (The quantity of tomato pulp varies with the juiciness and ripeness of the tomatoes.)

CHILI SAUCE
Mrs. W. J. Bentley

24 large red tomatoes
6 green peppers, chopped
4 large onions, chopped
1 cup sugar
1 tablespoon salt
1 teaspoon each white mustard seed, allspice and cloves
4 cups vinegar

Peel the tomatoes, and chop them. Chop the peppers and the onions. Mix all the ingredients together, and boil for two hours until the mixture is done, put in bottles, and seal.

DANISH ROE EGGS
Mrs. Rafferty

Hard boil the desired number of eggs, slice lengthwise. Take out the yolks, which should be smashed to a paste, and softened with a little mayonnaise and a few drops of Worcestershire Sauce. Cover with a mixture of tomato paste, thinned with mayonnaise until it takes on a pretty pink color. Then add some rich roe and spread over the eggs. Shad roe is especially good.

ENGLAND
SOLE WITH ANCHOVY BUTTER
Mrs. Donald Rafferty

    Sole (replaced with us by small
      tender speckled trout)
    egg
    cracker crumbs, very fine
 1 teaspoon anchovy paste
 ¼ pound butter

Split open the fish lengthwise, and tenderloin it. Roll it in egg and then in cracker crumbs. Fry in deep fat and serve with a ball of Anchovy butter on each.

Note: Anchovy butter is made by creaming ¼ pound butter with a teaspoon of anchovy paste which is then set in the refrigerator to harden.

ENGLISH CHOCOLATE PUDDING
Mrs. Donald Rafferty

 1 pint milk
 7 even tablespoons grated bread
      crumbs
 6 even tablespoons grated bitter
      chocolate
 3 eggs
 ½ tablespoon vanilla
    enough sugar to make very sweet
      (about 1 cup)

Separate yolks and whites of 2 eggs. Beat 1 whole egg and 2 yolks till very light with sugar. Heat milk to the boiling point, pour over bread and chocolate, add egg and sugar mixture, fold in beaten egg whites and add vanilla. Pour in buttered baking dish and bake in moderate over ¾ hour. Serve hot, sprinkle well with sugar.

ITALY
VITELLO CON ZUCCHINI
Mrs. Rafferty

    veal strips, cut very thin
    stuffing
    large potatoes
    summer squash (or cucumbers)
 ½ pound pork sausage meat
 1 cup soft bread crumbs soaked in
      hot water and drained
 1 egg
 1 cup grated cheese
    pepper, salt
 2 tablespoons flour

Cut the steaks in strips 2 inches square, spread thinly with well-seasoned stuffing, roll, and secure with toothpicks.

Make mashed potatoes, well-seasoned and smooth (bake, not boil, the potatoes for mashing, as they have more flavor so).

Zucchini, the small round pumpkin which stands in such high favor in Italy, is frequently not obtainable here. Mrs. Rafferty has resourcefully discovered that summer squash or cucumber makes an adequate substitute. Boil the squash, or cucumber, in salt water until tender and cut in halves (or cucumber lengthwise). Scoop out seeds and stuff with the filling of sausage meat, bread crumbs, egg, grated cheese and seasoning, all well blended together.

Put the meat rolls into hot lard in the skillet, with salt and pepper, and brown on both sides. Add hot water to half cover. Put the lid on the skillet and bake ¾ hour, basting occasionally.

Place the vegetable in the oven and bake ½ an hour. Heap the mashed potatoes in the center of the platter. Thicken the gravy with flour and pour it around the potatoes. Place the meat rolls upright against the mounded potatoes and place the vegetables around. Neither the gourmet nor the gourmand could demand much more for a dinner!

MINESTRONE SOUP, MONTEFORTE

A large lean soup bone. Cover with 5 quarts water and cook 4 hours. Add 3 quarts diced vegetables (be sure to include 2 potatoes, carrots, onions, some cabbage and other seasonable vegetables). Season with pepper and salt. After vegetables are cooked life out 1 quart of the nicely diced ones and set aside. Lift out the meat and puree the remaining vegetables back into the soup. Let cool and skim off fat. When ready to serve have ready 1 cup spaghetti and add with the quart of diced vegetables.

Serve piping hot and have passed a piece of Parmesan cheese and a small grater so each guest can grate the desired amount of cheese into soup.

(This is a Milanese custom. Each Milanese apparently has a different capacity for cheese. In lieu of the cheese en bloc, the already grated variety may be used. This recipe was given us by an old Milanese whose devotion to his city and its customs excelled his religion, so we have named it after him).

COURTBOUILLON GENOISE

Make a roux of 1 tablespoon lard, 1 tablespoon flour and 1 cup water. Add a finely minced garlic clove. Add 1 can tomato paste and can rinsed out with water. 1 teaspoon chili powder (made into paste). 1 tablespoon sugar. 2 bayleaves.

    pepper and salt
    let simmer a few minutes
    add squares of raw fish
    cover and cook till done

Add ½ cup of cooked peas and ½ cup diced carrots (also cooked). Serve surrounded by rice balls.

A SIMPLE CZECHOSLOVAKIAN DESSERT

6	peaches
2	whole eggs
1	egg yolk
½	granulated sugar
½	cup flour
	grated rind of 1 lemon
½	tablespoon lemon juice

Beat yolks till very thick and light. Gradually beat in sugar. Add rind in half the whites, then half the flour

Add 1 tablespoon gelatine, dissolve well sifted, then the other half of whites and remaining flour.

The success of this depends on the air beaten in the yolks, they cannot be beaten too long. Stirring must be avoided, only fold in. Line square baking dish with oiled paper. Pour in batter to depth of 1 inch. Arrange slices of peaches across top in curving, snake-like pattern. Cook in slow oven about 40 minutes, testing with straw. When cool cut in oblong squares and serve sprinkled lightly with powdered sugar.

AT SWEDISH SMORGASBORD THE FOLLOWING HEAD CHEESE WAS SERVED

3 pounds lean pork. Cut up and boil with onion, bayleaf, pepper, salt, till tender. Cut meat in ½ inch strips. Add some finely minced chives, parsley, sweet red peppers and a few small shreds of Tabasco peppers. Flake meat as finely as possible." Bring 2 cups of the meat broth to the boil.

Add 1 tablespoon gelatine, dissolve well and mix in the seasoned meat. Place in bread pan and put to set in ice-box.

When mold is firm turn out on bed of lettuce leaves. Place 3 hard-boiled egg halves (cut lengthwise) on top to represent lilies. Make an oblong bed on mold of finely ground pistachio nuts.

Color mayonnaise a delicate green and with cake decorator cover half of each egg in points to form calyx, add stems and leaves having stems join at base of not oblong. Also make a frame around the pistachio nuts with the mayonnaise.

FINLAND

In Finland all meals are served in the form of hors d'oeuvres and everyone helps himself. An average home has 20 small plates of all descriptions on the table, two times a day. We have counted as many as 52 dishes on a table at one time.

Among the common dishes usually present are dried fish, raw sliced marinated herring, smoked salmon or sturgeon, potato salad, vegetable salad with whipped cream dressing, various types of hard tack, whole cheeses, pickled beets, fish, mayonnaise, sardines, anchovies, caviar, thin sliced cucumbers soaked in sugared vinegar, etc. and usually hot soup, potatoes, meat balls or stew and the favorite puréed spinach in a very sweetened cream sauce.

A SIMPLE AND DELICIOUS FINNISH SALAD

It is composed of all seasonable vegetables, cooked and diced, such as beets, potatoes, carrots, beans, etc. to which are added some finely chopped-up fennel and nasturtiums.

Serve with a dressing of thin whipped cream unseasoned.

A simple French dessert consists of dried apricots and prunes, soaked and cooked with sugar, drained and soaked in white wine.

JAPAN

Tamiji Kattagawa, the distinguished Japanese painter now living in Mexico, and his apple-fresh little wife, Tetsko, have passed on typical Japanese dishes that are rapidly becoming naturalized American. As restaurants in New Orleans are known by their Bouillabaisse, so to the restaurants of Tokio, the famous Mikawa-Ya (in the district of Yotsuya-ku), Matsuki (in the district of Ginza) and Tokio-Kaikan (in the district of Marunouchi) are known by their Suki-Yaki.

The Japanese table service is as complicated and as ceremonial as is social life in general: the dishes have their casts: the Honzen, or main dishes; the Sanozen, or first side dishes, and so on. Rice, consommé, and salad are invariable accompaniments to any meal.

This recipe for Suki-Yaki, given by Mr. Kittagawa, is rapidly becoming a classic:
(Serves 3 or 4)

½	lb. meat
2	large Bermuda onions
½	cup Japanese sauce (to be had at the fancy grocery)
½	cup white wine
2	tablespoons sugar
3	or 4 raw eggs

The onion must be cut in slices, about ¼ inch thick. The meat must also be cut, across the grain, in slices as thin as possible, with a very sharp knife. Mix the Japanese sauce, the sugar, and the wine, in a greased saucepan (it must be iron, not aluminum) and let boil gently for a few minutes. (This is Wari-shita, the sauce for Suki-Yaki). Then remove the Wari-shita from the saucepan. A chafing-dish is set in the center of the dining-room table (in Japan, a little brazier with a charcoal fire is used). On it is placed the saucepan, and into it half the Wari-shita is put. When it begins to boil, first the onions, later the meat are put into it, and allowed to cook.

In front of each guest is set a bouillon cup with a raw egg in it. Each helps himself from the saucepan, to the meat and to the sliced onions, and, before eating it, dips each piece in the raw egg in his boullon cup. More meat, more onions, and the rest of the Wari-shita are added as the feast progresses.

(The idea of the raw egg, like that of snails, is at first repugnant but once admitted, it becomes a favorite).

TEMPRA

Tempra is the name given to breaded fish, another Japanese standard dish that finds favor in other lands. One may use filet of fish, oysters, shrimp, anything of the sort. The Koromo, or batter, is made of very fine white flour, salt water, egg, and baking powder. The salted water is stirred in well, but slowly, to the flour; the egg, well-beaten, is mixed in, and lastly, a little backing powder. The result is rather like pancake batter. (It should be handled as little as is compatible with good mixing). In a deep frying-pan put a good quantity of seasame oil, or camelia oil or (as must be in these United States) olive oil.

Drop the filet seasoned with salt and pepper (or shrimp, or other material) into the batter. When the oil in the frying-pan is piping hot, take the filets from the batter and drop them in—not too many at a time, as they should not crowd.

Turn the fish over rapidly but carefully, so that it will brown evenly on all sides, and remove to a thick brown paper. The process should be short and quick. Serve with Japanese Sauce, or Worcestershire.

MEXICO

The mention of Mexican cooking finds most Americans looking a bit askance, but a little travel in Mexico, where a thatched one-room house can often yield a delicious molé, often brings a change of attitude.

A good molé, a pungent individualist of flavor, the brown sauce served with meat, requires some 48 ingredients and almost as many hours of work, neither the ingredients nor the patience necessary can be found outside that unique country. But Mrs. J. H. Sutherland, whose shining little hotel in the beautiful mountain village of Tasco has become a mecca for Americans, suggests the following dishes as favorites of her clients:

CALABAZOS CON NATA
(Squash with Sour Cream)

	young tender squash
1	tablespoon lard (or half lard, half butter)
1½	tablespoons flour pepper, salt tablespoon minced parsley
½	red pepper, ground
1	cup milk
½	cup heavy sour cream

The squash must be so tender that the skin is not much thicker than apple peel. Dice the squash and boil till it is very tender. Then fry it a little and set it aside to keep warm. Put the lard, or the butter and lard in a saucepan, and when it is hot, stir in very carefully the flour until it is smooth (do not let it brown). Add the seasonings and let them cook until they are well blended, then add the squash, the milk, and the sour cream, and let all bubble gently 6 minutes before serving.

DULCE DE PANOCHA
(Brown Sugar Candy)
Maria Luisa

4 cups dark brown sugar
1 cup milk
2 cups nuts, finely chopped
1 teaspoon butter
½ teaspoon vanilla

Boil the sugar and milk together, stirring constantly until it forms a soft ball when dropped in cold water. Remove from the fire, put in all the other ingredients and beat thoroughly and quickly until the mixture begins to harden. Turn out the candy on a very wet biscuit board and roll it thin with wet roller.

Albondigas de Carne de Puerco Rellenas de Pass y Almendras (Pork Croquettes stuffed with raisins and almonds)

2 pounds fresh pork
  bay leaf thyme, parsley
3 green tomatoes
½ teaspoon salt
½ cup seeded raisins
½ cup blanched almonds
4 green peppers
2 cloves
½ pod red pepper, minced
2 hard-boiled eggs
1 large onion, minced

The meat is ground up with the herbs, 2 tomatoes, salt. A little more than half of the raisins and almonds are chopped up, and the eggs, and these are mixed well with the chopped meat, then shaped in croquette form, and sprinkled lightly with flour. Put the lard in a saucepan and let the albondigas brown slightly in it, then remove them for the moment and set them aside to remain warm. Let the minced onion brown a bit in the saucepan, then add the garlic, chopped green peppers, 1 chopped tomato, the red pepper, the rest of the raisins and almonds, chopped, a pinch of salt,

two cups of hot water, and the albondigas are replaced and set to simmer gently for an hour. It sounds rather startling, but is actually a most savoury dish, a great favorite with American visitors. An American modification that has found favor is that of wrapping each of the albondigas closely in a cabbage leaf for the simmering process

CHILES RELLENOS CON NATA
Amparo
(Stuffed Green Peppers with Sour Cream)

6 green peppers
2 boiled potatoes, minced
½ cup Parmesan cheese
3 tomatoes, minced
2 onions, minced
1 tablespoon lard
1 egg, lightly beaten
2 cloves garlic

The stems are cut off the peppers and they are wrapped in a thin cloth and set to steam. Then the thin skin is peeled off, they are opened, veined, and seeded.

Heat the lard in a saucepan and put into it ½ the onions to brown a little, then ½ the tomatoes and 1 clove of garlic. When these have fried a little they are removed and the saucepan set aside, while the contents are well mixed with the potatoes and the cheese, with salt and pepper. The peppers are stuffed with the mixture.

Next, they are dusted lightly with flour and rolled in the well-beaten egg, then put back in the saucepan with the rest of the chopped tomatoes, chopped onion and the other clove of garlic, to fry. Then the thick sour cream is added.

Cook gently for an hour before serving.

TABLE OF CONTENTS

TABLE OF CONTENTS

TABLE OF CONTENTS